JOHN PODHORETZ

SIMON & SCHUSTER
New York   London   Toronto   Sydney   Tokyo   Singapore

HELL

OF A

RIDE

Backstage
at the
White House
Follies
1989–1993

SIMON & SCHUSTER
Rockefeller Center
1230 Avenue of the Americas
New York, New York 10020

SIMON & SCHUSTER and colophon are registered trademarks
of Simon & Schuster Inc.

Manufactured in the United States of America

1   3   5   7   9   10   8   6   4   2

Library of Congress Cataloging-in-Publication Data

Podhoretz, John.
Hell of a ride : backstage at the White House follies, 1989–1993 /
John Podhoretz.
p.   cm.
1. United States—Politics and government—1989–1993.   2. Bush,
George, 1924– . I. Title.
E881.P6   1993
973.928—dc20   93-28819
CIP
ISBN: 0-671-79648-8

*For my mother—I manned the lifeboat;
for my father—to whom this is not, in any
way, a letter;
and for Tod Lindberg—a paragon of
friendship, wisdom
and good cheer*

Contents

CONTENTS

CONTENTS

a note on the structure of *Hell of a Ride*

This book chronicles the decline and fall of George Bush through the eyes of the people who worked in his palace court—the White House. It is told in alternating chapters. The "Freeze Frames" are portraits of specific unnamed White House staffers reflecting on the triumphs and troubles of George Bush over the course of the eighteen months between his near-universal popularity at the end of the Gulf War and his humiliation at the polls in November 1992 and following.

The remaining chapters explain that astonishing fall from grace by taking a close look at the inadvertently comic spectacle of a White House on the verge of total collapse.

Dead scandals form good subjects for dissection.
—Byron, *Don Juan*

FREEZE FRAME:

A BUSHIE WATCHES
THE BIG PARADE

JUNE 8, 1991

You can hardly see the Humvees and the Patriots—and, of course, the soldiers and sailors and airmen and Marines, let's not forget them, as they march behind and around the hardware that won the war—because the throng stands thirty deep off every inch of Constitution Avenue on this hot June day. You didn't even intend to come to the parade; you set out from your Georgetown apartment to go over to the White House and get some work done this Saturday afternoon. But the mobs everywhere in town, the giddy carnival atmosphere that is suffusing the city, drew you to the parade in honor of the nation's accomplishment in defeating Iraq and liberating Kuwait in Operation Desert Storm.

You keep going south, all the way down to the Department of Justice at Tenth Street, but there's simply no way to get a better view here among the civilians, and you wonder why you didn't do something last week about getting a VIP pass so you could have had a seat in a reviewing stand. What good is it to work in the White House, even in your relatively minor job, if you can't use what little pull you have to elevate yourself a foot or two above the mass of men? But actually being in the midst of things, you get a contact high. Never have you seen a mob like this—or at least not since the last big event in Washington, the 1989 inaugural of your boss.

You were high that day too, because the inaugural was the culmination of more than a year's work on the presidential campaign of George Bush. But you are even more elated than you were on January 20, 1989. It's like the mood around the White House these past few months, the complete and overpowering spirit of victory throughout the place. The day after the war started—when it became clear that it was going to be an amazing coup—you and everybody else began walking around with a purposeful gait, as though the focused determination expressed in the Oval Office and over in the West Wing had mysteriously infected you as well.

The day after the war's end, at the morning staff meeting—you don't attend it, but you heard about it the way you hear about almost everything, it's all in the air—White House chief of staff John Sununu announced in a quiet voice that a poll conducted by Bob Teeter's firm gave the president a popularity rating of 91 percent. Ninety-one percent, a number so astronomical that you might think the poll was a fixed election in Albania.

You work for the victor of world history's most lopsided military victory—not only work for him, but know him, and, even more important, he knows you. And all these people are here on the streets celebrating because of your boss, his triumph.

The ebullience of the crowd infects even your own customarily laconic attitude. Children riding the shoulders of their parents, teenagers actually climbing on top of police cruisers before they get pushed off by the cops, T-shirt hawkers selling graven images of George Bush kicking Saddam Hussein in the rear just like he said he would at $18 a pop.

Imagine that: George Bush adorning American T-shirts in the pose of a pop icon as though he were Axl Rose and this were one of the concession stands at the Guns N' Roses world-tour stop in Washington. Like Guns N' Roses, the president does have a youth following—a fan club of which you, at twenty-four, are a passionate member. You don't need a T-shirt because you have his likeness three times on the wall of your office in the complex of buildings over which he is the master—and in each of those pictures, shaking his hand, laughing at a joke, in a crowd of people at a meeting, is *you*.

Bush fans like you do not derive from the great wave of Republicanism that washed over the nation's youth in the wake of the Reagan revolution, when the eighteen-to-twenty-four vote became the most reliable "demographic" for the GOP. You and your counterparts don't care all that much about the things people fought about in Washington during the Reagan years. That's not the kind of Republican you are. Star Wars, Nicaragua, abortion, Bork: These issues of moral probity and geopolitical gamesmanship are in your case purely abstract. They simply don't speak to you. In fact, the people who are deeply interested in such matters—"the true believers," you and your friends call them, with some respect for their passion and maybe a little contempt for it as well—are people with whom you have almost nothing in common except party affiliation. They are embattled, humorless. It's exhausting to deal with them. They seem to have no fun; you never see them in the clubs you frequent, hanging out, dancing.

The true believers are ideological, polemical pains in the ass. A lot of them even used to be Democrats. You, on the other hand, are a Republican the way you are a Caucasian—born into it. And in this, as in so many other ways, you feel an affinity for, a commonality with, the president of the United States.

Actually, you worship the man. Yes, "worship" is the right word, ever since the 1988 campaign. You were just out of college and ended up in New Hampshire in the blackest days of the Bush candidacy, when it looked as if he might lose to Bob Dole. Your grandmother had been a Bush delegate in '80—her mother having been a childhood friend of Mrs. Pierce, Barbara Bush's mother. You hadn't really figured out what to do when you graduated in 1987, so when word came that available bodies were needed to canvass and leaflet and do scut work in New Hampshire for Bush that fall, you figured it would be fun and your parents said they thought it would be a good experience.

And it was fun, more fun than you had ever had. Kind of like what you imagine happens with people in the same platoon in war, only you don't have to go through basic training or live in trenches and tents. Mad, insane adrenaline, doing fifty different things at once, absolutely no sense of hierarchy or structure, getting to know the roads and byways of the whole of the state in the Subaru Justy you were given to use at college.

Vice-President Bush was around too, wandering through the same malls you had canvassed the day before with the information that he would be arriving. And just before he went out to Iowa for the week preceding the caucuses, you got your first chance to be in a room with him—in a holding room before he was to give a speech at a school. And it turned out that *he knew your name already*. Called you by your first name even before you had been introduced to him. Fifteen minutes before it was time to go on stage and there he was, focusing his light-blue eyes on you, and he started peppering you with questions—where you went to school, where you were from. And when he heard tell of your grandmother, his face lit up. Sure, of course, ah, she's a great lady. Give her my best. Even remembered your grandfather's Christian name.

You were cool. That's the virtue of being raised in a Connecticut family, you know how to remain composed. But you called your grandmother as soon as you could get to a phone, then your parents, then your girlfriend from school. "He is just the greatest guy," you said over and over again. "So . . . nice, he is so nice."

And though he lost Iowa and the atmosphere in the campaign was, as the vice-president said, "tension city," you marveled like everybody else around you at his unstoppable, unfathomable energy and his unfailing ability to turn on a dime and say hello to you, ask you how you were doing, pretty weird not getting so much sleep, isn't it?

And when New Hampshire was won, you went right to Washington to work at headquarters for the wildest eight months of your life.

You were all packed in like sardines at the Woodward Building on Fifteenth Street and just screwing your brains out. Because the girls arrived with the spring, and they were the finest flowering of female Republicanism, the Laura Ashleyed Southern belles and the Chaneled Northeastern preppies. The talent was everywhere. They were *all* beautiful, and I mean *all*. Skinny, either with the rail-thin legs of an anorectic or the defined arms of a part-time aerobics instructor. And you guys were not so bad yourselves, as well heeled as the girls but more scruffily dressed, carelessly fashionable. You were the better looking of the two presidential campaigns, and you knew it.

The convention was the best time. You hit New Orleans in a lunatic frenzy, working and drinking and getting laid, two weeks of unbelievable excitement culminating in George Bush's amazing "Read my lips" speech. Everybody knew it was over then, even though Bush had not yet caught up with Dukakis in the polls, and already all of you were trying to figure out what you might want to do in the new administration.

Here you are, two years later, what the books call a "White House aide." You make next to nothing—$26,000 a year—but you've gotten to see how the place works. You've settled into a routine that involves a ten- or twelve-hour day at work, most of which you enjoy, and you go out four or five nights a week, to the Spy Club (of which you are a member) or Sequoia overlooking the Potomac in Georgetown. You've got a girlfriend who also works at the White House. She's a staff assistant in the West Wing, whereas you are across the street in the Old Executive Office Building. So although she is actually at a lower rank than you, her gossip is better and she constantly sees the peripatetic president walking through the first-floor offices outside the Oval Office on his way to the Rose Garden for an event or into the Roosevelt Room to make a drop-by appearance at a meeting with congressmen. You don't often get a glimpse of him; when he does appear in the hallways of the OEOB, he's always on his way to give a speech in Room 450. And his staffers come out of their offices and actually applaud and cheer as he walks by. He waves as if he's on a campaign appearance, except that he throws names at people as he goes—"Hey, Bill . . . Joanne, hi!" And those folks don't just blush with pleasure, they nearly faint from it.

They have all had the same experiences with him that you have had—if they announce an engagement, in a few days they will get a handwritten note from the president congratulating them, with a P.S. by Mrs. Bush. And before the wedding, an elegant gift. If someone should have to go to the hospital for an operation, the president will again send a note, might even call the hospital room.

Little kindnesses, to be sure, but people who know politics say the president's behavior is unprecedented in their experience. Ronald Reagan barely knew the names of the people on his staff; senators and congressmen routinely abuse those who work for them. Yet this man, who bears the weight of the world on his shoulders, nonetheless has time to think about his staff, to consider them. It's an astounding quality.

So it's no surprise to you that the passionate loyalty he has earned from you is mirrored today in the emotional celebration of American triumph and the president's triumph in the war. But you take special pleasure in it when you recall what some Republicans were saying about the president right at the beginning of the administration. The White House staff included a number of Reagan holdovers then, who wandered around grousing that Bush was changing the way they had done things and it was perilously stupid to try to improve on a successful presidency like Reagan's.

The Reaganites weren't loyal to the new president, they were loyal to the old one. They complained constantly, especially about who deserved credit for the collapse of Communism. Bush, they whined, was perfectly willing to take credit for it himself, but what about *Reagan?*

Reagan, Reagan, Reagan. It's like these Reagan people woke up in the morning thinking about the guy and went to sleep thinking about the guy, who was by this point out in California staring off into the sunset.

The new president told his personnel chief, Chase Untermeyer, that he wanted an administration full of new faces, and he got it. He needed his own people in there because, as the Reaganites feared, he *was* going to do things differently. He said in his inaugural address that the people didn't send politicians to Washington to bicker, that he wanted to work harmoniously with the Congress. There's no question that, almost immediately, Washington had become a good deal more pleasant, less contentious, than it had been in Reagan's time.

In fact, most of the really serious tension in town these past two years came not from the Democrats but from the true believers, who began going bananas in June 1990. That was when, at the beginning of negotiations on a budget deal with Congress, Bush agreed to state publicly that new taxes were on the table in the talks. And when he outright broke his no-new-taxes pledge in a bold move to solve the deficit problem, the Republicans in Congress positively ignited and the true believers fed the flames.

Things got a little unpleasant for a while, but after the success in the Gulf most Americans seem to feel about Bush they way you do. The whole town is saying that the Democrats might as well give it up in 1992, that the Democrats who voted against the war in the House and Senate may well lose their seats in the next election, and that the supposed Republican majority claimed by Ronald Reagan will find its embodiment, in 1992, in the person of George Herbert Walker Bush, forty-first president of the United States, the most popular and powerful man in the world.

ONE:

OEOB, OR,
THE COURTIERS

Once upon a time, most of the executive branch of the government of the United States lived happily together in the Old Executive Office Building. The OEOB (say it "oh-ee-oh-bee") sits next to the White House across something called West Executive Avenue. West Exec, as it is known in the awkward slang with which everything is nicknamed in the federal government, was once an actual narrow street with actual street traffic and actual pedestrians on it. But in 1941 the Secret Service closed it off behind gates and barricades. Now it is comparable to a street on a Hollywood studio backlot, its sidewalks reserved for use by White House staffers and visitors who wear passes around their necks authorizing their presence.

Only White House personnel privileged enough to claim the coveted West Exec parking spaces, along with the chauffeurs of the White House's fleet of blue cars, actually drive on it. Still, staffers continue to refer to it as though it were a real live city street and not a boulevard in the Emerald City known as the White House that is separated from the common man by fences and guards—the late-twentieth-century version of a moat.

There is an East Exec, too, another shuttered road, which separates the Treasury Department from the White House on the mansion's downtown side. In 1872, when the OEOB opened, these three buildings occupying the west side of Pennsylvania Avenue between Fifteenth and Seventeenth Streets pretty much constituted the federal government. The construction of the Executive Office Building was made necessary because of the unparalleled growth of the executive branch as a result of the Civil War. During the war years and those that followed, the United States had become a military power and required a larger bureaucracy to manage the pensions paid to disabled veterans, as well as to widows and orphans. The EOB was built to house the burgeoning State and War departments.

Nowadays, the executive branch sprawls across Metropolitan Washington and has offices (courtesy of the Agriculture Department, also a creation of Lincoln) in nearly every county of the Union. There are fourteen cabinet departments, each with its own colossal complex, all around town, even across the Potomac, where the War Department ballooned into the horrific socialist-realist building called the Pentagon following another bureaucratizing war, World War II.

And, as the O added only twenty years ago to its name indicates, the OEOB is no longer big enough even to serve as space for the Executive Office of the President. Half a block up Seventeenth Street from the O, there sits the NEOB, a redbrick structure that just looks like the mid-1970s, when it was finished.

The Executive Office of the President is the general organization under which are performed all the labors and responsibilities of what this book (and everybody in government) calls "the White House." "The White House" is now merely a synecdoche. The physical construct with the columns that appears nightly as a colorful backdrop for network news reporters actually squeezes fewer than one hundred employees into its office space in its West and East wings.

Like the government, the White House itself has grown exponentially just in the past twenty years. Once merely the president's staff, the Executive Office now includes three semi-independent agencies. The NEOB is home to the Office of Management and Budget— although OMB's top people work in the OEOB. Across the street from the NEOB, at 750 Seventeenth Street, is a building (with a McDonald's in it) that houses the newest branch of the Executive Office of the President, the Office of National Drug Control Policy (also known as the office of the drug czar). Across from the OEOB is the Winder Building, in which resides the Office of the United States Trade Representative.

There are a few scatterings of the Executive Office of the President elsewhere as well. Until this year, across Pennsylvania Avenue from the mansion, on a street called Jackson Place that abuts Lafayette Park, stood the brownstone headquarters of the Council on Environmental Quality.[1] And somewhere deep within the bowels of Chinatown, half a mile away, are a couple of people who work for something called the National Critical Materials Council.

According to the government's organizational charts, all the people who work for these agencies are on the president's personal staff. Many of them (some OMB, drug czar and USTR people) are career civil servants. Everybody else is a "political appointee," known in government-personnel jargon as a "Schedule C." All Schedule C's serve at the pleasure of the president (although, again, a few people actually have to be confirmed by the Senate—the top two guys at OMB, the drug czar, the trade rep).

The people who really do work at the president's sufferance, the day-to-day, day-in, day-out laborers of the White House, work in the OEOB. The councils of White House power are held in the West Wing; it is rare to find a powerful staffer who does not have a West Wing office. There are always a few power centers in the OEOB, though; in the Reagan administration, the director of speechwriting was at the southwest corner of the first floor, and in the Bush administration the budget director, Richard Darman, and Bill Kristol, the vice-president's chief of staff, were up on the second floor.

The West Wing boasts a number of would-be great paintings on the walls, the press room where some of the nation's most famous media people work, and the legendary Mess, the executive dining room run by the Navy that is a wonderful aphrodisiac for a young staffer successful enough to have the privilege of eating there.

On the tours of the White House that staffers give late at night to

---

[1] The Clinton administration disbanded the council, only to rename it something else. It's still there.

impress the girls they are trying to sleep with (and that the married staffers give to friends and friends of friends), they like to talk about the "air of history" that hovers over the West Wing, the ghost of Lincoln wandering the halls and other such portents.

But of the two buildings, the OEOB actually looks and feels older. It is more handsome, more run-down, more lived-in, even though people actually live in that part of the White House called "the residence." Lincoln may have slept in the Lincoln bedroom there (the residence is one place White House staffers cannot take their girlfriends). But here in the OEOB, on the second floor, William Howard Taft had his office—Room 231—when he was secretary of war, and the amazingly portly Taft once took a full-gainer tumble down one of the building's eight semicircular staircases, which for some reason had no banister until that time. Here in his hideaway office (Room 180) Richard Nixon installed the taping equipment that would bring down his presidency. The White House is a place for men larger than life—Lincoln following the progress of Lee's army with stickpins or Harry Truman deciding to drop the Big One. The OEOB is where future presidents fall down the stairs and current presidents destroy themselves—where real things happen to real people.

The OEOB is also more architecturally impressive than the West Wing. The West Wing is a rabbit warren of beautifully kept common areas that resemble the hallways and staircases of a house, off which are undistinguished small offices far too compact to hold the volume of newspapers and legal documents and memoranda that sit piled up floor to ceiling in almost every corner.

The human scale of the West Wing is dwarfed by the insane American grandeur of the OEOB. The latter was conceived and built on a scale unimaginable today, as though the people of the previous century had not been a head shorter than we are but rather three heads taller and two hundred pounds heavier. The two parallel corridors that run the length of the building on three of its five floors are as long as football fields. They are, in width, about twenty feet. The ceilings are twenty-two feet high.

The thick marble tiles on the floor make an endless pattern of charcoal gray and white, charcoal gray and white, and as people make their way down the halls the heels of their shoes click and echo above and all around them. The sound of footfalls is the defining experience of the OEOB. Like the blind, staffers come to know the walking rhythms of the people they work with, can tell if the clickety-clack outside their door is the footwork of a friend about to pay a call or an unknown somebody passing by on his or her way elsewhere.

Behind the huge oaken doors that are cut into both sides of each corridor every ten feet are the common areas of the office suites, each occupied by three or four secretaries. The offices beyond are on average as large as a CEO's; the smaller ones would be appropriate for the manager of a small company while the larger ones rival the space demands of a *Fortune* 100 pooh-bah. They are also, many of them, quite glorious and run down, like a magnificent old Victorian house gone a little to seed. Wires for all the newfangled equipment invented since the building's construction—many offices have ten or twelve phone lines, not to mention cable television—snake along the floor and then up the wall in barely disguised fashion.

Beautiful parquet floors in fascinating patterns are covered with elegant Persian rugs long since frayed at the edges, huge battered desks bigger than the president's with huge black chairs that can lean back almost to the ground, and, over in a corner of a good office, not even taking up half the space, an entire living room: a couch, a couple of chairs, a large coffee table. Chances are the furniture will be undistinguished, but there is also the possibility that it will be antique and wonderful. Every now and then the restorers, who work in the White House on a never-ending quest to get the OEOB to look exactly as it did in the nineteenth century, get hold of an office and renovate it to its former glory. The stunning results are on every floor—the Indian Treaty Room, a riot of cherry floors and paneling; the White House library, unfathomably elegant and useless. Each renovation job takes a year or more and costs upward of a million dollars.

People who work in these offices tell one another not to get used to it—once their time in government is over they will never again have as nice a place to work. Nice, however, they don't stay. Over time, the sheer tonnage of printed matter that runs through every corner of the place—five or six newspapers a day, drafts of memos and working papers and speeches, weekly reports to the president or the vice-president on any number of matters—overwhelms even the most anal and well-organized worker. Paper spills off the piles on the desk and into piles on the floor around it. In-house intellectual James Pinkerton was such a pack rat he turned his cavernous office, 216, into a veritable maze of newsprint—little Towers of Babel all over the place. And as his next-door neighbor, health-care expert Hanns Kuttner, was taking leave of the office he had used for four years, a team of archivists had to take up residence just to make sense of the accumulated printed debris.

Some of this paper makes its way directly into the "burn bag," a special garbage receptacle for classified and embarrassing documents picked up daily by a Secret Service agent and soon after smoked into the atmosphere.

The better suites are occupied, for the most part, by commissioned officers. Like the Army, the White House staff comprises commissioned and noncommissioned officers, although in the White House the terms are basically meaningless. "Commissioned" is supposed to indicate someone with line authority, someone who runs an office or has direct access to the president, but many commissioned officers don't. These days, a commission is an honor, nothing more. A commissioned officer receives a piece of paper that is signed by the secretary of state and the president and is suitable for framing; in the Bush White House, a commissioned officer was allowed membership in the White House Mess. He also gets the words "The Honorable" before his name, a title whose use is by and large restricted to the Christmas cards and the party invitations sent by the White House itself.

The commissioned officers are either assistants to the president, deputy assistants to the president or special assistants to the president. Generally speaking, someone who runs one of the twelve offices inside the White House proper has the title of assistant. A whole bunch of people are, without rhyme or reason, called special assistant.

Most of the assistants and deputy assistants to the president are domiciled in the West Wing. They are more commonly known as "senior staff." In the Bush White House, people were senior staff if they were allowed into the 7:30 A.M. senior staff meetings in the Roosevelt Room on the first floor of the West Wing, meetings usually chaired by the chief of staff. Senior staffers also had entrée, along with members of the cabinet and the vice-president, to the executive mess, the smallest and darkest of the three dining rooms in the White House Mess.

Senior staffers were at the beck and call of the chief of staff, who directed them to get things done. Assistants to the president were the ones whose names were put on the president's schedule as the lead officials on events in which he was to take part, no matter how small. That was called "action"; people would always ask of specific events, "Who's got the action on that?"

Senior staffers directed their junior staffers—ensconced across West Exec in the OEOB—to do what the chief of staff had told them to do or to deal with the "action," chatting all the while about their skills at delegating authority, and about how delegation was really the key to good management.

So it was in the OEOB, land of the midlevel and low-level staffer, that the boring but necessary stuff was accomplished. Speeches were written; the five million pieces of mail that were received annually were answered; congressmen and cabinet secretaries and conservative groups and Jewish groups and Arab groups and their often bizarre requests were dealt with; policy wonks sat around thinking of ways to influence the policy being set three levels above them in the West Wing; economic advisers did whatever it was they did, running numbers over and over again to see whether they could get a nicer or better result to give to the president; and national security types tried to undo policies of the State Department or the Pentagon they didn't like.

The Bush White House was the palace court of the United States, and the OEOB was the domain of courtiers who hoped to be knighted later on, when they, too, could sit at the Round Table and watch John Sununu and Dick Darman work somebody over. They worked, uncomplaining, basically as apprentices, gathering and preparing materials, helping to manage the sheerly political aspects of the presidency and to tend to the complicated relationships between the White House and other governmental bodies: cabinet agencies, the Congress, the judiciary, governors and mayors. The courtiers spent their lives either on the telephone or in meetings with people from other White House offices and cabinet departments, as members of a "working group" on this issue or a "council" on that one.

Such meetings were in turn set up by yet other courtiers, who had to find a time for each meeting convenient to all attendees, then reserve one of the White House's few conference rooms, making sure there were iced Cokes on hand. This was a task fraught with peril, because inside every working group there was at least one murderous conspiracy. At least one member of the group always wanted it to fail—not hard to manage when any one of the ostentatiously busy people who worked in the federal government could gum up the works by claiming a conflict at every possible meeting time. Another common tactic of sabotage, available to the more important and senior members of a working group if they disapproved of it or felt it to be impinging upon their turf, was to call in sick or make some other excuse at the last minute. (EPA administrator William Reilly was famous for this one.)

Or they would refuse to attend unless the meeting were called by a personage of sufficient standing; Richard Darman would not go to meetings scheduled by officials he deemed his inferiors in rank and eventually went only to gatherings scheduled by the chief of staff or the president.

So if a courtier was not careful, he could involve his knight in the kind of White House calamity from which it was nearly impossible for a senior figure to recover: calling a B-List Meeting—a meeting attended only by lots of representatives of more important people but no important people themselves. Word of such a fiasco would travel through the White House like a virus, fed by the saboteur, whose purpose was not only to demonstrate the pointlessness of the meeting itself but to castrate the working group's leader. *Roger's working group was a disaster. Charlie called a meeting and absolutely nobody came!* And then, in lowered tones dripping with concern: *I really think this did Charlie some damage, don't you?*

Although the courtier's own reputation may not have been on the line, he was always convinced that his future depended on a good showing by his knight and so worried about the standing of his liege lord almost as obsessively as the knight himself. And small wonder, because the OEOB is a place where people begin their professional careers in politics. The Bush staffers who wrote the first drafts of history in the form of speeches and policy guidance were for the most part in their twenties and early thirties, young singles and young marrieds. To those here and abroad who consider the White House the center of the known universe, this may seem extraordinary. But working in the Bush White House did not so much represent an ambition fulfilled as the beginning of the path to future glory. Anyone who had reached his or her forties was either a secretary, a cleaning lady, or a member of senior staff. It was assumed that anyone past his thirties who would actually want to be a mere courtier in Bush's Washington was a loser, an also-ran. The place was therefore a parade of youth—not just the beautiful secretaries and assistants, both male and female, but those in positions of modest authority as well.

There were four types of midlevel staffer. There was the Reagan Holdover, of whom there were a very few (like deputy domestic policy adviser Charles Kolb, who had been in Reagan's Education Department), or a former official of the Reagan administration who had been there by virtue of his prior connection to Bush (personnel chiefs Chase Untermeyer and Connie Horner). Next there was the Protégé of a Bush Friend—someone who came recommended highly by one of Bush's two hundred or so close pals. The protégés could be located anywhere, from the cabinet (Treasury Secretary Nicholas Brady's pet, Ede Holiday, ran the Office of Cabinet Affairs) to the food business (one of Bush's secretaries, Nancy Huang, was the daughter of the owner of Bush's favorite Chinese restaurant in Houston). There was the Hill Aide, who had worked for one of the Republican members of Congress—particularly moderate to liberal members of Congress, since they were thought to be the more "effective" of the party's two ideological camps on the Hill (for example, OMB associate director Tom Scully, who had worked for Senator Slade Gorton). Most important was the Campaign Worker, who had given himself to the 1988 Bush effort. Campaign Workers made up by far the largest number, and were the chief residents and guiding spirits of the OEOB.

To get to work in the morning, staffers first fought among themselves for a strip of reserved parking spaces along E Street and then down the Ellipse, the long, flat area of parkland where the national Christmas tree is placed every year. From there they walked to the southwest gate, where they flashed their photo ID cards to gain entry. Those who took the Metro to work, or had no parking privileges, generally came in with the common run of White House visitors at the Seventeenth and G Street entrance, all the way on the other side of the building—here they had to use a computerized PIN number to get in and pass through a metal detector about five hundred times more sensitive than an airport's. A belt buckle could set it off, or a metal pen. A bored Secret Service agent had to come over with a hand-held metal detector and pass it the length and width of the visitor's body.

A visitor would be instructed to hang the metal chain of his appointment pass around his neck or, if he was given only a clasp, to pin it to his lapel. Staffers had passes in different hues—a blue pass gave a staffer access to all the White House grounds, while an orange pass restricted his movements to the OEOB.

The passes, temporary or permanent, posed a significant fashion problem for the superlatively well-dressed working crew of the Bush OEOB. Men who dressed in $750 suits with $100 shirts and $75 silk ties had to ruin the effect by hanging the pass's chain around their necks because the alternative clasp might have torn into the fabric of their jackets. Usually they tucked the pass into the breast pockets of their shirts (which meant they had finally found a use for that male accessory otherwise obsolete for those who did not smoke and would not dream of hanging a pen from it). Still, the chain hung dully down their fronts, spoiling the effect of their tailoring.

For some of the men, though, the chain served the same function as the stained blue tie badly knotted over the open collar in prep school—it was a nod to authority accompanying an aristocratically careless mastery of the rules of dress. The more nervous among them carried the chain in hand and played with it, whipping it about in their fingers as they walked like Orthodox Jews wrapping phylacteries at prayer time. But the entropic forces often got the better of them and the pass would go whizzing off, either through the halls or down the stairs like a Slinky (or William Howard Taft).

They could, of course, have simply put the thing in their pockets and forgotten about it. The pass existed only to show Secret Service guys that its bearer was permitted on the premises. But it was supposed to be worn exposed at all times—all staffers are told that by the Secret Service when they are issued the passes in the first place. As long as they are not libertarians, Republicans are very obedient folk and listen to men in uniform who tell them what to do. And anyway, truth to tell, the pass was a badge of honor, a secret decoder ring of the White House, the decoration given only to them and their three hundred colleagues.

For Bushie women, however, the pass presented a similar but nearly insurmountable difficulty. Carefully chosen outfits were hard to reconcile with the pass; some attempted to pin the thing to their purses, or on the insides of their jackets, but women were studied more closely by the Secret Service and their subterfuges were more easily detected. The compromise solution was to pin the pass to the top of a skirt, so that it fell unobtrusively at one's side.

Once staffers were inside, life in the OEOB required a great deal of sheer youthful energy. The work was grinding and ceaseless, and took at minimum sixty hours a week to perform, some weeks ninety or one hundred. And every assignment was urgent. The American people may have thought that George Bush did nothing as president, but the hundreds of members of his court ran through their paces like hamsters on speed. Staffers took their responsibilities with the utmost seriousness, as though the fate of the nation really did depend on their getting some piece of paper into the bureaucratic machine without a minute to spare.

The importance of an assignment would be conveyed by the invocation of some very high authority who might, at any moment, fly into a titanic rage. "Skinner said he needed that by two o'clock. He looked really pissed." Or, in a whisper: "Andy said that Sununu had to have that on his desk COB [by close of business], because the president is leaving at six for Camp [known to the rest of the world as Camp David, the presidential retreat]." Or "Baker was enraged when they didn't get that done." Some of this was accurate; most of it was wild exaggeration testifying to the fears of those delegating the work down the line that their lack of command over the matters under their authority might be exposed if they had to wing it, that is, to explain something without a piece of paper in front of them.

Staffers were so rushed that they did not even have time to speak English. Instead, they spoke Abbreviation, the strange argot of all government agencies and the officials who populate them. Abbreviation exists, like Pig Latin, to exclude those who have not yet figured out the code. It also signifies a conversation in a hurry, between two people who are all business:

> Staffer One (at urinal): How's it going?
> Staffer Two: God, I'm really pushing on something.
> Staffer One: COB?
> Staffer Two: No, ASAP. Staff Sec says it has to be cleared by DOJ,
> and then it's got to go right to POTUS.
> Staffer One (impressed): POTUS, huh?
> Staffer Two (out the door, acknowledging the coup): POTUS.

To translate: "ASAP" means "as soon as possible." "COB" means "close of business." "Staff Sec" is the staff secretary, the official responsible for managing White House paper flow. "DOJ" is the Department of Justice. It would be a faux pas of the first order to call it "Justice," or worse yet, "the Justice Department," while having a conversation in the men's room. "DOJ" is the department's officially sanctioned Abbreviation, and knowing each of these is key to demonstrating insider status. Often the Abbreviation is counterintuitive, just to keep the would-be insider from getting it right: The Department of Agriculture is "Ag," not (as many think) "USDA." The

Defense Department is "DOD," not "the Pentagon." The Department of State is "State," not "DOS." Transportation is "DOT." Health and Human Services is "HHS." The Office of National Drug Control Policy is "the drug office," not "the drug czar's office."

The "POTUS" about whom our two staffers had so much to say was none other than George Bush. "POTUS" (pronounced "POE-tahs") stands for "president of the United States"—which made his lovely wife, Barbara, "FLOTUS." "POTUS" did prove a most convenient Abbreviation, because it allowed staffers in informal conversation to refer to the president without having to call him "Bush," which was considered cheeky, or "the president," which often sounded pompous. Use of "the president" was reserved for suitably portentous discussions: whether a controversial document coming out of HHS might "embarrass the president" or whether a staffer would "best serve the president" by going on a fact-finding trip or staying back at the OEOB to coordinate.

John Sununu afforded his underlings a similar convenience when he insisted they address him as "Governor," even though his intention was vainglorious. Figuring out what to call the chief of staff has long been a White House problem. "Mr. So-and-So" always seems far too formal for a political organization, but first names seem impertinent. As a result, those who worked for Donald Regan in Reagan's White House and Sam Skinner, who followed Sununu in Bush's, never quite knew what to say. Senior staff usually got comfortable enough to be on a first-name basis, but if, for instance, a midlevel staffer called Skinner "Sam," he was stepping over a boundary line nobody had told him about.

Learning these rules, living under this kind of pressure, was the lot of the midlevel staffer. And the pay was lousy. Not by a truck driver's standards, but lousy given the standard of living in Washington—America's most affluent metropolitan area—and the consequent costs of goods and services and real estate. Midlevel staffers could barely maintain the mortgage on a condo with a Bush White House salary.

According to civil service ranking, the highest possible pay for a staffer was $125,000, and only three people besides the chief of staff received that. (One employee of the Office of Management and Budget parlayed a job offer from a law firm into a salary-and-bonus plan that ended up paying him $140,000—$15,000 more than his boss or the chief of staff.)

Salary levels are based on the amount of pay people received before they went into the government and on the civil-service ranking of their positions. For almost anyone in a position of authority in the private sector who might fit well into a White House job, a pay cut is required.

A bizarre miserliness came into play at the beginning of the administration as well. Rather than worrying about finding the best possible people for his staff and keeping them happy despite a relatively small salary, incoming White House chief of staff John Sununu, who had never worked or lived in Washington, decreed in 1989 that nobody in the place was going to be paid more than $52,000. If anybody complained, he said he would just hire some folks from his home state of New Hampshire who would be tickled pink to get such a salary. With this dazzling display of Yankee frugality of the sort that did New England in, Sununu began his glorious Washington career.

Weep not for the Bush White House staffers and their fellow Schedule C's in the government, though. One of the best ways onto the staff was by working on the campaign, where few people were paid more than peanuts. And since campaigns are full of young people who not only come cheap but don't exactly know what they are going to do with their lives (if they knew, they would be doing it instead of working on a campaign), the successful conclusion of the voting season meant an instant career and instant status. After college, almost any salary is acceptable.

And if a larger salary was needed, a Bushie could always bypass the White House and go directly to a job in a cabinet department or agency, where the pay was better. A White House staffer could parlay a relatively menial OEOB job into a position of authority outside the White House with a preset salary range tens of thousands of dollars higher—possibly, even, into what was known as a Senior Executive Service, or SES, job. That was like hitting the jackpot. In 1989, concerned that government workers in fields such as health research were deserting their posts for the private sector because their salaries were too low, the president and Congress agreed to a twenty-five percent increase in the salary structure of the SES. Suddenly, a management position in the government had a starting salary of $84,000—with *bonuses* every year. And that was just to start.

And so there were people working in the Bush administration—blocked Ph.D. candidates and Reagan-era secretaries and assistants who were still young—who had never worked anywhere outside the federal government in Washington and yet were earning salaries of $100,000 or more, money they could never have come close to being paid in the private sector. A fact many of them were to discover, to their horror, when the administration came to an end.

FREEZE FRAME:

WATER DAMAGE

NOVEMBER 2, 1991

"Honey, the president's on CNN," your husband calls to you, and you go into the living room on this cold Saturday afternoon to watch. Upstairs, your fourteen-month-old daughter is being entertained by the Filipino nanny. What you see is heartrending: the president, in a slicker, looking cold and forlorn, walking through the debris of Walker's Point, his Kennebunkport house. A freak storm has torn the place to shreds. "It's rather devastating" is all he can say.

You want to cry. It's just so unfair, especially after the disappointments and difficulties of the past couple of months: the continuing weakness of the economy, the slippage in the poll numbers, the terrible Clarence Thomas–Anita Hill hearing, the ruckus over the signing of the 1991 Civil Rights Act. The president looks like he's carrying the weight of the world on his shoulders—which, of course, he is, but usually he bears that weight with a happy face.

You also know he's carrying an extra burden these days—having to decide the fate of John Sununu, his chief of staff. Sam Skinner, the secretary of transportation, has been putting on a full-court press for the job, and the word around town is that before the beginning of 1992 Skinner will be in the West Wing and Sununu will be out.

You know people don't like Sununu. He doesn't suffer fools gladly; he loses his temper easily. But you're just crazy about him. He is just so amazingly brilliant it takes your breath away. The man can grab a ten-page memo, read it in thirty seconds, and grasp it all. He seems to know everything that's going on. And if you're good at your job and follow his instructions, he's really nice to you. Thoughtful. A good guy. When you went on maternity leave, he called you to keep you informed. He doesn't really ask for your advice—he never seems to need anybody's advice—but he lets you know what's going on. And you just feel so sorry for him, the way he's been getting dumped on day after day after day in the press from June onward.

So he took some private trips on government planes and in government cars. You would think from the way they're writing about it that he's some kind of axe murderer. It had been administration policy, set by Reagan's secretary of state, that the chief of staff has to fly on a government plane if he goes anywhere so that he can turn around and come back in a crisis at a moment's notice. So what is the guy supposed to do if he wants to take a couple of days off to go skiing?

And you would think, reading the papers, that he was driving to New York in some stretch limo with a bar and a TV in it to go to a stamp auction. The fact is that the White House cars are Chrysler New Yorkers, and the guy rode in his car to New York so he could do work on the way—reading papers, making phone calls. It was cheaper than taking the shuttle, and more efficient.

This is really too much. Here is Sununu, probably the poorest leading official in the administration, a man with eight kids who is used to New Hampshire prices, trying to make it in one of the most expensive cities in America on $125,000. That might sound like a lot to the American people, but in Washington it's peanuts, and with eight kids it's nearly impossible. You and your husband are doing all right only because he's a partner in a law firm. The idea that Sununu is living it up at government expense is just insane.

And who knows who is dropping these dirty dimes on him? You heard Lee Atwater's former deputy Rich Bond had an axe to grind, because Sununu screwed him out of the chairmanship of the Republican National Committee after the death of Atwater, the hard-charging forty-year-old who understood the concerns and interests of the American voter better than anybody else. Sununu got Bush to name, first, Bill Bennett and then, when Bennett said he couldn't, Clayton Yeutter. But if you try to talk to Sununu about it, he brushes you off with a smile and a joke.

He is confident as always, and serene when it comes to his own standing. And he is equally serene about the political future. He speaks amusingly of the "three K's" that are going to win the president the 1992 election in a walk—crime, quotas, and Kuwait. Americans know Democrats are soft on crime, and the administration is pushing a tough crime bill. Americans know Democrats want to institute racial quotas, and the administration vetoed the Civil Rights Act of 1990 because it was a quota bill. And the American people know that George Bush was the savior of Kuwait, while a majority of Democrats in the Senate voted against the war in January.

But it's starting to look as though the three K's aren't going to work. The Democrats refused to pass the administration's crime bill in September, even though the president had promised to make it a major issue in 1992 if they didn't go along.

And then quotas. The president was concerned about his standing in the black community after the Clarence Thomas–Anita Hill thing and instructed Sununu to see whether they could get a civil rights bill. Sununu talked to Teddy Kennedy, who gave in on a certain provision and made it possible for both Sununu and White House counsel Boyden Gray to say the Senate had answered the administration's stated legal objection to the 1990 bill. Just a few days ago, then, Bush agreed to the Civil Rights Act of 1991, a move that effectively took quotas off the table even though a bunch of people inside the administration said it was *still* a quota bill and the president shouldn't have signed it.

The president was all smiles about getting this bill, but then came the big screwup. The day before the bill was to be signed in a big South Lawn ceremony, some of its opponents in the White House worked together on a draft of the "signing statement"—a document of absolutely no meaning or value that goes into the historical record as an explanation for why the president agreed to the bill. The language in the draft signing statement had the president insisting that the act was not a quota bill but did in fact actually outlaw numerical affirmative action goals, and directed all federal agencies to comply with its provisions.

This might have seemed pretty simple and self-explanatory, but the people who had drafted it knew exactly the kind of storm they were brewing. The draft began circulating at 2:00 P.M., and by 2:45 P.M. the entire administration was up in arms. Labor Secretary Lynn Martin called in near hysterics because there was an entire branch of the Department of Labor called the Office of Compliance whose task it was to ensure that the federal government fulfilled affirmative action goals—in other words, a quota office. By 5:00, every network and major newspaper had the draft in its possession. By 6:30, when the newscasts began, the signing statement had been transmuted into an "executive order" outlawing affirmative action—an executive order being a document signed by the president that has the standing of law in the executive branch.

The leaders of the civil rights community, who had been stunned into silence and even praise when the administration did its turn-around on the bill, saw their chance to avoid giving the president the credit he seemed to want so much. En masse, they denounced the executive order that did not exist and boycotted the signing cere-mony the next day. So on the day of the signing, the nonexistent executive order and the black boycott became the story. The pres-ident got no credit for signing the bill, and at the same time eliminated quotas as an issue he could bash the Democrats with in 1992.

And as for Kuwait: Saddam Hussein's war on the Kurds in the north and the Shiites in the south of Iraq has taken some of the bloom off that rose, according to the polls. The American people are more than a little disappointed that Saddam Hussein, who Bush said was worse than Hitler, is still in power.

Earlier in the year, Sununu used the three K's to deflect efforts by conservative activists in the party to make a big push for their fa-vorite legislation. Right after the war, there was a lot of talk in Republican circles about a Domestic Desert Storm—an offensive against the Democrats, who were running scared because they hadn't supported the war and saw Bush with a popularity rating in the 80s while theirs was somewhere in the 30s. Republicans hoped to force Congress to go along with Republican legislation on everything from welfare reform to enterprise zones. But Sununu insisted that the president had already gotten almost everything he wanted out of Congress on the domestic front. He'd gotten the Americans with Disabilities Act, the Clean Air Act, the 1990 budget deal and Sununu's pet project, some child care legislation. True, he had failed to get a capital gains tax cut, but Sununu figured that capital gains was a loser going into an election year anyway, because it seemed to favor the rich.

So when it came time for the president to challenge Congress, the Domestic Desert Storm had been reduced to a manageable two items—a transportation bill and a crime bill. One of your deputies, an aggressive, tough-talking, ambitious guy, was disgusted by this and made no bones about it. He made fun of the president and Sununu by delivering a mock speech in your office: " 'My fellow Americans, we stand at the brink of an era that will reshape the world as we know it. So please pass my highway bill. Thank you very much, and God bless this wonderful country.' "

Your deputy was especially disappointed because he was one of the "empowerment" boys over in the OEOB. This was a crew of about ten or fifteen youngish men, led by deputy assistant Jim Pinkerton, the tallest person in the White House. Pinkerton, who is beloved by the press because he is quick with a clever quote, came up with the idea that there is a world-historical link between the collapse of Communism and the libertarian Republican interest in reducing the size of American government. He called it "the New Paradigm," and if that weren't grand enough, he sometimes talked about how George Bush was the leader of a "Fourth American Revolution" whose goal was the destruction of all large bureaucracies.

"The New Paradigm" was a way of giving an intellectual framework to various programs supported by the administration—school choice, welfare reform, deregulation, enterprise zones. But the term itself was quickly tossed out—too pretentious, besides which, nobody had actually read the book by Thomas S. Kuhn called *The Structure of Scientific Revolutions* from which Pinkerton had borrowed it—and was replaced by the word "empowerment."

The empowerment boys were all midlevel officials, below you in the hierarchy, who were just trying to advance the administration agenda. If the president had decided to go with the Domestic Desert Storm, you figure he would have had to go with the empowerment agenda. It was the only Republican game in town. But Darman's hostility to it and Sununu's desire not to fool around with the Congress he had such contempt for—not to mention the president's discomfort with some fancy pseudointellectual notion—made that impossible. Besides, Sununu and his ally Darman believed they had already achieved a Domestic Desert Storm—their beloved 1990 budget deal. Neither one of them was going to allow some grandiose legislative package to obscure that grand achievement. Your deputy quoted a friend of his over in Policy Development: " 'Sununu thinks he's Jupiter and Darman thinks he's Saturn, and they treat us like Uranus.' " You told him you didn't think that was funny.

But even though Sununu is serene and Darman is, well, Darman, other people you work with in the White House are getting uneasy. Michael Boskin, chairman of the Council of Economic Advisers, has announced that the economy is far weaker than he expected, as unemployment continues to go up and growth rates have begun to go down again after the upward blip in consumer confidence caused by the Gulf War.

Darman has attacked Boskin at senior staff meetings, wanting to know why he is so intent on putting a negative spin on the economic numbers, which could be read a lot more cheerfully. Boskin, who tends to get huffy, huffily replies that he won't cook the books or lie to the president. Darman says it wouldn't be a lie; he and Treasury Secretary Brady both believe the numbers are more encouraging, and maybe they should get their ducks in a row.

The president is going along with Darman and Brady. Things are going to get better. After all, thirty-nine out of forty economists polled by *The Wall Street Journal* back in June said the economy was going to come out of the recession over the summer. And that makes you confident too, because the president is just so amazing, so cool, so pleasant.

It's just a lull, Sununu says. The economy is on its way back, it's just going to take a little longer. And besides, what's the worry? That the president is going to lose the election? The man has just won the biggest military victory in history! Communism is dead! The attempted coup against Gorbachev was foiled! The president is about to announce a major Middle East peace initiative! All the major Democratic party figures are coming out and saying they're not going to run against Bush. Who's going to run? Paul Tsongas? That twerp?

Dan Quayle and his people have reported that conservatives in the party are becoming increasingly unglued. They were already outraged by the 1990 budget deal. They're up in arms about the signing of the Civil Rights Act. Their representatives in Congress, especially Newt Gingrich, want the president to keep Congress in session after Election Day and not let the members go home until they pass legislation Bush wants—they want him to treat the economic situation like a political crisis and try to score some political and economic points with it.

The conservatives? Sununu snorts. Where can *they* go? Are *they* going to vote Democrat?

Well, there is talk that Jack Kemp might resign from HUD and run in New Hampshire. Failing that, there is every indication that pundit Patrick J. Buchanan is going to run.

Buchanan? Sununu groans. He's a TV performer! He's never run a race in his life! This is all a joke. It's going to blow over.

Blow over like the storm at Walker's Point?

TWO:

THE WEST WING COCOON, OR, MEETING WITHOUT END, AMEN

The West Wing is the setting of countless works of fiction and non-fiction that reveal the supposedly shocking inside stories of Washington power betrayed and misused: decisions to lie to Congress, agreements to tap the phones of unsuspecting minor officials, astrological interference in the making of policy, and other high crimes and misdemeanors. The factoid-drenched anecdotes that begin these works—called "nuclear tips" by promotion-minded New York publishers looking for explosive scoops that will launch the books into top spots on the best-seller list—inevitably begin as follows:

At 7:53 Monday morning, July 22, deputy national security adviser [fill in name] strode purposefully down the hall of the West Wing's first floor into national security adviser [fill in name]'s office seven feet, three inches from his door. *Well, this is it,* he thought. He was so preoccupied he barely had time to wish his customary "Good morning" to the chief of staff's secretary, [Kathy, or Cathy—all White House secretaries seem to be named Kathy]. *The old man is going to blow,* she thought.

It had taken him several sleepless nights to make his decision. He went over it again and again. *He has to be told,* he thought. *The president must know.*

His tosses and turns had awakened his wife, [Nancy, or Brenda, or Alice], fifty-one, at 3:23 A.M. in their four-bedroom, two-and-a-half-bathroom McLean home, which they had purchased in 1967 for $32,000. *I hope everything is all right,* she thought. Down the hall slept their children, [Carrie, or Melissa, or Kristen], nineteen, a sophomore at [Brown or Wesleyan or William and Mary] with a major in political science and a minor in theater and [Scott or Kevin or Chip], fifteen, who his father hoped would follow in his footsteps and go to the Academy after high school. Neither child was thinking anything at the time; they were dreaming the dreams of the innocent.

Once the decision was made, he had no doubts or fears. He threw open the door. Inside, the national security adviser was huddled with [fill in appropriately WASPy name complete with nickname, such as A. James "Buddy" Cantrell], the director of central intelligence. He looked up. *Nobody barges into my office,* he thought. "Excuse me," he said loudly.

"It's over," the deputy national security adviser said. "I'm going to tell him."

"Don't you understand? *The president already knows.*"

The deputy couldn't believe what he was hearing. Surely it couldn't be true. "What?" he said.

"He's always known."

Oh, God, no, he thought. It all made sense. The president had always known. The time was 7:54:36—the moment this fifty-three-year-old man realized he had not lost his innocence charging Heartbreak Ridge during the Korean War. He had had a trace of it left. Now that, too, was gone.

The problem with these accounts is not that they exaggerate the passion of staffers in times of crisis, but that they give readers the entirely mistaken impression that this sort of thing goes on in the West Wing only when the very fate of the nation is at stake. In fact, the same feverish passion is spent with equal force every day of the week on just about everything.

West Wingers live at a level of intensity most other people achieve for only for a minute or so, during sex, say, or a really feverish racquetball volley. It begins from the moment they show up in the office in the morning—when, in winter, it is pitch-black out or, in summer, the sun is just coming over the horizon—and lasts until the moment they leave—again, in either the summer gloaming or the winter dark. They get into their cars, all parked at a 115-degree angle to the sidewalks of West Exec, pick up the phones installed therein and further discuss the day's obsessions journeying across the Potomac and west on Route 50 or along Connecticut and Massachusetts avenues northwest toward Maryland. The conversations continue until they pull into the driveways of their homes, where they sit for a couple of minutes inside the still-running autos as they wrap things up.

At last they go inside to say hello to their families, whereupon the telephone rings. The nasal voice on the other end of the phone belongs to the White House operator, who reports that Governor Sununu is on the line, or Mr. Skinner, or deputy chief of staff Andy Card. The White House operator is part of the remarkable secretarial service at the beck and call of all staffers; all any of them has to do is dial 202-456-1414 from any phone in the world and give the woman who answers with the words "White House" the name of someone somewhere on the planet he wishes to reach. Usually it will be another White House staffer or government official, but not necessarily. Thereupon the operator, who is employed by the legendarily efficient White House Communications Agency (known as WHCA, or "wocka"), will get the job done. She will ring people at home, leave a message, try the car, send a signal over a beeper, even track somebody down in a restaurant in another city or in another country. Even more impressive, senior staffers have special phone lines installed in their houses by the Signal Corps, which handles military communications. A "Signal drop" is a sure sign of status, especially since it gives those staffers who never served in the military the delightful experience of being called "sir" by the corpsmen who serve as the operators.

With the White House operator or Signal to work for him at night and a secretary or two during the day, a West Winger does not carry an address book, nor does he or she know a phone number. The White House operator is the true voice of the West Wing—the voice reminding the staffer that no matter the time, no matter the circumstances of his private life, he is on call twenty-four hours a day, seven days a week, to tend to the bottomless needs of the White House. Even when those needs are as apparently insignificant as determining the best way to respond to an unfavorable news story, how to fill a vacancy on one of the government's hundreds of advisory boards, or even the proper way to type up a memo or a fact sheet.

On very rare occasions, especially when the military might be put in harm's way, the decisions made in the West Wing deserve the hysterical attention they receive. These are the moments presidential biographers love to call "the burdens of leadership," conjuring up images of Lincoln murmuring "I cannot bear it" upon hearing of Union casualties in Fredericksburg. But like so many serious and studious words spoken and written about Washington, they are dead wrong.

Making life-and-death decisions is what politicians and their parasites crave. If, in the case of the military, they choose not to act, presidents and their aides celebrate their own restraint and the untold American lives they have saved. If, on the other hand, they choose to send in the troops, they have the cool thrill that comes from making a Very Big Call.

Politicians, like gamblers, need Action, presidents most of all. Presidents eat rubber chicken at a million luncheons and dinners, have boring conversations with untold numbers of rich people, smile sixteen hours a day and subject their wives and children and their psyches to a kind of scrutiny that would kill any sensible being just to get some.

The Action is one of the reasons presidents tend to focus on foreign affairs. The president of the United States doth bestride the narrow world like a Colossus. Even if he himself often feels hamstrung by congressional usurpations of his authority, in the eyes of foreigners he is an almost mystical figure, chosen as so few of them are in a national plebiscite and in charge of the most awesome military machine the world has ever seen. And, as Mel Brooks said, it's good to be the king.

Abroad are instability and danger and mass murder. There are always arms and economic treaties to consider. There is always somebody who thinks American troops should be sent into combat somewhere. And when all else fails, there is the Middle East, the swamp that mires all presidents given to the fantasy that they can in a few months' time solve problems that have been thousands of years in the making.

Whereas at home, things tend to run themselves even when the nation is in a rut. The president can't actually do all that much to help. Dealing with domestic issues is a mostly mundane task, involving tortuous negotiations with hundreds of fellow politicians and interest groups, and no matter what position you take, somebody is going to be really pissed off. There is little pleasure in this aspect of the job, and presidents are no different from anybody else: They try to avoid the pain and go for the fun. And who in their retinue of servants and hangers-on is going to gainsay them?

The mundane is what presidents abhor. Thus every West Winger must take what he does with a humorless earnestness bordering on the religious. And anyway, why should assistant to the president for national security affairs Brent Scowcroft have all the fun, making recommendations about what to blow up and when? Every other assistant to the president has a task to fulfill too, a staff to manage, and responsibilities to meet, and every one comes to believe that without his own crack work on the job, not only would the presidency be destroyed but the nation as we know it might cease to exist.

Sometimes staffers demonstrate the importance of their office by flexing bureaucratic muscles. When James Cicconi was staff secretary he proudly held up for three months some minor treaty the State Department had spent thirty years negotiating because he was a lawyer by training and was troubled by some of the "whereases" and "thereins" therein.

At other times staffers would insert themselves into policy and/or political matters over which they had no say but felt they should and because they had the bureaucratic weight to make their influence felt. Gregg Petersmeyer ran what happened to be the single least important division in the White House: the Office of National Service, more commonly known as the Thousand Points of Light. He got his job the old-fashioned way: He was rich, he was a boyhood friend of Bush son

Neil and he knew absolutely nothing about national service. He did have absolute loyalty bordering on the fanatic to George Bush, however, and when the president's political fortunes began to sag in early 1992, he took it upon himself to rally the White House staff. He sat down at a computer and came up with a very complicated gridlike document illustrating what he believed were all the accomplishments of the Bush presidency, as if oblivious of the fact that both a press office and a communications office already existed to do such things. Not to mention the fact that two blocks away, over on Fifteenth Street, there was a staff of one hundred people trying to figure out just how in hell to get Bush reelected. Petersmeyer had his grid, and the communications and speechwriting staff was compelled to hear all about it.

The staff gathered for Petersmeyer's exegesis of his grid—all the people in the White House who might reasonably be expected to know all about the president's achievements, since they were responsible for his talking about them endlessly on the campaign trail. At the end of his briefing, Petersmeyer looked up and said: "I have known George Bush since I was thirteen years old. He's like a second father to me. And my friends, our president is in trouble. We must help our president." Opinion is divided about whether tears actually formed in his eyes, but there is unanimity about the catch in his throat as he spoke.

"Helping the president" was what people in the White House, and particularly in the West Wing, did. Every decision was discussed in terms of whether it would be good or bad for the president himself, whether it would help him or hurt him, what it might do to his poll numbers.

For the West Wingers, it was a given that what was good for the president was not only good for them, but good for America as well. They saw almost no distinction between the two, which created a spiritual crisis in the West Wing when the ill winds began to blow. The nation that had liked George Bush—the America between January 1989 and August 1991—was, they believed, a country in good health. Surely it would understand that the recession was a passing thing about which a president could do little; surely the people looked to him as the magnificent world leader who had saved the world from Communism and had trounced Saddam Hussein. But when it became clear in the West Wing that America didn't see things that way, staffers derided the nation as angst-ridden, nutty, crazy, in the thrall of a liberal media, desirous of change for change's sake. The one word they didn't use, because Jimmy Carter had used it when *he* got into trouble, was "malaise," but they sure thought it.

And maybe, just maybe, in the end America was not as good and moral a place as it had been four years earlier. Maybe the rejection of George Bush was a sign that the liberals had been right after all—that America *was* in decline.

On Election Eve, George Bush called a senior aide from his room at the Houstonian Hotel, where he was having a drink with his favorite general, Brent Scowcroft. (Being a Mormon, Scowcroft was probably having orange juice.) "Brent and I were just talking," Bush said, "and we figure we've done all we can, and if things don't go well tomorrow, well then, the people out there just want a new generation of leaders and they just don't care about those old World War II virtues of trust and faith and patriotism that Brent and I stand for."

Aside from what it says about the state of Bush's humility on the eve of his greatest humiliation, this story is about what happens to a politician who spends his presidency happily wrapped in a West Wing cocoon made of people who generally adored him and thought of little else but him and his standing. The cocoon was impervious to the changes in the American political atmosphere during the final eighteen months of his ascendancy. Only an election could shatter it.

When a recession hits, a businessman will know it almost from its inception. If he owns a store, he will find himself selling fewer and fewer items at lower and lower prices. If he is a manufacturer, his customers will stop ordering goods from him. If he works in the service sector, his phone will stop ringing.

But the president of the United States, living in the West Wing cocoon, cannot tell the difference between one day and the next, between a day when his poll numbers are at 90 percent and a day when they are at 30 percent. He will certainly attend meetings at which the worrisome change in climate is discussed, but he will not be able to *feel* the difference. If he is George Bush, he will still have an hour of paperwork to do before his 8:00 A.M. intelligence briefing, the hour in which he dashes off the dozens of handwritten notes that are his stock-in-trade and signs the documents that require a president's signature. His time will still be doled out to visitors by his scheduler, Kathy Super, and his secretary, Patty Presock, in five-minute intervals. The people who meet with him will still be dazzled to be in the Oval Office, still concerned about his good opinion, and if the president asks how it looks out there, they will pull their punches.

When he slips out the side door of the Oval Office of an afternoon, the 150 civilians carefully selected by the Office of Public Liaison who come to hear him deliver boilerplate remarks about National Hispanic Heritage Month or the Excellence in Government Awards—the speeches known in White House lingo as "Rose Garden bullshit"—will always laugh at the jokes and applaud very loudly.

When he travels, he will ride in the same limousine, whose darkened windows do not afford him a good view of the surroundings. It wouldn't matter, anyway, since the Secret Service shuts all traffic down when the president travels.[1] He never opens a door for himself. He never drives, except a golf cart or a motorboat or a horse.

The West Wing cocoon removes a president so far from any semblance of a normal life that he loses the most important asset a successful politician has—his connection to the people who elected him. A congressman, a senator, a governor can tell how he is doing because he still does retail politics and can feel it in the hands he shakes and the conversations he has. A president becomes progressively more tone deaf; he cannot hear the music of the masses.

---

[1] When I took a trip with Ronald Reagan on *Air Force One* in 1988, we arrived at the Cincinnati airport ten miles east of the city in Kentucky at 5:00 P.M. Rush hour. And the highway between the airport and the city was shut down. In both directions. So that we could drive into Cincinnati *going the wrong way*. God only knows how many thousands of people were inconvenienced so that the Secret Service could pull off its favorite kind of security—"total geographic control." And I am sure that Reagan had no idea we were going the wrong way down a six-lane highway at rush hour. And I am sure Bush had no idea when it was done for him.

The West Wing cocoon explains, among other things, Ronald Reagan's failure to understand how serious a political blunder he had made in trading arms for hostages. And in George Bush's case, it explains why he stood by as the recession double-dipped in the fall of 1991 and did nothing—the act of omission that almost certainly cost him his reelection.

To be sure, in those critical months in 1991 stories were hitting the front page of *The Washington Post* about conservative proposals to keep Congress in Washington through the Thanksgiving and Christmas recesses for an emergency session to pass "growth" legislation. But those were voices allied with Bush's least favorite member of the cabinet, Jack Kemp (least favorite since the departure of his real least favorite, Labor Secretary Elizabeth Dole, wife of his bitter rival Bob). For all he knew—and the Evans and Novak column was certainly pushing the idea—Kemp might even bolt the cabinet and run against him in New Hampshire. So that took care of Kemp and his growth agenda. Anyway, when his closest economic advisers came to see him in the Oval Office—his best friend, Nicholas Brady, over at Treasury; his OMB director, Richard Darman; his chief of staff, John Sununu—they told him that it was all a tempest in a teapot, that if the administration did anything it would get in the way of a recovery, and besides, Senate majority leader George Mitchell would embarrass him by making it impossible for the necessary legislation to pass in an acceptable form.

Since the economic experts were so convinced, the only outside evidence he could rely on were those newspaper stories and the poll numbers. Polling, like astrology, is a wonderful thing because its users can either choose to believe that the numbers reflect a deeply held American conviction (a temptation often given into when the numbers are really, really good) or decide that they don't really describe anything but a momentary spasm (especially when they say something their subject does not wish to hear).

And as for news stories: For eight years Reaganites did nothing but complain that the liberal media were out to get the administration because of its revolutionary conservative approach to things. In its dark days, the Bush administration talked even more incessantly about media bias, but it had more than liberal bias to worry about. The conservative press was not exactly friendly to the president either. Bush felt especially oppressed by *The Wall Street Journal*'s editorial page and its Washington columnist, Paul Gigot, and John Sununu once upbraided White House counsel Boyden Gray for cooperating with Gigot.

How could George Bush really know just how very unhappy America was feeling? After all, *he* loved *his* job, and without question every single person who worked in a senior position at the White House absolutely adored his. This is true of all administrations; there is no group of employees more contented in the world, even when things are going badly. The proof? Nobody ever quits in disgust. Nobody. In fact, the *only* person to quit in disgust during the entire Bush administration was a lower-level foreign-service officer named George Kenney, who was unhappy with the State Department's Yugoslavia policy.

And certainly never does anybody walk away from the West Wing, in this administration or any other. West Wingers let go when their jobs are pried loose from their cold, dead fingers. On one of those extraordinarily rare occasions when a West Winger was fired during the Bush years, he never saw the writing on the wall, even if he was reading the writing printed in the pages of *The Washington Post;* both John Sununu and Samuel Skinner endured months of cruel leaks and invective before they were finally pushed out the door. And even then, underlings reported that they were surprised.

Political staffers who have made it to the West Wing have achieved a rare condition of soul: They do not wish to be anybody else, do not wish to be anywhere else. This is as good as it gets for people in politics who do not have it in them to run for public office and hold power in their own grasp. Real proximity to real power produces a special high, one made up of equal parts self-gratulation (I have finally made it) and anxiety (they'll figure out I'm really an incompetent nobody and come and take it all away). If parasites could fear, this is what their fear would be: expulsion from the host.

This might sound pretty awful, but people who reach this West Wing level are, generally speaking, not especially reflective. Washington ambition discourages reflection. If presidents and congressmen had it in them to do even minimal soul-searching about the compromises they were making, had to figure out whether what they were doing was for the common good or for their own personal good, the conundrums of conscience would make them ineffective and indecisive.

The same capacity for deliberately unenlightened self-interest characterizes just about everybody else involved in American politics. Just as politicians live for power—and after all, even the best of them are in it for the power, because they, too, need it to fulfill their special sense of mission—their parasites crave its proximity.

What does it get them? Aside from the chance to affect and indirectly control the lives of their fellow Americans and the fate of faraway countries of which we know little, it gets them recognition and respect, and certain psychic perks unattainable anywhere else. The trade-off and the reward are identical: total absorption in their work to the exclusion of most everything else.

That is evident from the punishing nature of the West Wing workday. The first official meeting of the day is the 7:30 A.M. senior staff meeting, at which attendance is *de rigueur* unless a senior staffer is out of town, in which case he is expected to send his top aide to sit in for him and hold his chair. At 8:00 the president gets his briefing on the state of the world, and he usually spends the rest of the hour cloistered with his chief of staff and whatever aides are necessary getting ready for the day ahead.

Every sensible Bush West Winger was in his office by 7:00 A.M., and usually fifteen to thirty minutes earlier. The hour between 6:30 and 7:30 was the only informal time in the day; once 8:00 A.M. rolled around the phone began to ring and never ceased. From then on, the day progressed with dizzying speed, and a senior staffer knew where he was going and what he was doing only because his scheduler gave him an index card that fit neatly into his breast pocket (there it is again, a use for the breast pocket). It listed the dozen obligations of the day before he could cut out, usually around 8:00 P.M.

As a rule, a senior staffer had both a secretary and a scheduler; few senior staffers could actually do something as complicated as setting up their own meetings. A senior staffer's wife often had to consult with a scheduler if she wanted to arrange a dinner party in her own home.

The staffer who arrived with the dawn could get a minute of John Sununu's or Sam Skinner's time to get the chief of staff to make a small decision he would otherwise have no time to get to. Sununu and Skinner would always be at their best and most cheerful right about then, their most accessible, their most pliable. And if a staffer was lucky enough, he might find himself part of Sununu's premeeting meeting in his office, where he breezily shot the shit with Darman, his chief aides, Andy Card and Ed Rogers, and maybe one or two others.

Dawn was the time that staffers got to know one another, exchanged what sparse gossip they knew about their own personal lives and began the White House's favorite game: the Leak Hunt. A staffer's main (unofficial) duty was to familiarize himself with the contents of the day's stories involving the White House in four newspapers— *The New York Times, The Washington Post, The Wall Street Journal* and *The Washington Times.* Every senior staffer was obsessed with the work of the reporters on the White House beat, especially the reliably bitchy Ann Devroy of *The Washington Post,* whose stories were rarely if ever concerned with policy and were almost always about personality conflicts and procedural mistakes in the West Wing.

Those stories were the focus of intense, Talmudic, almost pathological scrutiny. Which "senior administration official" described the president as "disengaged"? Goddamn it, whoever it was should be kicked right out the goddamn door, excuse the French! Was the source a White House staffer? Could be anybody in the administration. Perhaps it was someone in the cabinet. But every cabinet department had its own reporter; wouldn't a cabinet member or one of his aides feed their own press guys instead of Ann Devroy? No, it had to come from inside.

Okay, inside the White House then. Did the story have even a remotely conservative spin? Well, then, six to five it was Bill Kristol.

Was it a story with an economic focus? Figure on Dick Darman or his right-hand men, Tom Scully and Bob Grady, the Darmaniacs. Did the story bash Jim Baker? Look to his rival, counsel C. Boyden Gray.

Those in the president's or the chief of staff's favor were rarely the subjects of the Leak Hunt, on the highly dubious grounds that the teacher's pet doesn't put a razor blade in the apple. Certainly, there were officials who favored particular reporters. Evans and Novak channeled Sununu. Kristol was tight with *The New Republic*'s Fred Barnes, a fact the ethical Barnes made subtly clear in his stories. Darman favored Keith Schneider of *The New York Times*.

Bush loathed the practice of leaking with the passion of a man who had once been director of central intelligence. This attitude represented a major break with the previous regime. While the Reagan administration made a big show of its disgust at leaks, everybody in town knew that the key leaker in the first Reagan term was the chief of staff himself, James Baker. Reagan's people had raised the leak to an art form. They used leaks strategically, to advance the White House agenda, float possible policy initiatives, and hint to personnel in disfavor that it was time for them to go.

Despite its sometime usefulness, Bush really wanted to put an end to the practice lock, stock and barrel. He signaled the seriousness of his intent during the 1988 transition when he informed a longtime friend and aide that she would not be given a job in the administration because she had had unauthorized conversations with reporters. The example terrified White House staffers, and with the exception of the focused and controlled leaking campaigns against John Sununu and subsequently Sam Skinner, Bush mostly got his wish. It was rare, at least in the first two years, for policy disputes between the members of his senior staff to get a public airing. This was due in part to Ed Rogers, John Sununu's assistant, who was official Leak Inquisitor—if a staffer was told by his secretary that Ed Rogers was on the line, it would fill him with fear and trembling.

But more important than the Inquisition was the fact that so few officials were involved in determining policy, and those who were involved talked very little. In foreign affairs, Bush and Scowcroft and Scowcroft's deputy, Robert Gates, handled literally everything, and the rest of the National Security Council staff basically had nothing to do. In domestic affairs, Sununu and Darman and their trusted aides were the loop, and though Darman had been Leak Central during his years as Reagan's staff secretary, he kept himself mostly in check in the Bush White House.

As a result, the lion's share of the leaks were ill informed, at times dead wrong, and mostly small beer. The Bush leakers did the White House no damage—as opposed to the Reagan leakers, who loved to talk about controversies that would become major public-relations problems for the White House the minute they were published.

Bush's leak control was a major managerial success in one sense: He got hold of a problem that had been out of control in previous administrations and fixed it. Unfortunately for him, though, in the end the antileaking stance proved a colossal mistake. It was one of the reasons the American people believed the Bush administration had no domestic policy, which it most certainly did. But the president's people were robbed of the only surefire way to get the word out.

The Reagan team had perfected a method of getting their proposals and ideas in the news: They leaked them first, generally the day before the president was going to announce them. This strategy was beneficial in two ways. First, it was easier to get a story on the front page of *The Washington Post* or *The New York Times* by leaking it, because a leaked story has a luster that a mere report on a speech or a press conference doesn't have.[2]

Second, the leaked story served notice on other Washington reporters that something big, something they really should cover, was going to happen the next day. As a result, anything new coming out of the Reagan administration had at least two solid days of news coverage. And once something is in the papers or on television for two days, it will be there, on and off, for two years.

---

[2] Publishing a leak attributed to mysterious officials high up in the administration is part of the laughable attitude of White House reporters that they are engaged in old-fashioned, shoe-leather news gathering when in fact their biggest stories are spoon-fed to them by sources who have their numbers programmed into their voice-recognition car phones. "Name, please," says the disembodied computer voice of the phone. "Ann Devroy," says the staffer. "One moment, please," says the voice.

But in the leak-shy Bush West Wing it had been decreed that all White House news was going to be made by the president and the president alone. The press and the public would hear about administration innovations when the president spoke about them. Unfortunately for the president, that might be in some piece of "Rose Garden bullshit" the press corps didn't even bother to attend. And the speech would often be so uninspiring, and the president's delivery so distracted and lacking in enthusiasm, that there was little to quote and even less to show on television.

One very minor, but suggestive, case in point took place in October 1992. For a year, White House lawyers and a young policy aide named Jay Lefkowitz had been working on a simple proposal to reform the auto-insurance system, whose costs have been spiraling out of control in heavily urban states like New Jersey. It was one of the few White House plans pitched toward lower-middle-class consumers, and involved an average savings in New Jersey of $800 a year.

The idea languished in the White House version of what Hollywood types call "development hell"; it was always in the works, but never quite approved. Finally, chief of staff James Baker gave the go-ahead for its inclusion in a presidential speech in New Jersey on October 16.

Lefkowitz was, however, specifically enjoined from playing the strategic leaking game on the grounds that the president and only the president should announce his administration's initiatives. The speech was to be given on a Friday afternoon in New Jersey, and only on *Air Force One* about an hour before the speech was Lefkowitz allowed to brief reporters about the auto insurance plan—the briefing attributed only to "an administration official," since of course the ozone layer would melt if background briefings of this sort were actually given on the record and the briefer publicly identified.

The reform proposal was exactly the sort of thing that needed a leak to launch it, as its sad denouement reveals: As Bush got up to speak, some college kids began to heckle him. The president told the hecklers to sit down and shut up, and when they failed to do so, he complained to the crowd that "these draft dodgers" wouldn't let him finish.

That was it. The network newscasts had a field day with the

footage of the flustered president; the newspapers the next morning talked about how the president was spinning out of control. And a year's worth of work on auto-insurance reform was buried.

Lefkowitz did not disobey the antileak rule because he had already been a victim of it. In May 1992, a story by Fred Barnes about the workings of the Skinner White House appeared in *The New Republic*. It began with an anecdote: Lefkowitz runs into Skinner on West Exec. Skinner says, "Hey, Jay, what's up?" Lefkowitz tells him he's been working on a cause dear to conservatives—implementing a Supreme Court ruling that it was unconstitutional for unions to compel their members to contribute to political campaigns through the use of mandatory union dues. The decision had come down in 1988, but the White House had made nothing of it. Lefkowitz would like to get the president to publicly direct the Labor Department to comply with the decision.

"Great idea," Skinner says. "Follow me." He leads Lefkowitz to the keeper of Bush's schedule, Kathy Super, and says, "Jay here has a great idea for an event for this week about the *Beck* decision. Let's put it on."

Barnes wrote the story in a way that flattered Skinner—he was willing to make quick decisions, go with his instincts, be a can-do kind of guy. But farther down in the text, the story contrasted Skinner's quick yes with the temporizing way his policy aide, Clayton Yeutter, had been handling it for months. Yeutter was furious; he wrote a memo to Lefkowitz's boss, cabinet secretary Ede Holiday, informing her that "this petty leaking does the president no good." Later that week, Yeutter got Skinner to deny Holiday's request that Lefkowitz be given a commission and promoted to special assistant to the president.

Nor was that all Lefkowitz would have to suffer. On the day the article appeared, a *samizdat* parody of it began to circulate around the OEOB that began: "In 1787, Alexander Hamilton was crossing the green in front of the Philadelphia Assembly when he ran into Jay Lefkowitz, a bright young policy aide. 'Hey, Jay, what's up?' Hamilton said. 'I'm working on this idea I have for a constitution.'

" 'Great,' said Hamilton. 'Follow me.' " And the parody went on

with Lefkowitz talking Abraham Lincoln into the Emancipation Proc-
lamation, convincing Teddy Roosevelt to storm San Juan Hill, and so
on.

The authors of the parody—fellow midlevel staffers J. French Hill
and Todd Buchholz—were merely reflecting how deep the animosity
toward leaks and leakers ran. The irony was that Lefkowitz had not
been the leaker; rather, he had told the story to a couple of people
who in turn had relayed it to Barnes. No matter. Lefkowitz got the
blame.

But the truly obsessed Leak Hunter was not Sununu, not Yeutter:
It was the president himself. He went so far as to call reporters and
tell them to warn their sources that their president was on to them.
Bush had Sununu call *The Wall Street Journal*'s Paul Gigot several
times to complain that his conservative sources within the White
House didn't know what the hell they were talking about and started
throwing names around—clearly assuming Gigot would carry his
message back.

And when a cable from EPA administrator William Reilly during the
1992 Rio summit on the environment was leaked to *The New York
Times*'s Keith Schneider by someone Schneider described as an antagonist of Reilly's, Bush went on a tear. He ordered an investigation
of all outgoing White House phone calls and selected his favorite
suspect, David Mcintosh, a member of Dan Quayle's staff. On a
Saturday morning from Camp David, the president called Quayle and
began reading from the logs: At 4:09 Tuesday afternoon the staffer
had called Keith Schneider's office, and he'd better have a damn good
explanation. The staffer did; he said he had merely been returning a
call from the reporter. Maybe he was telling the truth; maybe he
wasn't; but after nearly twelve years in the White House George
Bush should have known that it is nearly impossible to pin down the
source of a leak.

And so it all blew over.

The Leak Hunt completed for the morning, and the informal business
taken care of, the West Wingers filed into the Roosevelt Room for
the 7:30 senior staff meeting. The Roosevelt Room is a handsome

space filled with memorabilia and paintings of the two Presidents Roosevelt—the Republican, Teddy, and the Democrat, Franklin. In Republican administrations, the painting of Teddy on horseback is given pride of place at the head of the conference table, while the portrait of Franklin is less prominent, on a side wall. In Democratic administrations, the positions are reversed.

Members of senior staff who were present sat at the table; others who had been deputized to represent their offices sat in chairs behind them.[3] There was one exception to the rule: National security adviser Brent Scowcroft always sat on a couch against the wall. But since Scowcroft was the president's closest ally in the West Wing, he could have seated himself anywhere he wanted to.

In theory, the purpose of the staff meeting was for its attendees to inform their colleagues on their activities and be informed in turn. That should have permitted some open discussion of administration policy, but in practice there was nothing of the sort. Under Sununu, Skinner and finally James Baker, the people around the table became practiced in the art of self-censorship, although for different reasons.

When Sununu was chief of staff, a strange form of public humiliation was practiced in the Roosevelt Room, as part of his overall strategy to maintain complete dominion over administration policy with the collaboration of his most trusted adviser, Richard Darman. Sununu sat at the head of the table and Darman at the foot, and the meetings were often merely games of verbal Ping-Pong between them, with the rest of senior staff serving as spectators.

And though Sununu was known throughout Washington for his spasms of temper, in the meetings he did not play his own bad cop. Darman did. Brilliant, witty and extraordinarily uncouth, Darman would demolish the contributions of other senior staffers—especially in his field of government spending and budget—hapless enough to

---

[3] Being "at the table" is a very big deal in Washington. In televised footage of meetings of the Bush cabinet, it was easy to tell just how important it was to be a designated member of the cabinet because you could see, clear as day right behind those who were "at the table," all the people who weren't among them. You could see drug czar William J. Bennett, who had been at the table as secretary of education in the Reagan years, cooling his heels behind Lauro Cavazos. It looked like a kind of staffer apartheid.

step anywhere near his turf. When called upon by Sununu at the beginning of a meeting, Darman rarely spoke. He usually saved his denunciations of others until after they had spoken their piece, using terms of abuse in a remarkably personal manner. This form of bureaucratic terrorism was called "being Darmanized," and perhaps its most remarkable expression came one morning in late 1989. Roger Porter, the domestic policy adviser, had given a nondescript speech on a trade issue the previous day. With Porter at his left hand, Darman said, "I would like to call everyone's attention to one of the *stupidest* things I have ever read," and proceeded to read from the text of Porter's speech without identifying its author. Darman finished by saying, "Whoever wrote this is a complete moron." Many at the table knew whom Darman was assaulting, and Porter's wimpish pallor gave the others an easy clue to his identity.

Sununu sat and said nothing.

"Stupid" and "moron" were just two of the words other staffers remember Darman using. Others were "ill-informed," "preposterous," "mindless," "impossible," "childish" and "naive."

Chances are, given the quality of the Bush West Wingers generally and the stunningly unimaginative Porter in particular, that Darman was right most of the time. It was not his conclusions that perturbed his colleagues; it was the violence of his *ad hominem* attacks. Yet despite press accounts about the president's and Sununu's insistence on collegiality in the White House, Sununu never upbraided Darman for his conduct. And so West Wingers understood that Darman was acting either at the behest of Sununu or with at least his tacit approval. They took the hint, and shut up.

At times, the two men turned the staff meeting into their own private comedy competition, since both men considered themselves wits and punsters (even though the latter is the lowest form of the former). In September 1990, one meeting turned to a discussion of deputy assistant James Pinkerton's policy concept, "the New Paradigm." Darman was suspicious of the idea and said, apropos of nothing, "All I can think of when I hear that is 'Brother, Can You Paradigm?' " (It was a line he was later to use in a speech that caused an enormous controversy within Republican ranks.) Upon hearing this, Sununu sat up straight in his chair at the head of the table, and for ten minutes, as the discussion continued, he was uncustomarily distracted. And then, as some assistant began droning on about the issue of maritime reform, he suddenly erupted with: "Here's a song title for you: 'What a Difference a *K* Makes: The Story of Jim Baker.' "

Get it? Neither did the people at the table. So Sununu had to explain that if Jim Baker's name had been spelled with an extra *k*, he would have been Jim Bakker, the evangelist.

Oh. Ah ha ha ha.

And thus did the two men who considered themselves the brightest and ablest people in the government spend some of their quality time with their fellow staffers. The end result was that at the meeting where the president's top advisers gathered to consider what counsel to give him, aides did not feel free, and were not free, to discuss, dissent from or make recommendations on policy.

When Skinner became chief of staff in December 1991, he was determined to end the reign of terror, but one of the unfortunate consequences was that he and everyone else descended into morning staff meeting purgatory. Suddenly people who had been silent in the Sununu years would start talking and never stop. Minor White House aides were dominating the meeting while the genuinely powerful ones (Darman especially) would sit in silence.

Science adviser D. Allan Bromley, universally considered the Official White House Bore, would talk for five minutes about how the General Services Administration was determined to move the National Science Foundation to a new building in northern Virginia and how this was a disaster for the president as the scientific community would take the move out of D.C. as evidence that the administration was not serious about science. Or Gregg Petersmeyer would go into more detail than anybody but Mother Teresa might want to hear about Point of Light Number 682.

Presently, instead of the hostile censorship of the Sununu years, there was the smiley-face, have-a-nice-day censorship of Campaign 1992. Bob Teeter and Fred Malek, the campaign chiefs, began coming to the meeting. Malek, who had been a CEO and therefore had read all kinds of management books and been to many management seminars, invariably reported that a campaign event had just gone wonderfully and all thanks and praise was due to speechwriting and Public Liaison for doing just a heck of a good job getting those retarded kids and their families into Room 450.

Deputy chief of staff Henson Moore would add his praise for something or other. Skinner and Yeutter would follow suit. And as the president's poll numbers refused to rise, Skinner gave almost daily reminders to the staff that the president was completely confident of his eventual victory, that he knew what he was doing, and that while Skinner and the president understood the anxieties of the White House staff, they should be cheerful. Everything was fine. No, everything was better than fine. And no complaining.

There was, said one senior staffer, an "easy totalitarianism" practiced at these meetings, and that was never clearer than on the morning of June 16, 1992. The president had just gotten back from his disastrous trip to Panama—where he got a dose of tear gas aimed at protesters—and the Rio summit. At the Rio summit, where the United States was discussed as though it were Nazi Germany on a bad day, the president had had to submit to the indignity of sitting on a platform while the last Stalinist on the face of the earth, Mr. Fidel Castro, made one of his stem-winding speeches about Yankee imperialism.

Bush's press secretary, Marlin Fitzwater, asked Skinner what he should say at the 9:30 briefing for the press about the president's journey abroad. Fitzwater's efforts to cast the previous week's activities in a good light had proved inadvertently comic: "It's been a very good trip, with the exception of the tear gas," he said upon leaving Panama. Clearly, he was a man in need of help.

Well, said Skinner, contrary to what the press had to say, the trip to Panama *was* a great success. The Secret Service did a terrific job, and he and the president would like to take this opportunity to thank the service for their excellent work down there. And as for Rio: Many people felt constrained from saying so in public, but in private they agreed that the president had said many important things in his speech about the need for economic growth and the need for everybody to plant lots of trees. And you know what? Those people in Rio were hypocrites; I mean, Fidel Castro got a standing ovation from them. And there were Jane Fonda and Bianca Jagger, standing cheek by jowl—applauding for a Communist!

Michael Deland, head of the president's Council on Environmental Quality, said it was really unfair that the organizers of the conference had made the president sit through Castro's speech.

Whereupon Connie Horner, head of presidential personnel, asked: "Why did that happen?"

"Well," said Deland, "they changed the agenda at the last minute and Bush spoke in John Major's place on the same program as Castro."

"Why," Horner wanted to know, "did we allow that to happen?"

"State knew about it," said Scowcroft, "and they didn't want to make a big stink over it. The conference was controversial enough as it was."

"But that meant the president of the United States had to sit meekly by and listen to our nation's sworn enemy Fidel Castro speak and receive a standing ovation. Doesn't this indicate that this was a corrupt conference? That perhaps it was more about America-bashing than the environment? We shouldn't be running away from it, we should be discrediting it," said Horner.

The tension level in the Roosevelt Room rose; this was the first interesting discussion in at least a month. So Skinner shut Horner up: "Connie has a good point," he said. "Let's talk about it later."

"Later" never came, needless to say. Those who, like the Ancient Mariner, had commenced to stoppeth one of three in the hallways saying, "Jesus Christ, we need to do something, something must be done, we're going down in flames," were being told they were bad campers who didn't play well with the other children. And so the meetings continued with discussions of maritime reform and a speech before the National Hosiery Manufacturers Association about our really exciting job-training package and a hearty congratulations to Bitsy Stewart in the correspondence unit because her cat had had a successful spaying.

When James Baker was brought over from the State Department

to be chief of staff at the end of August 1992, the senior staff meetings were usually chaired by his chief deputy, Bob Zoellick. Zoellick was a pallid and awkward man who had moved with his boss from the State Department with enormous resentment and let everybody around him know it every second of every minute of every day. He used the meetings to bark orders to a staff that, having been told only two months ago what a terrific job they were all doing, was now considered wildly incompetent.

The vaunted new Baker team—Zoellick and Margaret Tutwiler and Dennis Ross and Janet Mullins—had been rushed in, along with their boss, to save Bush from a looming electoral disaster, but they refused even to dine in proximity to the senior staff. They took over the wardroom, the private dining area of the Mess, for breakfast and lunch and plotted and strategized among themselves. Baker, with his customary warmth, had the couch removed from the chief of staff's waiting room so that nobody would hang around hoping to see him. And this team's highly regarded management skills led to the administration's final domestic triumph, the scandal over the illicit search of Bill Clinton's passport file.

These three chiefs of staff and all the assorted West Wingers were dedicated men and women who labored mightily and to the best of their abilities, however limited those abilities might have been. In the end, the defining character of the West Wing was not Sununu in his alternating personae of gruff charmer and raging monster, nor the get-it-done, sort-of-friendly-tough-guy Skinner, nor the temperate and distant and competent Baker. All these men did what their boss wanted them to do. The West Wing was fashioned entirely in the image of George Bush.

FREEZE FRAME:

JAPANIC

FEBRUARY 5, 1992

The last time you saw the president in the flesh, back in November, he looked well. You and your colleagues trooped into the Roosevelt Room for your meeting with him—the speechwriting and communications shop getting together with the Big Guy as the campaign to reelect him began. "We just need to get our message out," the president said, though he said little about what that message was.

But now, only two weeks before the Republican primary, all the polls are showing Republican challenger Pat Buchanan with amazingly strong support, hovering around 35 percent. When one of your colleagues asked the president about the threat of Buchanan back in November, he smiled with that goofy expression that brought your single-woman's dormant maternal instincts to the fore: You wanted to protect him, and you wanted to kill the people who wanted to hurt him.

"Don't worry about Pat," he said. "I've looked into his platform. The voters won't go for it. It's a wacky platform."

The memory of that moment is reassuring, especially since so little has been of late. You realize the most enduring image you have of the president these days is the long shot of him on television collapsing into the lap of the prime minister of Japan. You had been as concerned as all your colleagues in the speechwriting office about his health. But when you found out what he had actually done in Miyazawa's lap, all you could think of was: Hey, Mr. President, those are *my* remarks you threw up all over.

That horrific moment had taken place on January 8, and was the fitting end to a foreign journey that had, in the three months since its conception, metastasized into a miscarriage.

You had been intimately involved in the Asia trip because you had been given the special treat of going on the "preadvance" for it—a "preadvance" being the trip taken to places outside Washington by members of the White House staff for the purpose of planning the president's every move, where he lands, what sites he should visit, where he stays, how he gets from place to place. You were there on the trip in your role as researcher in the speechwriting office, gathering information and colorful detail for the speechwriters to weave through the remarks they would draft. *This ancient bridge was once the site of the great samurai battle of 1614. Now we meet, not in battle, but in friendship* . . .

The preadvance took ten days, from South Korea to Singapore to Australia and then to Japan. It was the sort of perk many staffers live for—flying around on a special military aircraft, getting treated like royalty by dazzled foreigners, out of bed by 5:30 A.M. taking a quick Cook's tour of the world, with a decent per diem and the chance to buy lots of local artifacts and baubles, the speed-freak thrill of being constantly on the go. Calling into the office from the crackling phone on the plane even though you had nothing to say to them. "Just checking in. What's up?"

You had not had a very good time, though; your longtime boyfriend had just broken off with you, you had been suffering through a bad cold, and your traveling companions had been advance men. And advance men are the loud, rowdy, sexist guys of a feminist's nightmare. (You are no conventional feminist, by the way—your taste runs to Camille Paglia and George Gilder.) On the one hand, they had constantly hit on you, and on the other, they had ignored you when you had wanted to get in on the goings-on.

You certainly had nothing against ordinary collegial flirtation—after the bust-up with your boyfriend, you immediately started going out with a new man who worked a floor above you in the OEOB, and after that had taken up just as quickly with a fellow down the hall—but the utterly retrogressive attitude of the advance men had been jarring. It's the only such experience you have had working in the Bush White House, in which men and women and boys and girls all work cozily together.

You had gone on the preadvance in October. The president's journey was supposed to take place at the end of November, a grand tour of the Pacific Rim in which the American president celebrated his close association with our Oriental allies who had played a crucial financial role in the Gulf War. But then, two weeks before Bush was scheduled to take off, his former attorney general, Richard Thornburgh, lost the Senate race in Pennsylvania; no, not lost, got creamed, after leading by 40 points in the polls two months earlier. The Washington consensus was that the election should be a wake-up call for the president, who was too concerned with foreign policy and not interested enough in domestic affairs. Bush and Sununu postponed the trip.

And you were upset and angry—why were they giving in to the Democrat idea that it was inappropriate for the president of the United States to be concerned about his country's foreign policy? Wasn't that the most important thing he had to do—preserve the Union against all enemies, foreign and domestic? Well, okay, so there weren't really any foreign enemies any longer, but still . . .

Or at least you *thought* there weren't any foreign enemies. But by the beginning of December, Sununu was out and Sam Skinner was in, and somehow, in all the confusion, Secretary of Commerce Robert Mosbacher was allowed to get his grubby paws all over the trip. Suddenly the tone and spirit of the thing were changed utterly, to focus on promoting American companies abroad and attacking unfair Japanese and South Korean trade practices. Mosbacher accused the Japanese of "exacerbating" the recession. The president said his upcoming trip was about "jobs, jobs, jobs." An administration devoted to free trade was starting to sound protectionist.

And how was Bush going to promote American jobs and American workers? Mosbacher had the inspired idea of inviting along the CEOs of America's big three car companies. You were at a meeting in the White House with the three men, one of whom got so agitated talking about the evil Japanese that he started bellowing at Mosbacher: "You better do something about this; this trip may be our last chance."

His last chance, maybe; everybody except the senior managers in the administration knew that Detroit was to blame for its own problems, fat-cat managers unable and unwilling to change the way they do business, making lousy cars and then blaming the competition for doing it better. Republicans weren't supposed to back these guys; the Republican party was supposed to be the party of entrepreneurs, those who bucked the system and figured out a better way.

First the Democrats attacked the president for planning the Asia trip at all. Then they attacked him for taking the Big Three Farts with him because they were not good representatives of America. Then they attacked him because they said he was going to Japan with hat in hand, asking an ungrateful ally that was trying to kill our economy for some trade handouts. And all three charges somehow seemed to stick in the public consciousness.

So when the president tossed his cookies into Miyazawa's lap at the big banquet, it seemed to sum up the whole three months of grief that the trip had caused the White House. But how unfair for you! You had gotten exactly one opportunity to write remarks for him to deliver on the trip—even though you were nominally a researcher, you knew you were a better speechwriter than practically everybody else in the office, but still you had to push and beg and plead for chances to write. This had been your chance, a little toast to Miyazawa. The cards were in the president' pocket as he leaned over and left his mark forever on the U.S.-Japanese relationship.

It wasn't just the president—everybody in the White House seemed to be losing it. Somebody—you heard it was Marlin Fitzwater—came up with the notion that the president could bolster consumer confidence by going to a JC Penney near Camp David and buying some socks. You knew the president didn't even carry money with him and hadn't for years; his personal assistant must have handed it to him in the car. The whole event had a Marie Antoinette, "Let them buy socks" quality to it.

Even the good news was turning into bad news. Almost everybody had been excited—and a little nervous—about the coming of Sam Skinner; the place had been in the doldrums ever since Sununu had gotten into trouble in the summer. But almost from the moment Skinner started working, people more senior than you were disappointed. He had a reputation as a can-do, no-bullshit manager, but that's not the impression he's been making. First thing he did was announce that everybody in the White House was expected to work a six-day week—which was, first, deeply insulting, because most White House staffers worked at least sixty hours by the time Saturday and Sunday rolled around, and second, kind of stupid because it violated federal workers' rights law. The edict was canceled almost immediately.

Then the French Breakfast Roll Man began wandering the halls. That was what people called Eugene Croisant, some efficiency expert Skinner brought in to help him restructure the White House. That *really* unnerved everybody. Skinner had, in essence, achieved a lifetime ambition of serving as the chief operating officer of the United States and he needed to hire someone who had never worked in politics to help him figure out how to organize his office?

The French Breakfast Roll Man was especially interested in the workings of your office, and you have to admit that things in speechwriting haven't been too great. The director of communications, Dave Demarest, has been fighting a cold war for months against chief speechwriter Tony Snow. The energetic and cheerful and talented Snow, formerly the editorial-page editor of *The Washington Times,* is nominally Demarest's deputy but came in as Sununu's pet the previous spring. His protected status didn't last long, because he proceeded to break every rule in the Bush White House book. He wrote a University of Michigan commencement address attacking political correctness; the speech made the front page of *The New York Times,* which was good, but Tony was named as its author above the fold, which was considered bad form. He also succeeded in angering national security adviser Scowcroft on Bush's swing through the former Soviet Union in the summer, because he was finishing speeches late. In addition, one careless phrase of Snow's uttered in an address in

Ukraine warning against "suicidal nationalisms" created an interna-
tional furor and came to be known as the "Chicken Kiev" speech.

At the end of the year, Tony was called away to devote all his
energies to the 1992 State of the Union address, which had become
an incredibly important speech: All the administration spin doctors
had told the press that the president was waiting until January 28,
1992, to announce all his great plans to stimulate the economy and
save America. Tony told you and everybody else that he was one of
only five people who actually knew what was going into the State of
the Union—the others were the president, Skinner, Darman and
pollster Bob Teeter, who was soon to take over the reins of the
reelection campaign.

It was going to be a revolutionary State of the Union, Tony said.
No laundry list of proposals, but rather a "thematic" address about
America and its future. The speech was so closely held that he did
not allow others in the office to make suggestions about sound-bites
and ideas. Nor did he deliver his draft until five days before the
president was to read it before both houses of Congress. The president took one look at the draft and disliked it. Whereupon Tony
called a rush meeting of his staff. "There have been some questions
raised about the draft that's circulating right now," he said. "I'd very
much appreciate your ideas and concepts for beefing it up, and if you
could have them on my desk in two hours, because I hear they've
brought in Peggy Noonan to work on it . . ."

Peggy Noonan. This was the ultimate Washington black mark—
Bush had gone outside to America's most famous speechwriter. You
and the rest of the staff wanted no part of this one, and gave him
desultory help, not more. Finally, the speech was touched up some
by Noonan, and it went . . . okay. Which meant, given the buildup,
that it was a failure. Things did not look all that bright for Tony's
future.

You find the missteps of the previous month simply unacceptable.
This is all a very serious business to you. You first came to politics
because you had become enamored of conservative ideas; as a
twenty-year-old Harvard student, you read R. Emmett Tyrrell, Jr.'s
The Liberal Crack-Up on a beach in Greece as you lolled about with

a Eurotrash boyfriend, and its portrayal of the American Left's decline changed your life. Your time in the White House has only deepened your sense of the Manichaean nature of American politics. George Bush is light, the Democrats are darkness. It might sound silly, but it's true. They have to be stopped.

The force of light who had sat at the head of the table in the Roosevelt Room back in November clearly does not understand how poorly he is being served by his new staff. He can't possibly understand; he's too good, he's too nice.

You keep thinking back to one thing he said in that meeting: "Now, listen, if any of you needs anything, wants to suggest anything, you come talk to me."

And he looked right at you as he spoke.

You were dazzled by his attention that day; now you are almost tempted to try to take him up on it. You pick up the phone to call over to the West Wing and realize how it would sound if you were to call Patty Presock, his secretary, and say, "Hi, Patty, listen, the president said if I ever needed to talk to him . . ."

You actually believe he would listen to you if you could ever get in the door. But you know you never could.

THREE:

STAFFING UP, STAFFING DOWN, OR, WHY THE WHITE HOUSE DIDN'T WORK

"It's the worst job in the world," said Sam Skinner. "Howard Baker said that when he was Reagan's chief of staff. The worst."

One month after Bush's defeat on November 3, 1992, and Skinner was in his Elba, eating three kinds of popcorn out of a tin cylinder eight inches wide and two feet tall. The tin was that year's omnipresent holiday offering; every Republican office in Washington was inundated with popcorn supplied by friendly lobbyists, every word processing keyboard stained with the icky orange residue of the cheese flavoring and the sticky brown goo of the caramel. Skinner's place of exile was a handsome office suite on the fourth floor of the Republican National Committee building on Capitol Hill. It had been his perch since August, when James Baker replaced him as White House chief of staff. Skinner had arrived at the White House just a year earlier, in December 1991. He was chief of staff for eight months, and in all that time he never had a good day. The first major event of Skinner's tenure was the president's trip to Japan in January 1992. That was followed in turn by the unsuccessful State of the Union address, and then Bush's first campaign trip to New Hampshire, in which he attempted to demonstrate to people that he cared about them by speaking the immortal words "Message: I care." And on and on it went, through an unbroken series of disasters and missed opportunities: the Rio summit, the Los Angeles riots, the great media flap over Dan Quayle's speech insulting "Murphy Brown."

Throughout these months, stretching into summer, staffers watched as their administration, once thought invincible, absorbed blow after blow and could not come up with a single thing that might improve Bush's standing in the eyes of the voters. They would gather and regather at the feet of OEOB staircases, huddling together in impromptu meetings by the men's-room door or on their way out at night, having what came to be known as the Conversation.

> Staffer One: Can you believe this? It's a nightmare.
> Staffer Two: Ninety percent in the polls less than a year ago. What happened?
> Staffer One: We're fucked is what happened.

The conclusion of the Conversation was always the same: It was all Skinner's fault, Skinner and the guys running the campaign. The one person who was not held responsible in these discussions was the president himself. The only acceptable way to criticize the president was to say that he was too trusting, too generous, especially about giving Skinner a chance.

They repeated the stories they had heard about how sure Bush was he was going to win, about how he had no doubts and did not want his people to worry. But the fact was, things weren't working well, and Only One Man Could Save Them. He was the Republican magus, James A. Baker III, Bush's close friend of thirty-five years, the man who had run every Republican campaign since 1976 and had won three of four.

Staffers would have been surprised to discover that Skinner agreed with them. By the summer he had come to be very much in favor of a Baker takeover; for months he had been saying Baker was the key to the reelection. But he had believed Baker either would be put in charge of the campaign or would come into the White House as a Super Counselor. Either way, Skinner figured he could keep his title and some of his duties. So he had been shocked when, on an August Wednesday right before lunch, the president informed him that come ten the next morning, Skinner was to be banished from the White House.

Skinner's innocence—or was it arrogance?—typified everything that had gone wrong in his time in the White House: his ignorance of the workings of Washington politics and his Panglossian faith that somehow things would work out just fine in the end.

Arriving back at the White House to take up once more the duties he had held in the first Reagan administration, Baker not only got rid of Skinner, as Washington rules required, but removed all traces of Skinner's tenure. He completely restructured the White House under four chief deputies. He dispatched Skinner's key hire, domestic policy czar Clayton Yeutter. And crueler still, he sent deputy chief of staff Henson Moore across West Exec to the OEOB and gave him titular charge of the office that served as liaison to the nation's governors.

This was easily the harshest fate the Baker people could have chosen for Moore. They would actually have done him a kindness by firing him outright instead of just removing him from his West Wing digs. West Wingers viewed the OEOB from a paternalistic remove; it was where the minions worked. West Wingers never set foot in the OEOB by choice. Even their secretaries, some of whom came to ape their superiors' condescension toward the OEOB, did not make the journey. Hard copy that needed to travel from a West Winger's office to his OEOB staff was delivered not by hand but by fax.

Moore, who was considered affable but startlingly fatuous by the White House staff, lost what little respect he had earned from them for meekly accepting his new assignment instead of leaving the White House with a shred of dignity left to him. The ghost of Moore's career haunted the OEOB hallways, the Jacob Marley of the Bush administration.

But Skinner's own evisceration came as a kind of spiritual deliverance to the White House staff, not because they disliked him but because their sense of justice had at last been satisfied. Things had gone horribly wrong and somebody was finally taking the fall for it. The president's decision to bring Baker on had confirmed their conviction that the problem lay in Skinner's faulty management. Skinner, and only Skinner, had been the cause of all the administration's troubles in 1992. Skinner's mistakes had created the conditions for a serious Republican challenge from Pat Buchanan, a serious Democratic challenge from Bill Clinton and a serious independent challenge from Ross Perot. Skinner's failure was not only a danger to the country's future, but an even more immediate threat to the livelihoods of the White House staff.

The Baker team played this opinion for all it was worth. In the myriad articles written about Baker's takeover of the White House, Baker's people spoke of little else (on background, of course) but the parlous state of the place in Skinner's wake. The clear implication was that if Bush did win in November, the credit would be entirely Baker's, but if he lost, Skinner would be the one responsible.

Skinner's vertiginous rise and fall—from Illinois pol of no particular distinction to secretary of transportation to White House chief of staff, all in about three and a half years—seemed a modern demonstration of the price of hubris. It was hard to imagine how a man could recover from so public a disaster.

But sitting in his Republican Elba on that December day, Skinner was actually one of the few Republicans in town cheerful and upbeat. He had just landed a $500,000 job as chairman of Commonwealth Edison. So while hundreds of his former employees awoke with night sweats trying to figure out how, as loyal employees of a disgraced administration, they were going to meet the mortgage payments, Skinner was returning to his hometown of Chicago perhaps a bit bloodied but basically unbowed. (Upon hearing of Skinner's hiring, one staffer immediately began calling around and with mock urgency advising his friends who might own stock in Commonwealth Edison to "sell short, for God's sake, sell short!")

Skinner had had the cold satisfaction of watching Baker's reputation as an unparalleled political operative sink under the weight of the investigation into his staff's participation in the search of Bill Clinton's passport file. In addition, insider accounts of the election year published immediately after the election were unrelenting in their portrait of Bush/Quayle '92—over which Skinner had been given no authority whatsoever—as perhaps the worst-run presidential campaign in modern history.

There was, in other words, plenty of blame to go around for the defeat. Skinner certainly thought so: He constantly cited the role of his predecessor, John Sununu, and campaign chief Bob Teeter while belittling the significance of his own eight months in the chief of staff's office. Those months had proved to be merely an interregnum between Sununu and Baker. "I was just an asterisk in history," he said, only he pronounced the word "asterik." It was, evidently, an important word to him; later, he dismissed a midlevel staffer's role in a key policy decision that year by calling her an "asterik" too.

What had made the job especially frustrating, he said flatly, was that he had inherited "the weakest staff in White House history" from Sununu. "You won't find anyone to disagree with that," Skinner said. "It was just hopeless."

Out of the mouths of babes: Skinner had stumbled onto the truth. The management problems of the White House preceded his time there and did not go away when he left. The management problem of the White House was George Bush, and the singularly inept way he structured his own political operation.

By dissing the White House staff, Skinner had merely put into words something that had been evident to people in the administration and elsewhere in Washington from January 20, 1989, onward. The White House staff, almost every member of which had been hired by Sununu himself, was astoundingly mediocre—politically shortsighted, ideologically deprived, inclined to inflate the importance of the trivial and discount the significant.

It is important to make clear the profound difference, unclear even to most people who live and work in Washington, between the White House, which the president runs, and the executive branch, over which he presides. To manage the executive branch, the president appoints officials who must be agreeable to the Senate. Those officials are in turn responsible for spending the money given to them by the House of Representatives. The money generally comes with all sorts of strings attached that channel it toward specific programs within each cabinet department and federal agency.

This means people in the executive branch don't have all that much discretion over their budgets. And anyway, 40 percent of the federal government's $1.7 trillion budget is tied up in entitlements, which both Congress and the executive branch are forbidden by law to tamper with.

Nevertheless, the executive branch actually does things: It administrates, it spends, it collects taxes, it sends people to jail, it regulates industry. Some of the millions of things it does are good. Most are indifferent. More than a million are really bad. But its employees actually get their hands dirty working the levers and pulleys of governance. Some 99.9 percent of federal spending goes to cabinet departments and agencies.

The White House gets the rest. The White House does not answer to Congress (although the three agencies within the Executive Office of the President do). Its staff does not testify before Congress, and Congress does not have the power to confirm White House officials (except for those in those three agencies). Moreover, the White House is only a little about governance; it is almost exclusively about politics. Its basic function is to conduct a permanent ongoing political campaign to protect, serve, burnish the reputation of and enhance the popularity of the president himself, and, if he has an agenda, to advance that too.

The White House, then, is supposed to work to maintain the president's ties to the people who voted for him, negotiate with Congress on his behalf, make sure that nothing goes on in the executive branch that might come back to hurt him and keep the public and the press informed of his activities and ideas through press spokesmen, press conferences and speeches.

When the Bush administration began, the White House was divided into twelve sections. Bush filled a few of the top jobs himself and left the rest to Sununu. The president's insouciance about the structure and order of his own political operation turned out to be a key indication of how he was going to pursue his presidency. Having spent eight years doing nothing but retail politics in his effort to get elected, he now wished to cleanse himself, to rise above it. He would leave all that to his famously brash and tough chief of staff and focus his attention on his consuming interest, foreign affairs (which he was to conduct in a manner startlingly indifferent to domestic political considerations, as in the case of his lukewarm response to the stirring prodemocracy demonstrations in Tiananmen Square and their suppression by the Communist government).

While he was hunkering down with national security adviser Scowcroft and Secretary of State Baker, Sununu was busy assembling a White House manned by senior staffers whose chief assets were that (a) they would owe extraordinary allegiance to the chief of staff for elevating them beyond their natural stations in life, and (b) they would pose absolutely no threat to his complete dominion over all aspects of White House policymaking.

The weakness of Sununu's staff was made manifest in the person of Fred McClure, a second-tier Washington lobbyist who took over the key office of congressional liaison. Legislative Affairs, as the office was known, is tasked with conducting the White House's difficult and complicated relations with the House and Senate. But Sununu had decided he wanted to be the White House personage who dealt with "the fools on the Hill," as he once called them. So he hired McClure, who had two credentials that won him Sununu's favor: First, he had worked in the Senate office of John Tower, Bush's candidate for secretary of defense and the president's fellow Texas Republican; second, and more important, he was black.

McClure was unable to do anything to reverse the Senate's rejection of his old boss Tower, the first time in modern history a former senator had been so rebuffed—an especially odd outcome considering the grounds, which were that he drank a little and sometimes fondled women in public. McClure departed the White House in 1991 and returned to Texas to practice law. When last seen, he was doing one thing he could do extremely well: singing the national anthem at the opening of the 1992 Republican National Convention in Houston.

Sununu had about an equal degree of success with the White House communications operation, which he had drastically downgraded from its previous high standing in the Reagan White House. A Reagan-era director of communications was either a celebrated or glamorous figure in his own right or soon became one—David Gergen was the first, Pat Buchanan the second. The director of communications supervised the dissemination of the White House's message through speeches, media appearances and, of course, strategic leaking.

Sununu's choice for the post was David Demarest, who had had the title during the campaign. But what he had done as director of communications for Bush/Quayle '88 was almost exclusively technical—setting up satellite feeds for candidate interviews, keeping track of which local media organs the candidate needed to hit on his relentless journey around the country. During the campaign, Demarest was not a speechwriter and did not participate in the making of policy, nor did he design a strategy to publicize and promote the candidate's ideas.

Sununu took advantage of Demarest's inexperience to gut the speechwriting operation, the most significant arm of the communications office. Now, the idea that a president didn't need especially good speechwriters might seem insane, especially when that president was George Bush, but Sununu and Bush had decided to pursue a communications strategy designed by press secretary Marlin Fitzwater. (The press office under Reagan and Bush was independent of the communications operation.) Fitzwater's recommendation was that Bush make policy announcements and speak to the American people not through speeches but in press conferences and informal interview sessions instead. Fitzwater was trying to help Bush define his own presidency, and the strategy was for Bush to differentiate himself from Reagan as much as possible. Reagan had had an adversarial relationship with the media; Bush didn't, and needn't, because he could think on his feet and throw lots of factoids into press-conference answers that would dazzle the White House press corps. Reagan excelled at giving speeches because he couldn't work without a script; Bush excelled at press conferences because he didn't need a speechwriter to tell him what to say and how to think.

In previous administrations, speechwriters had been considered important participants in the making of policy and had been treated as such. Speechwriting was given the nicest suite of offices in the OEOB, and whether they were commissioned officers or not, all speechwriters were given mess privileges. Speechwriters became celebrities either during or after every administration—Theodore Sorensen in JFK's; Peter Benchley and Ben Wattenberg in LBJ's; William Safire and Pat Buchanan in Richard Nixon's; Hendrik Hertzberg and James Fallows in Jimmy Carter's; Peggy Noonan in Reagan's.

Speeches were the central events in every modern president's public appearances largely for reasons of security. Ever since Gerald Ford had twice nearly been assassinated, the Secret Service decreed it was far too dangerous for the president to do retail politics—shaking hands with regular folk, exchanging a few words face-to-face with ordinary Americans. But as everybody who has ever written a speech for the man will concede, Bush hated giving one; he usually got bored in the middle, even if it was only two pages long. Clark Judge, who had written for him when he was vice-president, would deliver a speech to Bush and the first thing he would do was weigh it in his hands; if it was more than a five-minute peroration, he would say, "I don't know, this looks pretty heavy to me."

Though Bush delivered more speeches during the 1980s than any other person in America, he didn't like the whole business and much appreciated Fitzwater's idea that as president there was a better way for him to go. And Sununu, who understood the power and influence a good speechwriter could exert over policy simply by the agency of a really memorable phrase ("Read my lips," anyone?), was eager to eliminate yet another challenge to his own authority. He swung into action with an almost inspired gift for the petty. First, he kicked the speechwriting department out of its nice digs, and gave them instead to the deeply significant Thousand Points of Light office.

Following this, he decreed that speechwriters would no longer be allowed to eat in the White House Mess. What was more, no speechwriter would be paid more than $40,000. And finally, he forswore the résumés and skills of such first-rate former Bush and Reagan speechwriters as Clark Judge and opted instead for a crew of scribes who had mostly labored in the boondocks of the Reagan administration in the service of such Churchillian speakers as Secretary of Housing and Urban Development Pierce, otherwise known as "Silent Sam."

Sununu enjoyed plucking people from obscurity and placing them in some of the most senior positions in the most important political organization in America. For the director of the intergovernmental affairs office, the White House liaison with state and local officials, he found one Debra Rae Anderson. Anderson, who had no Washington experience whatsoever, was a legislator from that hotbed of political intrigue, South Dakota. Like McClure, she had one major asset, although in her case it was her sex, not her race.

To manage the advance work (i.e., the staging of presidential events), Sununu selected Steve Studdert, who had done a good job of it on the campaign. But alas, campaigns are not the same as White Houses, and three months into the presidency Studdert made a hilarious blunder. In a week devoted to Bush-the-education-president, the powers-that-were decided it would be a good idea for Bush to make a surprise visit to an area school, sit down and have lunch with some kids. Studdert chose a high school in Falls Church, Virginia, a few miles from the White House. The event appeared to be a success because the footage made the nightly news and the photo hit the front page of *The Washington Post.*

There was only one rather large big problem, as *The Washington Post*'s caption revealed: One of the little boys talking to the president was identified as Gary Studdert. It seemed that, without telling anybody else about it, Studdert had contrived to get his son into a photo op with the president. This was a cardinal sin for an advance man; these sorts of events are designed to fool the American people into believing the president really cares about them because he is willing to sit down with children just like theirs. When they discover, as they did in this case, that one of those kids happens to be the son of a White House employee, their cynicism knows no bounds.

A few months later, Studdert was back in Utah.

But of all Sununu's choices for the White House staff, easily the most consequential was Roger Porter. Porter was named assistant to the president for domestic policy. This is the title that had been given to Edwin Meese in the Reagan White House. Meese, perhaps

Reagan's closest personal adviser for twenty years, wanted to be to domestic affairs what the national security adviser was to foreign affairs—chief White House analyst and the check on the ambitions of power-hungry bureaucrats in the cabinet departments and agencies.

It never quite worked out that way. Foreign affairs are relatively easy to supervise from the White House because they are the responsibility of only three outside departments (State, Defense and Central Intelligence). Almost everything else is classified as domestic policy, and the sheer size of the federal government has dwarfed all efforts by domestic-policy assistants to achieve the degree of supervisory authority enjoyed by the national security adviser. (Meese had also gutted the position, when he left the White House in 1985 to become attorney general, by arranging to remain chairman of its two cabinet forums, the Domestic Policy Council and the Economic Policy Council.)

Even so, the position of domestic policy adviser was one of almost limitless possibility. Unfortunately, Porter proved a man of almost infinite limits. At a time when the Republican party was in a wild ferment of new ideas and policies in fields from education to welfare, Porter proved singularly uninterested in the ideas and instead obsessed over detail—not what to do, but how to do it. One of Porter's chief aides said he "was narcissistic about the paper on his desk"; he held up the release of documents from his office because he insisted on reading every word himself and sometimes complaining about the spacing of the tabs. In the summer of 1992, Judy Smith of the press office had to sit down with Porter's staff and tell them how to write a fact sheet on administration policy that would get the media's attention because Porter insisted on so many qualifications and emendations that his office's fact sheets were impossible to read. And, what was worse, were approved by him far too late in the process for anybody to fix them.

A visitor to Porter's office noted that pride of place was given to photographs of Porter himself in the company of none other than the first president he had served, Gerald Ford. Porter made frequent references to the Ford presidency, during which he had served as a paper pusher, as if that were the model that the present administration should emulate.

From the first day of the administration, Porter served as a kind of kid brother to the two actual domestic policy advisers, Sununu and Richard Darman. His status as an underling was confirmed when he accepted the job of taking the official notes at domestic policy meetings with the president. Porter's weakness led to the marginalization of the often creative staff of wonks who made up the Office of Policy Development under his tutelage—another set of thinkers and potential policy competitors disposed of.

The few choices Bush did make among the three-hundred-plus staffers in the White House were as telling in their way as Sununu's, for with one exception, they were people of no fixed opinions on the key issues affecting the country. They did not believe in anything very much except George Bush the man, and that was what mattered to the loyalty-crazed president.

He cited one of his first decisions in one of his final televised appearances before the nation, the second presidential debate. Asked what women he had as his closest advisers, he blanked for a minute and then spoke the words: "There's Rose Zamaria. Tough as a boot, saving the taxpayers' money." The comment provoked groans all over Republicanland and on the plane back from Richmond, Virginia, White House aides told each other that the "Zamaria debate" would go down in history as Bush's worst political moment. (A questionable proposition, given the wealth of choices.)

Zamaria, who had been Bush's secretary when he was a congressman in the mid-1960s, was not exactly the sort of high-ranking policy aide you might expect a president to name when asked about his closest advisers. But she was certainly close to him; he saw Zamaria every day, which gave her standing many other more important staffers lacked. She was the person Bush put in charge of West Wing administration, supervising the secretaries and in possession of the (theoretical) key to the supply closet. She appealed to one of the less attractive aspects of his Yankee upbringing—the parsimony for parsimony's sake that is a snobbish corruption of the Puritan emphasis on the godliness of thrift and the sin of waste.

To that end, Zamaria roamed the halls of the West Wing, accusing people of taking paper clips home with them from the office, making sure that her "girls" were not lollygagging, ordering people out of the Roosevelt Room if they arrived ten minutes early for a meeting by informing them that it wasn't a staff lounge, y'know. She would approach senior female staffers in the Mess and upbraid them for not wearing stockings like a lady should. In short order, Zamaria became the single most detested person in the White House (including Richard Darman) and probably the entire administration.

For Zamaria had another, more important duty as well: She was in charge of White House perks. There weren't many of these, but they were choice: Getting entrée into the president's box in the opera house of the Kennedy Center and obtaining cuff links and tie clips with the presidential seal and signature on them were primary among these. In the Reagan years, it had been a matter of course for staffers to get into the box; it was first-come, first-served, informal.

Unlike Reagan, Bush saw the perks as a political tool. Zamaria was administering the official White House favors because Bush wanted someone stingy to keep track of what he had done for his people. Gracious Bush certainly was, but never selfless. Every kindness on his part, or in his name, was considered payback for services rendered or an advance on services owed. This became clear in the aftermath of the 1990 budget deal, when John Sununu (with Bush's consent) took revenge against a Republican congressman who had voted against it by yanking his tickets to the presidential box that week.

Bush asked Marlin Fitzwater, who had been his vice-presidential press secretary before becoming Reagan's last press secretary, to stay on—the sole senior staff holdover from the Reagan administration was someone whose elevation in Reagan days was due to Bush alone.

Bush chose David Bates to serve as the cabinet secretary—the liaison between the cabinet departments and the White House, through whom all major decisions made outside the White House must be passed. Bates was a member of the august Bushie club known as the WBBIs—the acronym stood for "with Bush before Iowa" and referred to Republicans so firmly in the president's corner that they had worked for him even before his surprise victory in the 1980 Iowa caucus. Bates was a supremely competent bureaucrat who was there to ensure that Bush had someone keeping an eye on the cabinet, which was full of people Bush did not like very much and as a result did not trust.

C. Boyden Gray, a dryly witty, wealthy eccentric who had been Bush's counsel when he was vice-president, was tapped to run the important and very sensitive White House counsel's office—the internal law firm whose primary mission post Watergate is to keep the White House out of legal trouble. Gray, who looked eerily like a Jules Feiffer cartoon come to life, was another person who owed his political life to George Bush and George Bush alone, but among the qualities that made him a true original was his standing as the only true-blue conservative with impeccable Bushie credentials.

Bush did not choose him with that in mind, however; Gray had spent much of his career in the vice-president's office championing the very unconservative alternative fuel known as ethanol, a substance that owed its lavishly subsidized existence to the pork-barreling proclivities of Corn Belt senators like the hated Anti-Bush, Bob Dole. Gray came to feel so strongly about the combustible properties of maize that, when he was not taking the streets of Georgetown in his Porsche at a clip of one hundred miles an hour, looking the way Ichabod Crane would have in a sports car, he was rumbling his way to work in the only ethanol-powered car in the nation's capital.

And the ultimate Bushie got the ultimate Bushie job. Bush gave the Office of Presidential Personnel to Chase Untermeyer, who had served as an intern in the future president's congressional office in the mid-1960s. Bush considered the job so significant that he had Untermeyer start working on plans for it at the end of 1987, almost a year before his election.

It might seem odd that this tedious administrative position would so interest the president, but not when you consider that the purpose of the office is to find candidates for most of the 5,807 jobs the president was able to dole out. In addition to the 3,000 full-time Schedule C positions in the executive branch, Presidential Personnel handled the secretarial slots for its Schedule C's, not to mention ambassadorships and the highly coveted appointments to advisory boards.

Untermeyer's office had two major purposes: To pick out the real Bushies deserving of employ from the 23,000 resumes that crossed his desk, and to find as many racial and ethnic tokens as he possibly could from the wider world of nationwide Republicanism. He was also supposed to root out the Reaganites; Bush had given him a direct order to clean house, especially in the White House, and give the new administration a shiny new face.

Untermeyer, who had spent eight years in the Reagan administration, six of them working in the Department of the Navy, was the luckless Republican given the task of telling many of his friends and co-workers that they were out of luck because it was the time of the Bushies.

That gave rise to another problem: While he knew what blacks and Hispanics and women looked like, there was no set answer to the vexing question: Just What *Is* a Bushie? It had been relatively easy to define a Reaganite. A Reaganite earned the designation because of his opinions. That was why there could be such a thing as a Reagan Democrat—because party affiliation does not necessarily define what a party member believes in. To some extent, anybody who voted for Reagan was considered a Reaganite by the administration and its personnel office (though there was a clear bias toward Republicans, it was not insuperable).

But there could never be a "Bush Democrat"; there wasn't even a clear definition of a "Bush Republican" once you left Fairfield County, Connecticut. And you certainly couldn't call Bush voters "Bushies," because it was impossible to tell just why they were voting for him besides the fact that he was Ronald Reagan's chosen successor and he wasn't a Massachusetts liberal who let a crazy-eyed black killer out of jail to rape a perfectly decent white woman in Maryland.

Still, there were Bushies, and what ultimately defined them was this: They either worked for or gave money to George Bush. A *founding* Bushie was somebody like Untermeyer or Zamaria, who had worked for him back when he was a nobody. A *real* Bushie was someone who had worked on his campaign back in 1980. A *regular* Bushie was someone who had donated his time or his money to the 1988 campaign.

In other words, a Bushie was someone either directly beholden to Bush or someone to whom Bush was directly beholden. No Bushie, founding or real or regular, was without a handwritten note from the man, and many of them had pictures too. To clear the presidential personnel hurdle, Republicans had to demonstrate their personal loyalty to Bush with hard evidence. The forms that job seekers had to fill out asked candidates to specify their "Bush experience"—not their general Republican experience, perhaps working on a Senate race in Idaho or something, but their Bush experience solely.

Once identified, the Bushies all had to be taken care of before any job in the administration could be filled by anyone else. This determination caused no end of conflict with Bush's designated cabinet secretaries and agency heads, all of whom had to get their offices up and running and all of whom had their own Republican types they wished to hire, people *they* knew and trusted to be loyal to them as well as to the president.

Presidential Personnel played hardball on behalf of its people, but at the same time it didn't really care what they did or where they did it as long as the salary level was appropriate. For most midlevel appointments, getting qualified people was not the uppermost consideration for Presidential Personnel.

The hiring settled, Sununu's White House staff worked according to the wishes of its designer. Sununu had control of policy. He negotiated with Congress. He kept track of the status of the major administration initiatives, and did so with great efficiency. His appetite for the details of governance was inexhaustible; staffers who were engaged in issues and negotiations that interested him had complete access to him at all hours of the day and night and on weekends.

The day-to-day administrative details were left in the hands of Sununu's deputy, Andy Card. Sununu and Card had an unusual relationship for a chief and his second-in-command—Sununu was the scary one, while Card was the friendly face of the chief of staff.

Card returned his phone calls and got the paperwork done in a timely fashion. His general good nature made him almost pathetically popular with the rest of the White House staff, who tended to talk about "Andy" in the worshipful tones with which the other kids in high school discussed Ferris Bueller.

If Card was Sununu's fixer, Ed Rogers, Sununu's assistant, was his enforcer. Rogers, a disciple of hardball Republican operative Lee Atwater, was known for playing everybody in the place off everybody else—soliciting a private opinion from one staffer about the work of another and then telling the second staffer what the first had said about him.

Sununu's fall from power in 1991 came about not because Bush was unhappy with the quality of the White House staff, but because the press scandal over Sununu's travel had become a political liability at a time when Bush's sinking ratings in the polls called for some kind of major change. Since the president was not willing to introduce a major economic growth package, or even to apologize for having raised taxes in the 1990 budget deal, he had to make a personnel move. Sununu went. Skinner came.

Bush, however, refused to allow his new chief of staff to fix what was broken. Just before his arrival at the White House, Skinner gave an interview to *The New York Times* in which he suggested he might want to make serious staff changes—an understandable wish for a new manager who had been brought in because the previous management had fallen into disrepair. But Bush, always unhappy to see such things in print, scolded Skinner for speaking so publicly. Perhaps as punishment for the indiscretion, he told Skinner in no uncertain terms that the White House staff was his, Bush's, staff. He was not unhappy with their work. One or two major changes were as many as he or they could handle. Bush didn't want much to change.

Later, when not only was Skinner in Elba but Bush was soon to be in an exile of his own, Skinner made this point again and again—Bush wouldn't let him make repairs.

Actually, Skinner hadn't the least idea how to fix things in any case. His only idea was to enlist the services of New York management consultant Eugene Croisant, who also happened to be his best friend of thirty years. When he first took over as secretary of transportation in 1989, Skinner had called on Croisant and found him invaluable in helping to turn his disparate staff into a team. This goal had been achieved by means of management retreats for the department's senior aides, where they played games together so that they could learn to trust each other.

You might think that these touchy-feely, New Agey, post-1960s techniques would be anathema to Republicans, but you would be dead wrong. Management programs like Croisant's have become part and parcel of big-business culture, which believes that conflicts and even failures can be solved and resolved by a weekend at a really nice resort where people get to respect one another's space and emerge with a whole new collegial spirit they can take back to their corporate headquarters and proceed to use in running yet another major American industry into the ground.

Well, that sort of thing might have been all well and good at the Department of Transportation, but not at the White House. It made Skinner a laughingstock, and with precisely the people whose respect he both needed and craved.

Croisant wandered through the White House for three weeks, asking staffers what they did and why. In the end, he made two recommendations to Skinner that any mildly intelligent member of the White House staff could have given him in thirty seconds. First, he recommended that Skinner hire a new director of communications to replace David Demarest. Skinner then spent two pointless months trying to hire Jim Lake, who had been communications honcho in the '80, '84 and '88 campaigns, but after a month's jockeying Lake decided he could not afford to leave his lobbying business. Whereupon Skinner halted his search, explaining later that it was a very hard job to fill and he simply could find no other candidates among the 250 million residents of the United States of America who could do it besides Lake.

But he wanted to fire David Demarest, the White House communications director, anyway. Bush, who was very fond of Demarest, would not allow it. So instead Skinner gave Communications to Marlin Fitzwater, who already had more than enough to do running the White House press office. He made Demarest, who was no speechwriter, chief speechwriter. He then defenestrated the previous chief speechwriter, Tony Snow. But he didn't get rid of Snow either. Snow was moved across the hall from his office and was named director of media affairs, which basically allowed him to collect a salary, keep up his mortgage payments and keep his health benefits while his wife had their first child. So as a result of this first piece of management advice, there were speechwriters sitting around who weren't allowed to write speeches, a communications director who was too busy with his real job to supervise three different White House offices and a bunch of employees who were either overworked, unqualified or disgruntled—just the sort of thing you hire a management consultant for.

Croisant's second and more significant recommendation was that Skinner create a counterbalance to Darman's total control of domestic policy by appointing a new domestic policy adviser. His choice for domestic policy czar was Clayton Yeutter, chairman of the Republican National Committee, a nice man who was famous in Washington for emptying his in-box every day and having the most impressive collection of Rolodexes in a city that worshiped the Rolodex as an aborigine worships his totem. But nobody ever accused Yeutter of having an idea in his head, which is what a domestic policy czar is supposed to have. And rather than counterbalancing Darman, Skinner merely enraged him and then backed down from his intention of marginalizing the OMB director.

To begin with, on the very day of Skinner's arrival at the White House he was quoted in *The New York Times* as saying, "Dick Darman is a smart guy and he will be one of—and I stress one of—the president's close advisers." Sununu and Darman had been so close that their offices had special phones that rang directly between them; Skinner had Darman's "drop line," as it was called, removed. Darman lay low until three weeks later, when Skinner was quoted in a *National Journal* article calling Darman "a nice young man."

For reasons only a psychiatrist could understand, this remark drove Darman (who was only three years younger than Skinner) into a frenzy. He raged like Lear to his two closest aides, Tom Scully and Bob Grady. He was going to get Skinner. He was going to cut his balls off. That pip-squeak didn't know who he was dealing with. He was going to call Junior—"Junior" being the misappellation for Bush's son George W., who served as a back channel to the president for select staffers.

Darman got hold of himself and called Skinner's office. The chief of staff was traveling that day, so Darman passed his message on to Skinner's assistant, Cam Findlay. If Sam wants to fire me, that's okay, he told Findlay—knowing full well that because he was a presidential appointee confirmed by the Senate, the chief of staff did not have that power, only the president did—but this sort of public humiliation is unacceptable. And Darman proceeded to read through all the statements Skinner had made about him to the press, citing each one by newspaper or magazine, page number, column number and paragraph number. "I am not going to allow my reputation to be destroyed," Darman told Findlay—a remark Findlay found completely reasonable.

Skinner and Darman ended up that afternoon in the deputy chief of staff's office and had a "full and frank discussion," as the State Department briefers in the 1980s used to describe heated negotiating sessions between the U.S. and the Soviets. Skinner acknowledged that he should not have dissed Darman in print but asserted that he wanted a domestic policy operation in the White House independent of the OMB director.

He didn't get one. Yeutter was not equipped for the task, and in any case had only twenty people working for him while Darman had two hundred career analysts working for him at OMB who could run numbers and come up with a report about a hundred times faster than the Office of Policy Development.

And so Skinner found himself again in the same situation he had been in over the directorship of communications: Although he had hired Yeutter, Bush would not allow him to fire the previous domestic policy adviser, Roger Porter. So there were two domestic policy advisers in the place, both of whom had call on the same underlings.

Skinner blew another chance to get the political operation in order when he found himself with an opening in the Office of Public Liaison. Public Liaison, a subordinate operation within Communications, was another important Reagan-era operation that Sununu had trashed. A Reagan White House innovation, Public Liaison was the office of outreach to interest groups—the crucial link between the White House and conservative activists. The Reagan people understood that it was necessary to treat these activists with respect, to give them a forum and a friendly ear—especially since most of the time the administration could not and would not do what they wanted it to do beyond giving their causes lip service. Public Liaison kept such volatile groups as the prolifers and the gun nuts informed and happy. It made the anticommunist organizations waging ideological war against Castro's Cuba and Ortega's Nicaragua feel that their causes were not being neglected. It listened with sympathy to the ideas, no matter how kooky, of the families of POWs and MIAs.

Sununu, mistakenly thought of as a member of the Republican party's ideological hard Right, had declared himself chief White House liaison to conservative groups just as he had declared himself chief White House congressional negotiator. He reduced the number of officials in the office who dealt with conservatives to one, and expanded Public Liaison's outreach to include *all* interest groups, not just Republican ones.

By the time Sununu had left office, he had done such a sterling job that conservatives were trading stories about being treated with condescension, disrespect or even viciously profane threats by the man who had told them he would be their "best friend in the White House." ("I'm going to cut your balls off with a chain saw," he screamed at Chamber of Commerce chief Richard Lesher when Lesher criticized the 1990 budget deal on a television show.) He had fired his conservative liaison, Doug Wead, because Wead had made a stink when another official, liberal Republican Bobbie Kilberg, invited a gay-rights group to the signing ceremony for a bill on hate crimes. Wead had leaked the news to the "Inside the Beltway" column in *The Washington Times,* and the next day he was ousted. Wead's replacement was the exuberant Leigh Ann Metzger, a Georgia peach by way of Phyllis Schlafly's Eagle Forum, who served as the dream date of the New Right. She did a great deal to heal the breach Sununu had caused.

As for Skinner, rather than reorganizing the office to hire more Leigh Ann Metzgers who could successfully stroke alienated conservatives and thereby stanch the bleeding inflicted on the president by the Buchanan candidacy, he came up with a peculiar Machiavellian scheme. He hired Sherrie Rollins, an ABC News spokeswoman of no particular ideological leanings who had worked for Bush when he was vice-president. Aside from the fact that she had "mainstream" credentials to go along with her Bushie past, she was married to Republican political consultant Ed Rollins. And Rollins was proving to be a major irritant to the White House; he had been feuding with Bush ever since the 1990 budget deal, when as head of the Republican congressional campaign committee he had advised GOP House members to oppose the package if they wanted to win reelection. Because of Bush's fury with him, Rollins left the job after the 1990 election, and following that the telegenic consultant had been taking to the airwaves as an analyst and warning of impending Republican disaster in November.

Skinner thought Sherrie's position in the White House would shut her husband up. His scheme was so successful that only a few months later Ed delivered a stunning blow to national Republican unity by agreeing to serve as Ross Perot's campaign chairman. Three days of headlines and countless news stories later, Sherrie resigned and Skinner's best-laid plans had gang a-gley once again.

Finally, even Bush had to act. So Baker came to the White House and Skinner was out. Five days after his firing, while he was still technically chief of staff, Skinner was in Houston at the Republican National Convention. It was Tuesday night, August 18, 6:30 P.M., in front of the J. W. Marriott Galleria hotel, and it was time for Republicans to head out to the Astrodome. Cabinet secretary Ede Holiday and her aide Jay Lefkowitz emerged from a small cocktail party hosted by Dan Quayle looking for Holiday's car. Holiday's driver told her the authorities had insisted the car be parked in a lot around the corner and not in front of the hotel to keep the streets clear. As a result, nobody's car was where he expected it to be; Boyden Gray was pacing in front of his hotel, looking confused and a little desperate. Holiday and Lefkowitz and driver headed down to the corner, where they bumped into Skinner and his wife, Honey.

Holiday and Honey blew air kisses at one another as an unsmiling and preoccupied Sam said, "You have any idea where the cars are?"

"We're going around the corner to see if our car is there," Holiday said. They continued along the cobblestoned sidewalk, Honey's high-heeled shoes losing the war with the cobblestones. As they turned the corner, there was only the one car, Holiday's, in sight.

"Well, I don't see ours," Skinner said.

And Ede Holiday, who only six days before would have ordered Lefkowitz to go find Skinner's car or made the supreme sacrifice of insisting that he take *her* car—only fitting for a man who only six days before played a gigantic role in her professional and emotional life—now merely said, "Okay, good luck, Sam. See you later, Honey."

As they crossed the street to the lot, Lefkowitz murmured sadly: "Jesus, the guy can't even get a *ride*."

And as Holiday's car drove by the hotel, there in front, taking a few steps this way and then a few steps that way, gazing backward and forward, stood the man who was still the chief operating officer of the United States of America, aideless and therefore helpless. For the last three and a half years he had probably never even opened a car door for himself, and now as the general chairman of the Republican National Committee he couldn't find a car whose door he *could* open.

FREEZE FRAME:

THE LONGEST DAY

JUNE 11, 1992

The squawk box has just gone dead. The president was about to speak in Panama City, you were sitting in your OEOB office ready to listen, there were a few disturbing noises and then—silence.

The squawk box is a little speaker installed in the White House press room and various offices around the complex that pipes through the sound of the president's formal appearances primarily for the benefit of the members of the White House press corps who cannot be with the president on some occasions when he's speaking.

The box came on without warning, as it often does, broadcasting the sounds of an event before the event's real beginning—people rustling past an open microphone, which is tied into the satellite feed that brings it back from wherever the president is right into the White House. You were a little startled, but continued to work at your computer. Then in the distance you hear three staccato claps, POP POP POP, and then the transmission immediately cuts off, as though somebody has pulled the plug on the box.

You rise from your chair, go around the desk and into the wide OEOB hallway. As you appear, so do a few other people. You exchange looks, nobody wanting to say what you all dread, which is that the president has been assassinated.

"Weird," you say, and one of your colleagues nods in assent.

"I'm going to call the press room," another says, and goes inside. A minute later she emerges. "It's okay," she says. "It was just that there was a big demonstration, and they had to use tear gas to break it up."

"Oh," you say, momentarily relieved—until you figure out what has happened. The president has gone to Panama so he can take an easy victory lap there. He has not been to the place since U.S. forces invaded and deposed Manuel Noriega back in the fall of 1989, and given how badly things have been going, you can understand why he would reach back to a past triumph to make himself feel better.

You could have told them. Hell, you *did* tell them. When you heard about the trip, you wrote your boss a memo, dated 6/4/92:

> I am a bit concerned about the perception that the Panama stop will be an all upside "victory lap." Panama is not Czechoslovakia or Poland. [President Guillermo] Endara is not Havel or Walesa. There is widespread public sentiment that the U.S. has forgotten about Panama. These factors raise the possibility that the response to the president's four-hour visit will be less than enthusiastic. According to our embassy, we can in fact count on protests, of what size and scope remains unknown. One last note regarding the weather: It is now rainy season in Panama—sudden torrential downpours every third day. Maybe we should pray for rain.

Nobody paid any attention to your memo, but at least you will get to show it to people afterward and say, "See?" Although there's no great percentage to being a prophet of doom in the White House these days.

Only a little after noon, and already the day has become a political nightmare. This morning, just before the president left the country, word came back from Capitol Hill that the proposal to amend the constitution to require a balanced budget had been defeated by the Senate. Then the president got on his plane, arrived in Panama City and got teargassed at his own party. Now he will get back on the plane and head on down to the UN's Earth Summit in Rio de Janeiro, where he will arrive in just a few hours to the catcalls of the world.

After flirting with the idea for six months, the president has agreed to attend the Earth Summit—even though he should know what is already clear from the press coverage of the mood in Rio in the week leading up to the conference: He and the United States are being cast as the supervillains, evil *norteamericano* polluters intent on destroying the world. The heads of state and government of 128 nations are going to be in attendance, but all the world wants to talk about is America—it's as though Bush himself climbed a ladder over Antarctica and, while nobody was looking, tore a big hole in the ozone layer and scampered down again.

You don't buy all this global warming talk anyway—they've been hammering away at this ever since you were a teenager, declaring this or that to be an environmental hazard, scaring the world half to death before it turns out there is no threat. Remember the dioxin scare? The Environmental Protection Agency forcing the people of Times Beach, Missouri, to flee their homes in 1983 and then determining, eight years later, that the dioxin levels were perfectly safe? And now the EPA, under William Reilly, is really getting out of control, trying to get the president to agree to all sorts of world environmental treaties that give Japan and Europe a whole mess of competitive trade advantages because they use nuclear energy and we don't.

And who is in Rio, anyway, aside from those noble heads of state and Reilly, dancing around like the "global rock star" John Sununu once said he was? Just the surviving worldwide remnant of the Woodstock Nation has trooped to the foot of Sugarloaf, with their sickeningly sentimental one-world, anticar, vegetarian, anticapitalist neosocialism. Scratch the surface of the Earth Summit and you find the one persistent theme of world leftism—the United States is to blame for all the planet's woes.

Disgusting. It's stuff like this Chicken Little attack on capitalism and the West and this mushy Woodstock Nation culture that turned you to the Republican party. You come from a family inclined toward libertarianism—after all, your grandfather was a rumrunner during Prohibition, and what was that but an attempt to evade needless government regulation?

Why is the president submitting to this America-bashing, especially at the hands of nations in the third world where people are dying not from third-level environmental toxins measured in parts per billion but because there is no clean water while there are golden sinks and toilets in the homes of high-ranking government officials?

The president is the very image of an American patriot; he actually chokes up when he talks about his wartime experiences or about the flag, you have seen him do it, have seen him object to a touching passage in a speech draft because he says he won't be able to get through it without breaking down.

So why is George Bush, this example of everything that is good and noble in America, sacrificing the national dignity on the altar of the Rio summit?

You know perfectly well why. All his friends are going to be there. Mitterrand, Major, Mubarak, the people you have come to think of as "the allies," as though Desert Storm has supplanted World War II. Brent Scowcroft thinks it wouldn't look right, the leader of the United States refusing to attend. Scowcroft has it completely backward, in your view. By attending, the president of the United States is giving sanction to a host of ideas that are inimical to the very things he and the Republican party stand for: free markets and free trade and economic growth.

He should have stayed home and given a speech about it. Said *I am not going because the Rio summit is a corrupt assault on America and I won't stand for it.* Reagan often stood alone against the United Nations and the American people always supported him because, given a choice between their own president and a bunch of foreigners, they go with the prez every time. But it was not, of course, the obvious play. There were risks involved. Couldn't predict how it would be covered. President had to go.

A tough speech was too much to hope for, especially given how difficult it was to get language into the Rio draft that would have the president say he will not sacrifice American jobs on the altar of no-growth environmentalism. Bob Grady is one of the senior officials in Rio, and every time a draft is faxed to him he takes the tough

language out. Grady has been playing administration environmental-
ist this week.

Grady is the number two official in the Office of Management and
Budget, a smart and lively guy in his early thirties whose politics are
a strange mixture of Ayn Rand libertarianism and big-government
liberal Republicanism. You can always spot Grady from the back in
the OEOB, because he's the only man there with long hair, which he
occasionally gathers into a little ponytail. You really like him, he's
terrifically smart and lively, but you do find his office a little discon-
certing. Its walls are covered with every award he has ever received,
dating back to high school, not to mention two dozen photos of
himself shaking hands with every dignitary he has ever met—not only
the traditional photos of Grady with Bush and Barbara and Reagan,
but also Grady with Jesse Jackson, Grady with Arnold Schwarzenegger, and Grady with God knows who else.

In the end, your faction finally won the battle to get the strong
language in, but it was small comfort. The very fact that the president
is in Rio at the conference invalidates the language altogether.

Oh, God, what a horrible day this is. The morning's news about the
balanced-budget admendment's failure has disappointed you more
than you thought it would. It came so close. Seven of the bill's
cosponsors actually ended up voting against it because the Democrat
leadership on the Hill twisted their arms so hard. Now it's just another administration failure. You have to give Senate majority leader
George Mitchell credit—he knows how to play politics. If the amendment had won, it would have been an astonishing victory for the
president.

But neither Bush nor you even gave it much thought until about
three weeks ago. Of course, the balanced-budget amendment has
long been a favorite Republican campaign ploy, dating back to the
mid-1960s, and the president is on record as favoring it. But he
hardly ever talked about it until Ross Perot entered the race in April.
Almost immediately, every speech the president gave mentioned the
balanced-budget amendment. It was decided to force a vote on the
Hill, and there was real hope that the craven bums down there might
be too afraid to vote against it.

God, what a coup that would have been! What a great thing! Finally, after years of playing corrupt budgetary games and blaming the president (who cannot spend a dime that Congress hasn't given him) for deficits, Congress would finally be reined in. No more pork. No more Big Government. And all because of Perot.

You hate Perot, needless to say. Everybody at the White House does. First ignored him, then hated him. Everybody assumes he got in the race because he has some psycho vendetta going against the president. It's a Texas thing, like those T-shirts around town that read: "It's a black thing, you wouldn't understand."

The few voices of disaffection inside the Bush camp, like Jim Pinkerton and Bill Kristol, were strongly advising the honchos to take Perot seriously, but Skinner and Teeter airily dismissed them. Then Teeter, who has the spine of Jell-O when it comes to his own political prognostications, made a 180 when he saw that Perot's poll numbers weren't falling. In the middle of March, the president's popularity rating started dipping below 40 percent, and Perot was hovering between 25 and 35, with Clinton down around 15. Clinton started climbing, Perot stabilized in the mid-30s and the president wasn't moving at all. Not a bit.

Teeter's focus groups were talking about how they wanted "change." So Teeter supervised a speech Bush delivered March 20 in which he used the word "change" twenty-four times. No joke. As if just saying the word over and over and over again would convince people that he believed in it. *We need to CHANGE it's time to CHANGE we are the CHANGE I believe in CHANGE. CHANGE! CHANGE! DID I MENTION CHANGE?*

But when the president got an opportunity to endorse real change, he did not take it. That came with the outbreak of the riots in Los Angeles on Wednesday, April 29, following the not-guilty verdict in the Rodney King case. The sight of whole neighborhoods burning to the ground focused every mind in the White House on the place momentarily. While the Democrats and the black leadership were talking about racism and the coming revolution, the empowerment folks (like you) awakened from your slumbers and thought that maybe this was the opportunity to make the presidential campaign a referendum on the best Republican proposals and ideas.

The whole idea behind empowerment, after all, is to free the urban poor from the state's suffocating embrace. School choice, which could free kids and parents from really bad inner-city schools by forcing public schools to compete. Real welfare reform, which would give people incentives to work and prosper instead of incentives to stay forever on the dole. And more.

But at meetings with the president to discuss the new "urban agenda," Bush would start looking out the window to the Rose Garden, and would then snap back into focus and say, "I really have to engage on this." It was no use. The whole empowerment thing was really too abstract for him.

Fortunately for the president, Los Angeles did not represent a new revolution—not unless you were a Korean grocer whose store was burned down while cops stood there and watched and did nothing—and the whole issue faded as the Democrats dissolved into factions about what sorts of goodies they might get to buy off their special interests. The president moved on. To the balanced-budget amendment. And his trip to Panama. And Rio.

You have worked in the White House since the beginning, in 1989. You have gotten to know the president a little bit, seen him in action. He has even become a role model for you. You have recently married a woman with two small kids, and you are so committed to being a good father to your two new stepchildren that you drive the thirty-four miles back and forth between the White House and the kids' school to go to their games in the middle of the day.

That would have been almost impossible during the Reagan administration, in which you also worked. But now you are working for Bush, and you know how important family is to him. You know what a good father he is, what a good family man. You feel that by working to get close to your kids, you are fulfilling his mandate. You do not feel guilty—well, not much—about taking the two hours away from the OEOB and making them up later.

You are upset at the political decisions being made, upset at the way things are going, but it makes you a little mad when you hear some people in the place talking about Bush in a way you consider disrespectful. It's not his fault. He's being ill served. It's just so obvious.

FOUR:

IN AND OUT OF THE LOOP, OR, THE GNOMISH GNOSTICS MEET SKULL AND BONES

Washington is a city that produces nothing but information. And information is treated as though it were a rare and precious jewel because, by its very nature, there is never enough of it to go around. The key to a culture based on information is that the act of hoarding it becomes second nature. Not only second nature: It has become the basis of a bureaucratic religion. And the acknowledged high priest of that religion in the Bush years was Richard Darman, who was both the director of the Office of Management and Budget and the most powerful staffer throughout the four years of the Bush White House.

Darman cut a fascinating figure. His graying hair was always disheveled, as befit a man who was his own barber—a fact he never failed to mention to reporters who wrote profiles of him, since it made him seem without vanity. But on an afternoon one week before he and everybody else were to be sent packing from the White House for good, what was most interesting was his trousers, which were easily two inches too tight around the waist. He wore his pants without a belt, and they folded in on themselves at his midsection. The last four years had not exactly done wonders for his figure.

He was complaining about the industry that was cropping up in the wake of the Bush defeat, an industry whose sole purpose was the assassination of his character. The two White House aides with whom he had feuded most publicly, deputy assistants to the president Charles Kolb and James Pinkerton, were both writing books, he had heard, and he knew he was going to be the villain in both. Kolb and Pinkerton were going to make it sound as though he were personally responsible for the presidential defeat.

But what, he wondered aloud, could two relatively lowly members of the senior staff have to say about the administration that could possibly be of any interest? Their own boss, Roger Porter, paid them no attention, did not bring them into policy discussions. Anything they wrote, he said, would be wrong—ill informed and ignorant. "They didn't know anything. They weren't one of the five people in the meetings. They weren't even one of the twenty-five. They have no idea what went on."

He paused. "Which, I guess, is part of their point, that they were kept out of the loop. But still, they just have no clue."

What Darman was saying was this: Only administration insiders would ever really know the truth—the reasons things happened the way they happened. Which meant that anyone not "in the loop" was not competent to judge the decisions that emanated from inside "the loop."

Darman's dismissal of his critics was holy writ from the altar of his, and Bush-era Washington's, true religion: Gnomish Gnosticism.

The original Gnostics were early Christians who believed there was a hidden meaning to the words of Jesus only they could decipher by mystical knowledge with which only they had been endowed by God. That particular band of Gnostics was branded heretical and died out, but the intellectual perversity they represented has survived well into the twentieth century and flourishes in Washington today.

The Gnomish Gnostics are gnomish both physically—for some reason the Gnomish Gnostics tend to be stout and often short—and intellectually—since they affect a worldly wit that is at once seductive and condescending. The gospel of the Gnomish Gnostics holds that the public statements, public decisions and public actions of politicians are at best meaningless and at worst deliberately misleading. The truth is known only to those who know the secret codes and are in possession of the truth that is kept veiled by those with the power.

According to the Gnomish Gnostics, decisions can only be understood "in context"; it is unfair or illegitimate to criticize decision makers unless you were there, with them, at the time. It does not matter to the Gnostics that those private decisions have profound public consequences, and are a matter of fact no matter how they were reached.

The Gnostics need little outside counsel; instead, they conduct their business in secret and then present their grand designs to the world without warning. They assume that their knowledge of the mysteries of the Washington universe will dazzle and humble all those below.

The ultimate triumph of the Gnomish Gnostics was the 1990 budget deal, reached with Congress after five months of secret negotiations at Andrews Air Force Base. The budget deal was set before a stunned political world by its designers with the simple presumption that the nation would have no choice but to accept the purification ritual of higher taxes and fewer services the Gnostics had, in all their wisdom, devised.

It was the budget deal that focused the wrath of Republican Washington on Richard Darman. Its details were a matter of public knowledge; its passage either had no positive effect on the nascent recession or in fact caused the economy to remain in the doldrums for two years; and everybody in America knew that Bush had broken his no-new-taxes pledge to sign it. And still, two years later, Darman was completely convinced that Kolb and Pinkerton could have nothing intelligent to say about it because *they weren't in the loop.*

This Gnostic attitude so suffuses official Washington that it functions as a convenient way to control and censor discussions and disagreements. Those "in the loop" can always trump those who aren't merely by making reference to the secrets they know but cannot reveal.

Darman was right; his critics weren't in the loop. They were not privy to the private discussions of the White House brain trust—a group that never numbered more than ten people. That means ten people were doing and deciding and managing *everything* in the White House's purview. Especially in the two and a half years of Sununu's stewardship, and Baker's five months, White House staffers merely carried out policies made without their participation and often in contradiction to the publicly stated goals of the administration as delineated in the campaign many of them had worked on. When aides like Pinkerton and Kolb made uncertain attempts to insert themselves into the policy-making process, they were told in no uncertain terms to get the hell out.

But Darman's dismissal of these staffers as ignorant when they were deliberately kept in the dark and out of the meetings was an illustration of how completely the Gnostic religion controlled the Bush White House.

The Bush White House certainly did not invent the loop. There has always been a loop, especially in intelligence matters, because the leak of a secret bit of intelligence could mean the death of the agent supplying it. In the modern presidency, there has always been a loop and there will always be one.

But never before had the loop mattered quite so much.

Darman found a fellow Gnomish Gnostic in John Sununu. The two of them attempted to duplicate in domestic policy the extraordinary teamsmanship of Richard Nixon and Henry Kissinger in foreign policy. Just as it was with their predecessors, the domestic policy loop they formed was the White House equivalent of the Computer Club. They were nerdy guys fully grown, who retained from their high school years the special blend of arrogance and awkwardness that gets nerds beaten up by the nice but dumb jocks they scorn.

Sununu and Darman shared with Nixon and Kissinger a clinical and unemotional evaluation of power and policy; they brought to domestic policy the approach Kissinger called "realpolitik." They were managers of the world as it was, not as they believed it should be. Sununu and Darman were empiricists, not ideologues: Sununu constantly used the terminology of his engineering background to describe his view of politics. And Darman brought to the team an encyclopedic knowledge of the machinery of the executive branch.

The Gnomish Gnostics offer a politician a no-lose deal: They promise him he can cut lots of deals—a pol's favorite activity—and stand tough and firm all at the same time. Gnostics promise that any deal they make in the name of their elected boss will be the best one possible.

This was how Darman and Sununu sold Bush on the 1990 budget pact, which traded tax increases for a restructuring of the way the government spends its money. They told Bush the deal would protect defense spending from liberals lasciviously eyeing Pentagon riches at the end of the Cold War and compel them to offset every dollar in new spending with a dollar in spending cuts.

It was a seductive pitch: The tax increase will sting for a little while but it's basically a gimme because we've gotten an amazing deal out of the Congress. Total control over spending! A revolution in the way government spends money! We've actually got Congress by the balls! It's beautiful! No more runaway spending, no more threats to the defense budget, no more raiding of the Treasury! By giving in on this little matter, Mr. President, you have won a victory far larger than anybody could possibly have anticipated!

In other words: It may look like you lost, but actually you won! A remarkable piece of Gnomish Gnostic logic, and too clever by half. Because, actually, the Bush White House lost and lost big. Not only was the violation of the no-new-taxes pledge a political catastrophe for the Bush presidency, but the deal's benefits proved illusory. The deficit would not be cut in half in five years, as Darman promised; there was never the slightest chance that increased revenues from taxes would be met with significant cuts in spending. Congress doesn't work that way. Congressmen, unlike Gnomish Gnostics, have to face the voters rather frequently, and what they do is say, "Look how much I got for you!"

So just as Kissinger had his Paris peace accords, Darman had his budget deal. Just as Kissinger won the Nobel Peace Prize and the North Vietnamese won the war, so Darman won an extraordinary bureaucratic victory and helped his boss lose the 1992 election.

The domestic policy loop was concerned with one thing and one thing only: how to deal with Congress. Indeed, probably no White House has ever been quite as obsessed with Congress, not even Lyndon Johnson's.

Ordinarily, the issue of executive-branch relations with the legislative branch is just one of several confronting the White House, and by no means the most important. Every cabinet department has an assistant secretary dedicated to congressional relations with a staff larger than the entire White House legislative affairs operation. When things are working right, these specialists outside the White House should be handling most of the business between the executive branch and the Hill.

A successful White House is much more concerned with controlling the atmosphere and issues in Washington and the nation through a combination of outreach and public relations. When the White House manages the national agenda, Congress can be compelled either to follow or to fight a defensive battle against an active and energetic presidency. The Bush White House, all four years of it, mistakenly believed that its primary job was to work with or work against Congress—not to lead Congress, but to enter into partnership with Congress. "I don't think about the word 'mandate,' " Bush said at his first press conference as president-elect. "I want to work with Congress to determine the will of the people."

Wrong. As one of the two nationally elected officials (the other is the vice-president) the president is the person in Washington best equipped to judge "the will of the people." That is why we have a president instead of a prime minister; his direct election is the sole source of his constitutional authority. Congress is supposed to represent parochial interests. The president is supposed to harness the factions of Congress together so that it will fund projects that serve the nation as a whole.

The president can control Congress only by reminding its members over and over that he got fifty million votes while most of them were lucky if they received one hundred thousand. He does that by using the office to conduct an ongoing conversation with the American people to which no other politician is invited—stirring speeches, symbolic public appearances and leaks that reveal the supposedly "private" passions of the president about the behavior of his rivals. The Reaganites called this "going over the heads of the establishment directly to the American people."

"Leadership" is the word often used to describe this aspect of the presidency. Actually, it's a form of consultation. The president is not the leader of the American people, but their employee. They are the stockholders, he is a CEO with a four-year contract, and he'd better let them in on the action and get them excited about it if he wants to get his contract renewed in the next leap year.

That is why a successful White House gives much more thought to its relations with the coalition that elected the president and to public opinion in general than to Congress. But everything was backward in the Bush White House. Bush was uncomfortable serving as the tribune of the people. He didn't understand them and felt very little connection to them. The only person in the loop who might have been able to convince the president to intensify that connection was press secretary Marlin Fitzwater, but Fitzwater's interest was purely parochial. He was not concerned with ways of advancing the president's agenda, and what few ideas he did have weren't especially good ones. His primary concern was how best to answer embarrassing questions from the Washington media, which was always an exercise in defense, a form of damage control.

And while Bush had little to say to the American people, he believed he had a lot to say to the 535 members of Congress. Like them, he was a professional politician who had served on the Hill. Like them, he had left the real world for Washington as soon as he was able and never went back. And like them, he believed politics was the art of the deal.

Bush was always opposed to bashing Congress, even though Democrats controlled both houses of Congress and Congress-bashing never failed to wow the crowds. What is more, during his administration Congress was rocked with the Barney Frank call-boy scandal, the House post office money-laundering scandal, the check-bouncing scandal, the Teddy Kennedy–in–Palm Beach scandal, and the scandalous treatment of Anita Hill (if you were a liberal) or the scandalous treatment of Clarence Thomas (if you were a conservative). Congressional misbehavior was material for Jay Leno; why not the president of the United States?

But Bush always balked at it because as he read his speeches he saw the face of his friend Danny Rostenkowski, the ultimate House wheeler-dealer and chairman of the Ways and Means Committee. He did not want to hurt Danny's feelings, did not want to get Danny mad at him. "Danny won't like that," he said again and again, striking caustic sound-bites about Congress time and again.

The administration described all its successes in legislative terms: It got a Clean Air Act, an Americans with Disabilities Act, a transportation bill. Sununu spent an extraordinary amount of time in direct negotiations over legislation, even traveling to the Hill for meetings. He was on the floor of the House during the dramatic all-nighters in October when the thirteen bills that made up the government budget were passed. No chief of staff had done that before—chiefs of staff are supposed to sit in their office and run the White House, not write the budget.

The Gnostics even swaggered over the president's power by citing his thirty-five successful vetoes, a string unbroken until October 1992. The vetoes were the iron fist within Bush's velvet glove, and were considered a mark of the administration's willingness to get tough with the Congress. But that strategy proved unintentionally damaging; Congress would pack a fiscally irresponsible bill full of things the White House had said it would not accept, vote on it favorably and then send it to the White House for a veto. Thus saved from the costs of their own action, they would fail to overturn the veto and simultaneously blame Washington's paralysis and gridlock on the inflexibility of what was in truth an all-too-flexible White House.

Granted, the Bush White House faced an extremely difficult situation when it took office: both houses of Congress in Democratic control, as opposed to 1981, when Reagan not only had a Republican Senate but a conservative voting bloc in the House until the 1982 elections.

But rather than playing to the president's strengths—the 54 percent of the electorate that chose Bush in 1988—he played to Danny and Tom (Foley) and George (Mitchell) instead. Bush permitted his administration to become a political and ideological hostage to the whims of a Congress in hostile hands.

His conciliatory attitude finally convinced Senate majority leader

George Mitchell that his presidency was hollow. Mitchell clearly decided he was simply going to play Herman Melville's Bartleby the Scrivener until November 1992 and say "I prefer not to" whenever the White House wanted something. And bereft of his teammate in the effort to determine "the will of the people," George Bush began to fall apart.

The Gnostics did not do *everything* by themselves. On individual issues, they would bring in White House specialists to do some of the spadework on Capitol Hill. These specialists were invariably fellow Gnostics, or Gnostics-in-training. None of them was a Sununu appointee.

The two favorites were Darman's chief aides, Bob Grady and Tom Scully—whose presence did not really represent a widening of the loop, since both men were serving at Darman's pleasure. Both were thirty-one at the beginning of the administration, and like their boss they proved almost frighteningly competent. "Competent" was the watchword of a true Gnostic, and the two men were both proud of their own skills and utterly contemptuous of others they could not apply the word to.

The Gnostics deputized Quayle chief of staff Bill Kristol to work with conservatives, especially regarding the controversies that were raging at the National Endowment for the Arts. Kristol, the voice of the New Right in the White House, had many things in common with the Gnostics and was therefore accorded some respect by Sununu and Darman, who loathed everybody else in the place with his views. Sununu, unsurprisingly, had played no role in hiring Kristol at the White House; Kristol could have filled a variety of jobs, but Sununu could never have countenanced so able an underling.

A brilliant manipulator of the press, an aggressive bureaucratic infighter possessed of a terrific deprecatory wit, Kristol was the only Reaganite success story of the Bush administration. He was a latecomer to the Washington scene, having been an Ivy League academic until he was brought to Washington by then–Education Secretary William J. Bennett to be his chief of staff in 1986.

It was a remarkably fortuitous move, for at the age of thirty-five,

Kristol was single-handedly to disprove George Bernard Shaw's maxim: "He who can, does. He who cannot, teaches." He helped Bennett turn a backwater department into a lightning rod for the educational reform movement and the center of conservative ferment in the second Reagan term. The Washington Kristol was a man of action, not introspection, and he took to his labors with the infectious glee of a kid who loves to jump in the mud puddles in the clothes his mother has just washed. At the same time, he was immeasurably strengthened by his previous intellectual life because it had given him a respect for the hidden power of ideas and the subtle way they can affect the culture and the country. He was unusual among the Reaganite true believers because he was as interested in *how* Reaganite ideas had penetrated the American consciousness and how they could continue to do so.

In this respect he shared the Gnostic view of the Washington roundelay. He was able to maintain a certain distance from his own machinations; he understood it was all a game. At the height of the controversy between Dan Quayle and Hollywood over "Murphy Brown," for which he had been responsible, he was able to explain away the fact that neither he nor Quayle had ever actually seen the show with the knowing and ironic quip: "We're too busy watching reruns of 'Ozzie and Harriet.' "

But unlike the Gnostics, Kristol did not use his bureaucratic skills for the perpetuation of his own bureaucratic prerogatives within the administration. Instead, he worked to perpetuate and strengthen his position as a leader of the conservative movement that existed both inside and outside the White House. He and Quayle determined that the key to saving and restoring Quayle's horrifically reduced reputation was promoting the vice-president as the conservative's conservative within the White House. It worked; when campaign chairman Bob Teeter launched an all-out assault on Quayle to get him kicked off the ticket before the Republican convention, the principal reason his gambit failed was that it would have caused utter consternation among the movement conservatives—just the people whose support the campaign knew it needed to solidify at the convention if Bush was to have any hope at all in November.

Quayle's defense of conservative principles was complemented by Kristol's defense of conservatives themselves. If some movement conservative—anyone, in any agency—had a problem, or if a conservative journalist needed a favor, the words that came to everybody's lips were: "Do you know anyone who knows Bill Kristol?" Even that was unnecessary; Kristol returned all his phone calls and listened to everybody's sob stories.

Darman got his way with the cabinet; Kristol helped his movement allies. And at the close of the Bush administration, Darman had become a pariah while "the buzz" had Kristol as the obvious candidate for the next Republican president's chief of staff.[1]

Following the work Kristol had done getting conservatives on the Hill to cool down about one of their particular bêtes noires, the National Endowment for the Arts, he was allowed into Gnostic paradise: the informal pre-senior-staff-meeting meeting with Sununu, his aides Andy Card and Ed Rogers, and Darman, just before 7:00 every morning. That, more than anything else, testified to Kristol's almost unprecedented power in the White House, for when Bush had been vice-president, his chiefs of staff, Craig Fuller and Dan Murphy, had no standing in the West Wing.

Kristol did his duty. He went to the Hill at Sununu's insistence to urge conservative Republicans to vote for the budget deal—his argument, which turned out to be true, was that if they rejected the first version, the second one was going to be far more tilted toward the Democrats. But he told them he thought the very idea of a deal was a calamity; even if he hadn't, it would have been political suicide for him to back it when his own constituency among the conservatives viewed the deal as the American domestic version of the Munich pact.

---

[1] Quayle himself had unusual standing in the White House. Bush kept him informed, and Quayle felt free to express his views on a wide variety of matters. But there is no question his effectiveness was hampered by the constant beating he took in the press. The administration was obsessed with poll numbers and news coverage; for the first three years Quayle was the only consistent negative for the White House in those two categories. Sununu was careful never to challenge or exclude the vice-president, but the ceremonial duties of the office and the constant traveling it required conspired with the natural proclivities of the chief of staff and the OMB director to make policy without him.

Sununu had taken such a beating on the budget deal that he was at his most Nixonian in the six weeks following it; nobody liked it, everybody hated it, he'd had to twist arms to get the deal's second and weaker version passed. His temper was roused and his standing in town plummeted. Fortunately, the president's attention was completely devoted to the coming war with Iraq, and Sununu wanted it that way.

Which was why Sununu got so upset on the morning of December 6 when he saw the front page of *The Washington Times*. "Conservatives Say Sununu Must Go," read the headline on the story by Paul Bedard, which went on to quote "senior administration officials" bashing Sununu. The story promoted Kristol as his potential replacement as chief of staff.

Kristol knew the story was trouble when he saw it on his doorstep in McLean, Virginia, at 6:00 A.M. He was not the "senior administration official"; he had never actually met Bedard and had only spoken to him once before. Moreover, the whole central conceit was utterly preposterous: Kristol knew that (a) the president would not fire Sununu because of conservative pressure, and (b) even if he did, the last person he would hire for the job was Kristol, whom he did not like.

Kristol arrived at the White House a little early, hoping to laugh off the whole business, but when he entered Sununu's office he found a murder board facing him. He made a joke and Ed Rogers said, "We don't think this is funny." He denied his involvement; Sununu glowered at him; Andy Card looked uncomfortable; and when he left the office that morning it was the end of his time in the Sununu loop.

Another potential powerhouse who found himself delooped was Boyden Gray. Gray was the sole member of the senior staff aside from Sununu who truly had Bush's ear and his confidence. Gray was also the only person in the place aside from Darman who had hired a truly crack staff. Staffers from other offices at times amused themselves discussing which of Gray's three top aides—deputy John Schmitz and associates Lee Liberman and Nelson Lund, all former Supreme Court clerks—was the most intellectually prodigious person in the White House.

In addition to the president's confidence and a great staff, Gray had a fine mind, but he was not much of a bureaucratic politician. Early on, Gray made a dangerous enemy of the person in the White House who was the manager of the loop. He was Jim Cicconi, the staff secretary.

Cicconi was Jim Baker's man on the White House staff; he had been Baker's aide-de-camp in the first Reagan term. Like all Baker people (including Darman), he was a terrific bureaucrat and was remarkably loyal to his mentor. And when Gray and Baker found themselves at daggers drawn, Cicconi was one of the instruments of Baker's revenge.

The story begins during the Reagan-Bush transition, when reporters thirsting for news were badgering the press spokesmen for information on what the new administration was going to do. Bush's communications people had nothing to say, especially given the fact that in his first press conference as president-elect, Bush specifically denied he had a "mandate."

The image of an incoming president with no agenda began to emerge in the press coverage, and it is the job of a communications staff to alter negative images and retouch them into positive ones. One day, press aide Alixe Glen was in Boyden Gray's office and saw at the top of his in-box a memo from Wendell Willkie IV, a Reagan administration lawyer. Willkie's memo recommended that the new administration make a big show of its concern with ethics. The Reagan administration had taken a beating in the press in 1988 for supposedly lax ethical standards that led to the convictions of several former officials for lobbying violations. Willkie argued that talking tough on ethics was a clean and easy way for Bush to distinguish himself from Reagan.

Glen grabbed the memo and called Steven Holmes of *The New York Times*. "Here's our first hundred days," she said, and the next day Bush's new ethics focus was a front-page story. Despite the fact that it had been leaked, Bush went for the idea in a big way and appointed Boyden Gray administration ethics czar. Gray was to examine officials and their financial records with a microscope to ensure that they could not profit from their government labors.

Bush got his favorable publicity out of it, but taking a holier-than-thou attitude on ethical matters in Washington can be near-suicidal. The policy's implicit criticism of the Reagan administration infuriated Reaganites, who believed the accusation to be politically motivated and grotesquely unfair. It was the first real indication they had received that the Bush people intended not to praise their predecessors, but to bury them.

And guess who was the first violator of the ethics rules? None other than Boyden Gray himself. At the beginning of February 1989, stories mysteriously appeared in *The New York Times* revealing that Gray was on the board of Summit Communications, Inc., the $500 million family business, and had received $86,900 in outside income from Summit in 1985 and 1986.

This was a phony issue. Gray was not being accused of anything but Washington's favorite new crime: the *appearance* of a *possible* conflict of interest. Not a conflict of interest, mind you; a *possible* conflict of interest. Not even a possible conflict of interest, but something perfectly explicable that to an untutored eye might *appear* as though it *might* be a conflict of interest.

As White House counsel Gray would probably deal with matters involving communications; normally in such a situation an official can simply recuse himself from the matter. But in the maniacal atmosphere the "ethics presidency" had created, that was insufficient. Gray immediately resigned his position and put all his holdings into a blind trust, a move that cost him $100,000. But he did not move fast enough; the news hit all the papers.

Gray was convinced that the leak about his problem came from the White House camp, which was still loyal to Jim Baker. And why? Because at that very time Gray had discovered that Baker, Bush's closest adviser, was *also* in violation of the ethics principles—and in a manner far more suspicious than Gray.

Baker, Gray had found out, held $250,000 worth of stock in Chemical Bank. Moreover, Baker had held on to the stock during his service as treasury secretary from 1985 to 1988; his most noteworthy act in the job was his ambitious proposal for reducing third-world debt and American bank exposure to it. Chemical Bank was owed $10 billion by third-world countries staggering under the debt burden. Baker had put his money in a semiblind trust—he had no authority to manage his own funds, but he knew where they were. As Bush's secretary of state, he was still in a position to affect the third-world debt problem. But he did not sell his holdings.

Gray believed Baker or one of his people inside the White House had betrayed Gray to the press to distract attention from Baker's own concurrent problems, which had not yet made their way into the papers.

But just one day after Gray's story appeared, the Baker problem was in all the papers as well. Eventually, Baker agreed to sell his stock at a loss of at least $100,000 too. And he was (sources reported) "furious" at Gray because (sources reported) Gray had leaked the stories about Baker to deflect attention from *his* own concurrent problems.

In other words, in best Washington style, Gray had believed Baker had leaked a story about him and in retaliation had leaked a story about Baker, who then leaked back his "fury." Bush, who only a week earlier had insisted, "My emphasis on ethical public service is not some fad or passing fancy. It's something I would like to see our administration institutionalize as best we can," found two of the people he most trusted in big trouble. And that, as well as the ethics talk swirling about the pension arrangement Health and Human Services Secretary–designate Louis Sullivan had made with the college whose president he had been, finally put an end to the ethics-for-ethics'-sake that was threatening to consume some of his favorite staff members.

"I want high ethical standards," he said at a March 6 press conference, "but I don't want to have it so it goes so far, bends over so far backwards, that a person that knows something about a subject matter is disqualified from serving, or a person that has some means is disqualified from serving, or a man that worked his heart out building a black medical college is made to feel that there's some perception of immorality if he keeps a pension that he's earned. I worry that I may have created something that's—certainly I know it needs clarification. . . . And secondly, I hope I haven't created something that just carries things too far."

Everything was settled, at enormous cost, just because the transition needed to feed a positive story to *The New York Times*.

White House staffers were convinced that Gray was a dead duck—he had gone after one of Washington's most vicious infighters, Baker, one whose relationship with the president was nonpareil. Or so they had thought. It turned out that Bush's vaunted friendship with Baker was a very complicated thing, made up of mutual rivalry, dependency and history. Baker, whom Bush had brought into politics, had been a far more powerful person than his old friend in Reagan-era Washington, and now that Bush was president he was not about to do Baker's bidding in a turf-and-leak war. Gray was safe.

The Baker-Gray feud erupted again in March 1989 when Baker shocked conservative Washington by striking a deal with the Congress that offered the Communist rulers of Nicaragua an end to all contra fighting in exchange for an election in early 1990. The true believers who had passionately supported the contras—easily the most polarizing issue of the past decade and one that had destroyed several careers and threatened prison for several people the Reaganites viewed as American heroes—felt betrayed. They did not believe in making deals with Communists (or Congress), did not believe Communists (or Congress) could hold fair elections and did believe that Baker was selling out one of the signal elements of the conservative cause (for Congress).

Those conservatives found their White House voice in an entirely unexpected quarter: the heretofore low-profile Gray. Gray gave an on-the-record interview to *The New York Times* in which he said the agreement seriously troubled him. His major complaint was that his office had not been shown the agreement before its announcement and it seemed to him an infringement of the president's constitutional authority over foreign affairs.

In short, he was complaining that Baker had left him out of the loop, which Baker most certainly had. The interview, which was an almost unprecedented public airing of an internal policy dispute because Gray had refused to take refuge behind the usual "anonymous source" designation, landed the White House counsel in what George Bush had once so famously referred to as "deep doo-doo." Sununu yelled at him loud enough for people to hear it two offices away. Fitzwater said in a press briefing, "I just can't tell you what was in Boyden Gray's mind. I mean, that's more than I can handle."

Gray's damaged position allowed Baker to effect the revenge previously denied him by the president. His man, Cicconi, got Sununu's agreement to reduce Gray's access to the White House loop. For years it had been White House policy for the general memos, speeches and statements that circulated around the White House to be cleared through the counsel's office. The lawyers received as much paper as the chief of staff did for the perfectly sensible reason that they needed to make sure the legal niceties were being observed. But Cicconi decreed that henceforth Gray and his people would receive only those documents that dealt specifically with questions of law. It was a spectacularly tacky gesture, but Gray's efforts to involve himself in a policy issue practically demanded that Sununu perform a bureaucratic castration.

Cicconi could not have delooped Gray without Sununu's consent, and the chief of staff's consent revealed that he thought of the deeply conservative Gray not as an ideological ally but as a potential rival. Reaganites often made the mistake of believing the ideologically illiterate mainstream press's portrayal of Sununu as a member of the party's hard Right. In fact, he was a technocratic policy wonk with a bias toward free enterprise. About one issue he was staunch: A devout Catholic, Sununu was theologically opposed to abortion. Even so, when he had his chance to lead the country against *Roe* v. *Wade* at the time the administration got its first chance to fill a seat on the Supreme Court, he and fellow New Hampshirite (and moderate Republican) Senator Warren Rudman cooked up a scheme to appoint fellow Granite State nobody David Souter, whose chief virtue aside from loyalty to his mother was his complete lack of an opinion on the issue.

The choice of Souter was an example of Sununu's technocratic thinking. (1) There was a problem getting a conservative jurist through the Democratic Senate. (2) A bloody fight on the matter would do the president no good. Therefore, the administration should (3) find someone unknown, whose views could not be discerned.

Souter was a gimmick, an engineer's clever shortcut solution to a political tangle. And like most gimmicks, it only worked for a little while. Souter turned out to be a supporter of the abortion status quo when push came to shove: He ruled in favor of *Roe* v. *Wade* in 1992 and consistently ruled against the administration in pursuit of his standing as a member of the Court's "middle." Boyden Gray had wanted Edith Jones, a more controversial Texas judge who might not have made it onto the Court—an interesting question, in light of the Anita Hill hearings—but whose selection would have demonstrated fealty to a set of principles and kept a sizable segment of the administration's constituency happy. No matter. Sununu had found his brilliant gimmick. And he had long since eliminated Gray—who was in charge of administration judicial selection—from the loop even on a matter as central to the legal issues facing the White House as the Supreme Court.

From its most junior levels to its most senior, the White House staff in the Sununu years served only as logistical support for the Sununu-Darman loop. Wags said that Sununu's preferred title would be governor of the United States, and Darman's director of the United States.

In many ways, Sununu was a good chief of staff. His White House did work. Things got done. Decisions were made. And for those who understood that his bouts of temper were not to be taken personally, he was a fair boss, informal and straight-shooting, likable and thoughtful. But the airlessness of the closed loop was over time destructive both to the spirit of the political enterprise and to the give-and-take and openness to ideas that characterize any successful political organization.

Every administration needs a Sununu or a Darman. They are the guys who know where everything is, who can always be counted on to remember the details and finesse the numbers and do the thousand different unpleasant tasks that Big Thinkers cannot handle. They were both superb in their own way.

But when you have *only* Sununu and Darman, when the bean counters and the technocrats are allowed to run the White House by Gnomish Gnostic principles, the extraordinary limitations of their vision and their stunning ignorance of the basic rules of political life will inevitably take their toll.

The act of delooping was not restricted to White House staffers. Sununu and Darman did their best to marginalize most of the cabinet as well. Once again, they were following the lead of Nixon and Kissinger, who joined in a conspiracy to turn Secretary of State William Rogers into a powerless figurehead. But that was only one cabinet secretary and one department; Sununu and Darman tried the same thing on no fewer than ten. Sununu would, whenever he felt the need, simply dictate policy from his office; Darman would, on the other hand, assert White House dominance and limit cabinet prerogatives by fiddling around with department budgets.

They were successful enough at this to wrest control of the economy away from Treasury Secretary Nicholas Brady—which might have seemed a major feat, since Brady was not only treasury secretary but Bush's best friend in Washington.

They found it easy to dominate Brady because it is never difficult to outwit a dimwit. When a rumor circulated around Washington that Brady was dyslexic, his people hotly defended him by saying, No, it wasn't true he was dyslexic, he just had to read things really slowly because otherwise he couldn't understand them. The dyslexia rumor gave rise to one of the meanest cracks of the Bush era: The president took so long to acknowledge there was a recession because Brady was the person who drew the charts.

In 1988, the outgoing Reagan administration had allowed Bush to pick James Baker's successor at Treasury when Baker left the department to run Bush's campaign. Brady was therefore Bush's first real presidential choice, and the quality of the selection was a portent of his administration to come. Brady was a Wall Street investment banker whose previous Washington experience had been vouchsafed to him when he was appointed senator from New Jersey after the sitting senator had been convicted and sent to jail. His political career eerily resembled that of Bush, who had won two elections in the 1960s and had spent the subsequent twenty years losing races and going from one appointed job in the executive branch to another.

Throughout his administration, Bush filled his cabinet in much the same way that Sununu had filled the White House staff—unimpressively. His taste ran to aged and undistinguished congressmen, like Representatives Manuel Lujan (at Interior), Ed Derwinski (at Veterans Affairs) and Edward Madigan (at Agriculture).

He also grudgingly made a gesture to his leading 1988 presidential rivals by giving Bob Dole's wife, Elizabeth, the Labor Department and his conservative presidential rival Jack Kemp the Department of Housing and Urban Development. They were the two people in his administration he could not bear having around him, and not coincidentally they were given the two departments he considered the least important.

When a good secretary made his way in, it was simply a happy coincidence. His best cabinet choice, Dick Cheney, got the job because ex-senator and weirdo John Tower couldn't get confirmed by the Senate—and the country might well have started rooting for Iraq in the Gulf War if the extremely dislikable Tower had been doing the briefings instead of the extremely personable Cheney.

When the president finally bit the bullet and allowed Sununu to fire Education Secretary Lauro Cavazos (officially, he resigned), the first choice for the job, former New Jersey governor Tom Kean, turned it down. Only then did Sununu turn to the exceptional Lamar Alexander, who had almost single-handedly invented the national educational-reform movement while he was governor of Tennessee.

Bush also had a fondness for losers—literally. He replaced Elizabeth Dole with Lynn Martin, a former congresswoman from Illinois. The shrill Martin was a great favorite of the Bushies, largely because she was a prochoice moderate who didn't go around bashing the prolifers. (Prochoice Republican women did badly in 1988 but well in the Bush administration; another, Susan Engeleiter, lost a Wisconsin

Senate race but became chair of the Small Business Administration.)
Bushies liked Martin so much they gave her a prime-time speaking
slot at the 1992 Republican convention, where she gave a talk that
made Bill Clinton's famously endless 1988 keynote seem like the
Gettysburg Address.

Even worse was Bill Bennett's successor in the job of drug czar,
defeated Florida governor Bob Martinez, who may have set an all-
time Washington record for fastest political suicide. At his first cabinet meeting, Bush introduced Martinez warmly and asked him to
share his thoughts on the drug problem. Martinez began spinning an
obscure story about how controlling drugs was like controlling thiev-
ery at the restaurants he owned in Florida. Unfortunately, he got lost
in the thickets of his own ganglia. He could not find the conclusion to
his tale, and he rambled on for more than ten minutes. There were
sighs, the clearing of throats, and a giggle or two, and when he finally
shut himself up, he and everybody else at the table knew he was
finished. He stayed on for two years, though. Like most of his fellow
Bush administration appointees, he had nothing better to do.

Sununu played an important role in many of these appointments,
and it is hard not to draw the conclusion that, as he had inside the
White House, that he chose weak people deliberately so he could
control them. Control them he did, although with so heavy a hand
that in six months' time he had made quiet enemies of nearly all of
them. One of those enemies was Transportation Secretary Sam Skinner, and it was a mark of how deep Skinner's disdain for Sununu was
that when he came on board as chief of staff he had not a single
conversation with his predecessor about how to run the place—even
though Sununu had been kept on for four months to "consult."

By keeping the loop tight, Sununu had forced people in the White
House to be excessively preoccupied with the perks attendant on
their positions—namely, offices and titles. And it was Sam Skinner
who would pay the price; his hope of expanding and loosening the
inner circle upon his arrival in December 1991 led to warfare without
end. When he let it be known that Clayton Yeutter was to be the
domestic policy honcho, that naturally bothered Roger Porter, assis-

tant to the president for domestic policy, who believed that he himself was domestic policy honcho. (Actually, there was no way he could believe that, since it had never been true. But it *was* part of his title.) What was worse, the only office appropriate for Yeutter belonged to none other than Roger Porter. And while he was peevish about the title, Porter was positively up in arms about the idea of moving offices. He wrote Skinner memo after memo, and talked endlessly to Skinner aide Cam Findlay about how important it was that he remain where he was. He lost, but the fight took three weeks.

At the same time, Skinner was giving Yeutter control of the White House's Economic Policy Council.[2] *That* prompted a major protest from Treasury Secretary Nicholas Brady. He, Brady, was the chief economic adviser to the president. (Well, once again that had never been true, but he was treasury secretary, dammit, just like Alexander Hamilton!) He insisted that the word "economic" appear nowhere in Yeutter's title. Again, it took three weeks for Findlay to come up with a title that would satisfy all parties (the ever-pleasant Yeutter never complained): counselor to the president.

But the main instrument for expanding the loop during Skinner's tenure was not his new appointments but all the meetings. Now all there were were meetings. Endless meetings morning, noon and night. Scheduling meetings and communications meetings. Campaign meetings and Policy Coordinating Group meetings. Like a character in a movie by Buñuel, a staffer would enter the Roosevelt Room for a meeting and find that he and his companions were prevented by some mysterious force from rising and leaving the room.

That mysterious force went by the name Henson Moore. Moore, the deputy chief of staff, had been a House member from the great state of Louisiana and then had served as deputy energy secretary.

---

[2] The Economic Policy Council was a forum for cabinet-level discussions of economic matters. It had a director and an assistant director who had worked previously for the cabinet secretary (first David Bates, then Ede Holiday). It was distinct from the Council of Economic Advisers, chaired by Michael Boskin, which served as an internal think tank and number-crunching firm.

He was used to being the boss; or, more precisely, he was used to having a lot of people around him in his direct employ. When he came to the White House for a briefing on his job from the outgoing deputy, Andy Card, Card showed him the small office on the West Wing's first floor in which he would work. Moore looked around and said, "Great. Where does my staff sit?"

"You don't have any staff," Card said. "You *are* the staff. The chief of staff's staff."

Well, Moore certainly fooled Card. He got Skinner's permission to bring over his personal aide, a twenty-six-year-old who had recently graduated from law school. Because of his exemplary legal standing, the aide was given the title "senior counselor to the deputy chief of staff."

When people weren't in those meetings, they were parts of "working groups," in which representatives from each White House office would come together to serve as the building's brain trust on individual issues. There were working groups on everything. Child care. Health care. Urban policy. Medicare restrictions. The family.

There had been working groups in Sununu's day too, but they had been for show. Now they *were* the show—everybody in the White House could now become part of some loop, any loop. But they had no direction, and Yeutter was incapable of championing the recommendations of any working group. In addition, some of them were riven with ideological disagreement and could never come to consensus.

One thing Skinner had in common with Sununu: He, too, failed to understand the important dictum set down by James Baker during his time in the Reagan White House: "The chief of staff is still staff." He is not supposed to serve as the deputy president, but rather as the manager of the administration's *political* apparatus.

Sununu hadn't understood that he was not supposed to be a policymaker, but a policy adjudicator—the person who helped determine whether a given action would help or hurt the president. If something will help the president, the chief of staff's job is to see to it that the entire White House squeezes every last bit of political advantage out of it. If, on the other hand, something is going to hurt him, the chief of staff must try to figure out how to either minimize the damage or transmute an unpopular piece of business into a winner.

As for Skinner, he thought of himself as the hands-on subordinate of the nation's chief executive officer. It was just a matter of getting the place organized.

And he soon came to discover how unruly a large loop could be. He got so bored and annoyed by the ditherings at the morning staff meeting that he resolved to restructure it by reducing the number of those in attendance from twenty-five to ten, and then created a weekly session called the "chief of staff's meeting" to give senior staffers something to hang on to.

One by one, the senior staffers who had been disinvited came to Skinner. Media adviser Dorrance Smith said he really had to be at the morning meeting because otherwise how could he best advise the president on his media appearances? And Skinner, perhaps mindful of the fact that Smith played tennis with the president twice a week, relented.

Gregg Petersmeyer said he really had to be at the morning meeting to coordinate the efforts of his national service office, which did "interface" regularly with the public out there. And Skinner relented. Over the course of a month, almost everyone who had been disinvited from the senior staff meeting somehow made his or her way back into the room, until only two or three were left out—excluded, stewing, offended. The senior staff *meeting* had proved more powerful than the chief of staff *himself*.

So it was that Skinner, the organization man, was hardly competent even to organize. But even if he had done a crack job, the White House would still have been in crisis because nobody—not the president, not his three chiefs of staff, nobody—knew what the administration was about. Nobody—including the president—knew what Bush believed. And as a result, nobody knew what to do or what to think.

In a White House motivated at least in part by ideas—as the Reagan administration was, and as the Johnson administration was—every staffer could feel he was a part of the policy process because he understood the philosophical and theoretical outlines of administration policy. In the Reagan White House, the outlines were quite simple: Reagan was philosophically opposed to the growth of government, the growth of taxation, and the spread of Communism. He was prolife, anti–gun control, opposed to judicial activism.

With this ideological outline in mind, White House staffers from assistants to the president to secretaries in the New Executive Office Building could go about their business with little confusion. They would know without having to ask when somebody floated a proposal to ban assault rifles that it was dead in the water. There was no way the Old Man would go for that. No need even to bring it up, to consider the issue for more than a minute, unless it was to come up with the best possible argument against it.

But in the Bush White House, it was very difficult to feel a part of things in the same way, because staffers had no idea from one day to the next where the administration stood on *anything*. Policy was an ever-evolving thing, always under negotiation.

In successful administrations, there is always a dialectic. The ideologues and visionaries come up with all sorts of schemes that make the Gnomish Gnostics suspicious, the Gnostics attempt to undercut and sabotage the ideologues, and when the smoke has cleared, an uneasy alliance has formed. The ideological fever is tempered by the realities of the political situation, but at the same time efforts are made to change the political dynamic to make it more receptive to the ideas.

There is a simple explanation for the administration's failure in that regard: George Bush's notorious problem with "the vision thing" and his own preference for the airless loop. George Bush, the first member of the ultraexclusive Yale secret society Skull and Bones to reach the Oval Office, turned American foreign and defense policy into a boys' club.

Pennsylvania Avenue's version of Skull and Bones comprised Bush, Scowcroft and deputy national security adviser Robert Gates, with Secretary of State Baker coming in from the outside. Baker, in turn, had his own subclique of Undersecretary of State Lawrence Eagleburger and the Gang of Four who later joined the White House with Baker: Margaret Tutwiler, Dennis Ross, Janet Mullins and Robert Zoellick. There were hundreds of political appointees, and foreign-service officers at the State Department were rarely, if ever, consulted.

When defense matters were in play, Secretary of Defense Cheney and Joint Chiefs chairman Colin Powell joined in too. And that was it. Scowcroft's National Security Council staff, which had its quarters on the third floor of the OEOB, was amazingly uninvolved in policy, especially considering the fact that in the Reagan years the NSC had run roughshod over the government. It might be fancied that the NSC staff's exclusion from the loop was a response to the Irangate depredations of Ollie North and company, but that would be wrong. The truth was that Scowcroft was a control freak capable of retaining extraordinary amounts of information and detail, and did not need or want his staff's help.

Scowcroft's secretive nature had its basis in three major influences: the character of the president he served; the character of Henry Kissinger, who had been his mentor; and the character of the Church of Jesus Christ of Latter-Day Saints, of which he is a member and whose president he might be someday.[3]

Bush's own secretive qualities are certainly understandable if, as the stories say, he actually lay down in a coffin in the Skull and Bones house in New Haven and either (a) publicly masturbated or (b) related all his sexual fantasies and his complete sexual history. We will never really know what happened, because the power of Skull and Bones is such that no one who has ever been initiated has *ever* revealed the secrets of the society. Good training for a future director of the CIA.

Terrible training for a future president. Bush's political life was inextricably linked to the social skills he acquired as he made his way through one boys' institution after another: affability, self-confidence,

---

[3] Bush and Sununu liked Mormons; there were two other Mormon assistants to the president, Roger Porter and Steve Studdert. There was, by contrast, not a single Jew among the original fourteen assistants, and by the end of the administration the number had risen so profoundly that the percentage increase was mathematically incalculable—from zero to one.

deference to the people above him on the ladder and magnanimity to the people below.

Achieving the state of grace known as "popularity" is the consummation most devoutly to be wished by gawky teenage boys who are forever shaped by the delusion of grace and style presented by a Poppy Bush as he makes his cheerful way round and about the campus of Phillips Academy in Andover, Massachusetts. Like all the most popular preppies, he was hesitant to give offense and careful with his manners, never going too far this way or that, relying on an "after you, Alphonse; no, after you, Gaston" set of principles in which he neither raced too far ahead of the general consensus nor languished far behind.

At Andover, he earned the lifetime devotion of one Bruce Gelb when he saved the awkward and strange young Bruce from a bully. Four decades later, Bush dipped back into his Andover past to give the awkward and strange middle-aged Bruce the position of director of the United States Information Agency, where he called staff meetings and, pointing to a stain on his couch that an FBI test later determined was chocolate, demanded to know who on his staff was having sex on his couch.

The Texas oil business Bush joined as a young man was itself one gigantic clique, and there could have been no tighter clique in the world than the tiny circle of Texas Republicans. Bush's tenacious efforts to save the nomination of the Lone Star State's John Tower as secretary of defense is testimony to the ties that bound two members of a minority nearly thirty years before. The Republican party was itself a family matter for Bush, who was the son of a Republican senator.

Bush is the spiritual opposite of Groucho Marx; he never knew a club that he *didn't* want to be a member of. Club members get privileges, but only the most successful club members know that the best way to exercise your privileges is to make yourself beholden to other people so that they in turn will be beholden to you.

That explains Bush's fascinating decision in 1970 to take on Democrat Lloyd Bentsen in a Texas Senate race he had not much chance of winning. He knew that Richard Nixon, who had put pressure on him to run, would take care of him, and Nixon did. It could well be said that the presidency of George Bush was born in that defeat; he became a good soldier for Nixon and Ford serving honorably and dully at the United Nations, at the Republican National Committee, as ambassador to China and finally as director of the CIA. Those credentials made him a viable presidential candidate in 1980; that viability caused Ronald Reagan to select him as his vice-president; and Reagan's success led to Bush's triumph in 1988. As president, he believed he could rely on the spirit of Skull and Bones to carry him to glory as it had in the past.

But America is not a Yale secret society.

In the end, the Gnostics and the Skull and Bones types (Bush, Brady and others) had a strange symbiotic relationship, like an alliance between the nerds and the jocks at some Ivy school.

The Skull and Bones boys went off and made the big plays in the big games in Panama and Iraq. The Gnomish Gnostics did the jocks' homework (domestic policy), and when even that wasn't enough, they went into the computer system and changed their C's to A's. As a reward, the Gnostics got to go to the fashionable parties and fool around with the uglier women.

The scheme didn't work. The headmaster figured out the subterfuge of the Gnomish Gnostics. And as the last week of the Bush administration proved, when Bush had to throw another $5 billion in ordnance at Saddam Hussein, the Skull and Bones boys may have made a couple of big plays in Iraq, but they never won the game.

FREEZE FRAME:

THE BUSH BARBECUE

AUGUST 3, 1992

Dressing for a weekend in the White House is an exercise in forced informality, a matter requiring the most rigorous sloppiness. You don bum's attire as a way of acting like a normal American person, a way of saying, "Jesus Christ, I work hard all week, I deserve a little time off, a little rest, it's not like I don't have a life, I most certainly do have a life, a life in which I can look as much like Fred Flintstone as the next guy."

If you are the type who must appear at meetings on Saturday mornings, as many in the White House are, then by all means you must (if you are a guy) arrive unshaven. You must wear a collage of short pants and pastel shirt in the summer, and jeans and a beat-up sweater or sweatshirt with college insignia in cooler temperatures. (Women, by contrast, are never acceptably dirty—they must appear casual, but neat.)

On weekends, you are expected to curse a little more, joke a little more. The pressure is off, and often more work gets done precisely because the quiet surroundings and informal trappings make it appear as though rather less is at stake. It is, almost always, more fun to work on the weekends than it is during the week. There is an easy-going camaraderie, and the mere fact that the telephone doesn't ring every forty-five seconds is a great inducement to clear the in-box and experience the always joyous feeling that you are in control of your job, not that your job is in control of you.

Henry Kissinger once said power was the ultimate aphrodisiac, and while he was talking specifically about getting laid, you know what else he was referring to. Being in the White House complex, being in close proximity to power, is hypnotically compelling. In her book on the White House, Peggy Noonan says everybody there is happy, but not everybody is good. Well, you don't know about happy or unhappy, but you do notice that you and people who work with you can hardly bear to leave the premises once you arrive there at 7:00 A.M. Acquaintances and friends and journalists want to take you out to lunch—which means leaving the complex grounds—and the thought fills you with vague anxiety, as though they'll cancel your access when you come back and strip you of the all-important blue pass with your photo on it. At the same time, the thought of leaving, even for an hour, seems pointless and foolish. After all, you can always go grab lunch at the staff table in the Mess, where you can sit around and gossip and feel that delicious feeling you can never quite get over that you are Inside the Inner Circle, that you are part of the hottest clique in the world. And in the Mess, the Navy men who serve you call *you* sir, like you outrank them, when in fact you probably wouldn't have made it through week four of basic training with them.

Your own job is your aphrodisiac. You are hypnotized by yourself, by your work, by your responsibilities, even if they seem petty and stupid to you much of the time. You have been permitted access to the sanctum sanctorum, even though outside the complex you are just another Republican dweeb, attacked by the media, demonized by the popular culture. Only your beeper, indicating a call from the White House operator, stays at your side to remind you that You Are Somebody. You miss it when you are away, and are thrilled, even when the pressure is intense, to arrive at the gate in your car (since you have one of the coveted spaces inside the complex), have your trunk searched for a bomb and then get waved through with a poker-faced expression by the Secret Service guys. You feel the calm that comes with the sense that you have attained one of life's ambitions.

Still, you are required to complain about the demands of a job that requires you to sacrifice your weekends. The act of dressing down is a symbolic expression of this complaint, but in the past twenty years it has itself hardened into a Style, so much so that your ordinary White House staffer would be teased within an inch of his life if he wore a tie or even dress slacks (although a sports jacket is acceptable because it might mean you need an extra pocket for your Sharp Wizard or Casio Boss or checkbook). This sartorial sarcasm is *de rigueur,* this knitted insistence that yes, I do have a life, even though everybody in the White House knows full well that he doesn't have *a life*, not really. People who work, on average, ninety hours a week do not have a life in the normal sense. You are, instead, a casual visitor to your own private life.

White House Republican men may praise the importance of fathers in families, but with your family is the last place we will find you. Your real life is your work life. Your friends are mostly friends from the campaign that turned into the staff job that turned into the senior staff job. Some of your colleagues have deeper and longer connections to George Bush (or Ronald Reagan before him) than to their spouses, whom they may have met at the White House or on a political campaign, in which case their marriages, too, are just offshoots of their political lives.

The White House is where you invest your passion, your hopes, your fears, even your true devotion. In a cult of personality, which is what the White House is, the demands of the flesh—your flesh and blood—are as nothing compared to the calling of the higher being—the president you serve. He gets your attention, your support, the occasional anger and frustration that any god invokes in his devotees, but what do the wife and kids get? Screwed, basically.

In the White House, people seem to get married and have children for the sole purpose of having smiling faces that stare out at visitors from picture frames on desks—or on walls, if their families have been fortunate enough to be snapped in proximity with the Bushes or the Quayles. A wife is to take to the staff Christmas party. Children are born to be borne to the South Lawn for the Easter egg roll.

A harsh condemnation of the Republican male ethic? Perhaps, but the putatively more feminized males of the Clinton presidency will live exactly the same lives; the modern-day White House requires nearly monastic dedication and a corresponding inattention to the person who may well have to fasten your Depend when you grow old and incontinent. Consider the story of Stuart Eizenstat, Carter's man, who got into the backseat of his own car on the day after the inauguration of Ronald Reagan because he mistook his own wife for his longtime portal-to-portal driver. The condition of White House Male is unchanging, and being married to it will require sacrifices.

Of course, the result of all this distance is . . . guilt and more distance. It's not only that you're never home; it's that when you are home, you don't really have a defined place there. Long ago your children learned that you will not make it to their Little League games, will go on a hastily scheduled trip on the night of a parent-teacher conference. They have come to expect their mother to serve not only as the comforter, but as the disciplinarian and the car service. A lack of familiarity with the lives and behavior of children breeds . . . not contempt, really, but incompetence and discomfort. You don't know what to do with them when you *do* have time to spend with them.

So you are actually relieved to leave the house after a decent night's sleep on Saturday morning, because on Saturdays the kids are underfoot, whereas on weekdays you are generally out of the house before they are even up. There's noise from the cartoons on the television, they want you to pour juice for them, a fight breaks out between your daughter and son while you are reading the latest assault on the White House staff by Ann Devroy (it's a slow news day) and about Clinton scoring points off the president on Bosnia, looking tough while we look vacillating. The noise and the fighting and the generalized sense of dread occasioned by even the most rudimentary glance at the paper jangle your nerves something fierce. You are a visitor in your own home, and the place is a nuthouse. Time to go to your real home.

So when you arrive at 9:30 for the morning meeting on this unexpectedly cool weekend, you find solace in the crowded byways of the West Wing and discover that, actually, there isn't really a meeting to be had because of course everybody is up at Kennebunkport and all they're talking about is foreign policy, which means Scowcroft and Bush and Larry Eagleburger in a room blathering away without anybody else knowing what the hell is going on. So you and three or four other aides basically stand around, doing the office-door-to-office-door thing, leaning against the jamb of each successive portal as this impromptu ferry service deposits each staffer at his door with a clear shot at emptying that in-box.

The mood is surprisingly cheerful—surprising because Bush is still at least 20 points down and though unemployment improved a little last week, that's happened before, and you've been on too much of an emotional roller coaster to allow your mood to be boosted by such an evanescent phenomenon. But at last there's been some shake-up in the staffing—the speechwriting office went through a Tuesday night massacre, four speechwriters fired all at once.

Meanwhile, there's something in Bush's manner that is heartening, the sound of a firmer resolve, and despite your contempt for the White House staff leadership, you are nonetheless rather pleased that Mary Matalin, who worked on the campaign, got kicked in the ass for her stupid, sophomoric effort to bring up the Clinton "bimbo" issue. Her enemies in the West Wing say she's one of the campaign people who's done nothing but dump on the White House through anonymous leaks to her pals in the press, but it's not as though she has any ideas of how to run things; in fact, her chief substantive contribution to the debate in the last four months was to whine and complain about Quayle's speech on single mothers because she was somehow offended that a conservative Republican politician like the vice-president might actually defend a traditional value or two.

But you're a little afraid to say you're getting cheerful, because it's not only Saturday, the day for complaint; it's also become a matter of routine to be mordant and mocking with your close comrades about the ruinous state of affairs. To act as though you are in a state of good cheer would be to start seeming Pollyannaish, insufficiently realistic. The whole attitude reminds you of a movie you once watched, insomnia ridden, on HBO in some hotel during the '88 campaign, called *Clockwise*. John Cleese is this very precise English guy who needs to get somewhere by 5:00 and every possible disaster befalls him on the way, but none of them quite so disastrous that it becomes completely inconceivable that he could actually make it on time. Two thirds of the way through, Cleese says, apropos of nothing, "It's not the despair. It's the hope I can't stand." *It's the hope I can't stand*: perfect words for the mood this Saturday morning. You almost dread the hope.

The day passes quickly, because on those Saturdays when the president is in Kennebunkport things are even more quiet, and you keep going, finishing the in-box and even drafting a few quick memos on your own even though it's now well past 1:00 and you told your wife you were going to be home by now to have lunch with the kids. Still, she knows better than to expect this. But you do need to be home by 3:00 because, in your never-ending effort to prove that you do have a life even though you don't have a life, you told an old friend from the Reagan days who is now at a think tank that you would bring the clan to a barbecue out somewhere the hell in Reston, and you need to add extra time for getting lost.

When you attend a party on the weekends, probably a barbecue or something where you can bring the kids and ditch them with other kids so that, once again, you do not have to spend all that much time with them, you do not dress like a bum but you are still very casual— Dockers and polo shirts, which get tighter as the months go by because you really don't get a chance to get to the gym and those cookies in the Mess are really first-rate.

The party, this studied concession to the idea that you are a real person with a real life, proves to be mostly work nonetheless. For you find you must uphold the good and the true and the beautiful about George Bush even in these few hours of mindless socializing.

These parties have usually been a pleasure because, let's face it, you are a big shot in the eyes of people who do not work in the White House. Even though you know that you don't have any real power, that you are just a paper pusher, that the real power in this administration is closely held by about five or six people at the top, in Washington even the proximity to power is an aphrodisiac.

You are not immune to the deference paid you, however slight and subtle—the fact that people don't interrupt you when you are speaking, the fact that people ask you questions the answers to which they really seem interested in. You get that impressed "Really?" when you drop a little tidbit of information, a cute little detail about Michael Boskin actually raising his voice and shouting at Sam Skinner in a morning staff meeting—just the kind of gossip that you know is going to be spread around with great seriousness, as the people you told it to tell others, "Well, somebody at the White House knows the economy is in trouble, because I hear that in a staff meeting Boskin actually screamed at Skinner about the GNP figures!"

What goes around comes around. There's a guy at this party who was a senior official in the Reagan Defense Department and is now a consultant. When you were working at one of the less significant Reagan departments and encountered him at a party, he did that looking-over-your-shoulder-to-find-somebody-more-important-to-talk-to thing. Now he's standing in the semicircle that has formed around you, a supplicant for information and gossip. For it's not only who you know in Washington, it's what you know, and when. If a civilian gets hold of some White House dirt that hits the papers four days later, and manages to tell several people about it before the *Post* publishes it, his stock will rise meteorically. Evans and Novak say Boskin yelled at Skinner—*Oh, yeah, I heard that*, the civilian can say. And he says it with worldly ennui, as though it is tough to be so knowledgeable, so incapable of surprise.

Parties and barbecues are therefore pleasurable stroking sessions for you. But this one early on takes a vaguely disquieting turn. As usual, those in attendance at the party want to grill you about your work, your life. But you are now working for a man who is daily the focus of stories about impending political doom, and if you feed the crowd your own dissatisfaction or fears you may be feeding a fire you really want doused. You do think the odds are your boss is going to lose, and these people are supposedly your friends, and you've been through the wars with them to some degree. You knew them from Reagan days, when Washington really felt like a battleground. But their questions and interest do not comfort you, as friends should. They are outside the inner circle, and as they press their inquiry you start to get the sense that they might not be sympathetic at all.

You may be giving aid and comfort to the enemy, or at least to people who do not wish George Bush well. And not wishing George Bush well is, ultimately, to wish you ill, because if he loses on November 3 and you are not a lawyer but rather one of those Republicans who is, basically, a professional Republican, bereft of fungible skills, you are in deep, dark trouble.

In fact, it seems as though there is a certain glee in the countenances of your friends as they speak of the political calamity befalling the administration. They may even float the notion to you that it might be better for the party if "we" lost the White House for a while. Time to regroup, let the Dems fall on their asses, screw up the country, and when the party has recovered, the GOP can swoop down and take not only the White House, but at least one chamber of Congress as well.

And you want to shout, "What do you mean 'we,' white man?"

Look, you are a conservative too. You believe in less government and you believed in fighting the Commies. You're not one of those Bushies, those softies who like to hug a tree as long as it protects their pristine view of the ocean from their North Carolina estate on a bluff. You are disappointed with Bush too, with the tax-raising and the Americans with Disabilities Act. But let's get a grip here! These guys act as though Bush is somehow responsible for every woe that has befallen America, including the rain that bollixed up his effort to start hitting the Democrats at a picnic outside Chicago last weekend.

Conservatives are behaving as if they're actually rooting for a Bush loss and a Clinton victory! It's like these columns and editorials by conservatives recently that have been calling on Bush to step aside at the convention. Who wrote them? George F. Will, the longtime antagonist of George Bush's? Paul Gigot of *The Wall Street Journal,* another enemy? *The Orange County Register*'s Ken Grubbs, who is a libertarian in conservative's clothing? Richard Viguerie, the fundraiser who went broke raising money back in the 1980s? Burton Yale Pines, who was let go by the Heritage Foundation?

These people are using their loose ideological affiliation with George Bush to express a loathing and contempt for him that is, actually, of very long standing. They're playing the media game, pretending to have been in the Bush camp when, in fact, most of them secretly would just as soon have lost in 1988 too!

So these conservatives, these folks who view the media with roughly the same admiration they felt toward the Soviet Union, are perfectly willing to let the "liberals" use them as a stick to beat George Bush with. When it comes to Republicans putting down other Republicans, the media are only too happy to listen, aren't they? Haven't Republicans spent years complaining that policy wonk Kevin Phillips is always described as a Republican when all he does is spout Democratic platform bullshit? Essentially, guys like Pines are perfectly happy to allow themselves to be called Republicans when what they're up to is bashing the king of the Republican party in 1992, the very president of these United States!

How else could Burt Pines get himself on "Face the Nation" and "Larry King Live" all in the space of three days at the tail end of July and the first few days of August? This is a guy who nowadays doesn't represent anybody but himself. And here he is, this man without a country, without a think tank, without a constituency, just some Washington blowhard making himself famous by advocating the self-immolation of George Bush! This is something that isn't going to happen, especially if he hears Burt Pines, of all people, calling for it, Burt Pines, who once said of George Bush that he was the worst president since Herbert Hoover—and this even before the budget deal of 1990!

Since they know Bush isn't going to step down, all they are doing is adding to the general sense that the president is crippled. They are not merely commentating, but are confirming the basic precept of the Heisenberg Uncertainty Principle: Their supposedly helpful observations from the sidelines actually affect the course of public opinion. They will not affect Bush's own opinion. The guy is running; if he didn't want to run or serve again he would have gotten out eight months ago. So they are objectively helping the Democrats with their portrait of Bush as hapless, out of touch.

They're being shortsighted and narrow-minded, blinded by pride. Their pride has been injured because they feel the president has refused to take them seriously, to treat them with the deference and respect they are due. More specifically, he didn't offer any of them a job, and they can't even pretend that they have lots of friends working on the inside from whom they can get skinny and feel like they have some role to play. This is their revenge, and to you it seems pretty petty. Of course, you *have* a job, so you would think that.

But their shortsightedness is disgusting, you think. After all, no matter how bad a Bush presidency might be in their eyes, a Clinton presidency will be calamitous. He'll start revivifying the activist judiciary. He will get at least two and possibly three Supreme Court nominations in the next year or two, and reverse the painstaking effort we have made to get that out-of-control unelected legislature under some control.

And that's not even to begin to speak of the wild shit that will come down with Clinton and a Democratic congress. Okay, so Bush agreed to the budget deal, and that was bad. But that was $131 billion in new taxes. In the four years of a Clinton administration God only knows how high taxes will go. God only knows what kind of legislation they will pass—anathema to even middle-of-the-road Republicans, like national health insurance, gay-rights stuff, federal funding for abortions, the full-scale rebirth of the Democratic taste for social engineering and experimentation with the lives and pocketbooks of ordinary Americans. Bush, whatever his faults, has served (as Reagan did) as a firebreak for the worst of Democratic obsessions.

Every American problem is a crisis to the Democrats, with a legislative solution that costs billions of dollars and will violate the central Hippocratic precept: Above all, do no harm. These people spent twenty years toying with the incentives and behaviors of the American people, almost all to the detriment of the family, the inner city, and the body politic. So it's obvious that for the health of the fragile country conservatives believe America to be, it is essential that George Bush get reelected *because he is the lesser of the two evils.*

Burt Pines would no doubt object that he is merely stating the obvious; as he told Larry King, Bush is going to crash like the *Titanic,* and somebody must yell, "Iceberg, iceberg!" But that doesn't account for the almost joyous way he is playing Cassandra. Cassandra didn't actually seek the destruction of Troy.

Of course, the folks at this barbecue are not the same as Burt Pines; they're not bashing Bush and calling for your unemployment in the national media. Your friends will even laugh with you at the foolishness of these calls for Bush to step aside when *of course* he would never ever do such a thing. But there is, no mistaking it, real *Schadenfreude* in these conservatives. They weren't invited to this dance, so it makes some sense that they would be pleased when the dance turned into the prom from hell at the end of *Carrie*.

But they mask their pleasure with a tone of intimate concern, as though they too might have jobs to lose and no visible means of family support. And you find there is something ghoulish about this, as though they are eagerly anticipating your funeral. For that is what is about to happen, your funeral, because this administration is going to be completely discredited if Bush loses, as Carter's was in 1980 and Johnson's in 1968. The people who worked for it are not going to be in much demand as political figures for a really, really long time. And executive-branch politics is all you know how to do.

So you find yourself starting to get defensive, starting even to sound "upbeat," starting to sound like Republican National Committee chairman Rich Bond on CNN. "This president isn't about to let these kinds of scurrilous attacks on him go unanswered," you say, you who just two days earlier stood outside the men's room at the rear of the second floor of the OEOB with the fellow you shared an eight-by-eight office with during the Bush campaign and said, "What the fuck is going on over there we didn't fuck around like this in '88 if Atwater were alive if Baker were here already if if if if . . ."

You start praising the president's vast foreign-policy experience, and the fact that if Congress had only done what he asked them to do America would have been saved from all the woes that have befallen her lo these many months. You talk about Clinton's poor environmental record in Arkansas. In other words, you turn yourself into a Bush robot, mindlessly spouting the lines you've heard the Bushies for whom you have contempt spouting in meeting after meeting.

And why? Because, like it or not, they are comfort food to you now. The Bush people are now your people.

Suddenly the day, which began with such promise when you arrived at the office proudly displaying your stubble in a T-shirt with a caricature of the senior senator from Massachusetts and his controversial nephew William Kennedy Smith emblazoned with the words "Will and Ted's Illicit Adventure—Be Sure to Cover Up!" occasioning much laughter, having emptied out your in-box and fought the impulse to be excessively cheerful, must end your Saturday in the car, silent, the kids asleep in the back, driving through the dusky streets of Washington and noting, with more than a hint of alarm, that the Previa is losing some of its pickup and there are still twenty-five coupons in that car book before you can claim you own it, but it's already out of warranty. And while your wife can deal with the hassle of repairing it, you have to deal with the fear of what happens if the goddamn car needs to be replaced.

"Honey?" she says. "I think I'm late."

Panic.

FIVE:

ADVENTURES IN REPUBLICANLAND, OR, BUSH CONTRA REAGAN

On November 15, 1989, the official portraits of Ronald Wilson Reagan and his wife, Nancy, were unveiled in a ceremony in the East Room of the White House. About one hundred people attended, including President George Bush. Press secretary Marlin Fitzwater, who had held the same position in Reagan's last year, was there. So was personnel director Chase Untermeyer, who had served in the White House and the Navy under Reagan.

But Office of Management and Budget director Richard Darman, who had been staff secretary in the Reagan White House from 1981 to 1985, didn't show. Nor did chief of staff John Sununu. Nor did thirteen other assistants to the president in the Bush White House, who all had better things to do that morning than pay their respects to the man whose eight-year presidency had transformed the GOP from a crippled enterprise into the first serious threat to the fifty-year Democratic dominance of American politics—and whose triumphant White House tenure was primarily responsible for their employment in it on November 15, 1989.

Fast forward to January 13, 1993, the day before Bush began a long weekend at Camp David, his final such weekend as president. In his last official public event, President George Bush presented former President Ronald Reagan with the Medal of Freedom, again in the

East Room. It was a final gathering of Republicans inside the complex that had been their party's domain for twelve years. And for many in attendance who had worked in the Reagan White House, it was the first time they had set foot inside the complex since January 20, 1989.

Caspar Weinberger, the longest-serving Reagan official, now newly pardoned by Reagan's successor, was there. So was Ed Meese, Reagan's most loyal lieutenant, whose reward for his twenty years in service to the president was to be kicked off the board of the Ronald Reagan Presidential Library by the ever-gracious Mrs. Nancy Reagan, she whom young Reaganites called "the dark side of the Force." Most surprising, in light of Nancy Reagan's iron control of the guest list, was Donald Regan, who wrote the most devastating kiss-and-tell book of them all about her after she deposed him as chief of staff in 1987.

Bush placed the medal around the neck of the frail, stooped old man who had been so robust and apple-cheeked throughout his seventies, even after the bullet that nearly killed him, a man who startled visitors to the Oval Office because he was so *big*, more strapping than he appeared on TV, his shoulders so surprisingly broad and his chest so bulky. The years had caught up with Reagan even in the months since his last major appearance at the 1992 Republican National Convention—he finally looked his eighty-one years, the wrinkled face and pompadoured hair eerily like the editorial cartoons that had mocked him during his time in office.

The lean and hungry Bush, who often looked slight and even a little sickly next to his old boss, choked back tears in the midst of his remarks (he was publicly choking back tears quite a lot in those days). During the ceremony, he finally uttered the words in the White House that he had said publicly only once before, at the convention: that he believed Reagan was due the credit he and his staff had mostly given themselves for the happy conclusion of the Cold War.

This time, all along the back wall of the room, straining to fit through the doorway and hear the proceedings at front, were dozens of Bushies from around the White House. They had been drawn to witness this remarkable scene: a successful president who had dominated the American political landscape as no other figure had in the postwar era and his failed successor, who was basking in the reflected glory of his old boss one last time.

What happened between these two occasions was the failure of George Bush's administration, a failure due both to the high-handed way Bush and his people handled Reagan's supporters and to Bush's misguided effort to do things his way and not Reagan's, even though Reagan's way had won him two elections and probably won Bush a third. To tell this story, we have first to understand who Reagan's people were and are.

The Reaganites—the true believers who came to Washington to work in and around the Reagan administration—may have been part of a popular and successful political movement, but they always felt out of it, self-conscious in the Washington whirl, as though they had been invited to a chic party and expected at any moment either to be laughed out of the room or asked to leave.

Even though they spoke the language of American populism and believed they represented the heart and soul of the nation, the Reaganites were actually members of the nation's most subversive counterculture. Unlike the more conventional counterculture types— hippies, gays—they had chosen to join a movement that placed itself foursquare in polemical opposition to the dominant intellectual and cultural tendencies of its time. They had taken to heart William F. Buckley, Jr.'s *cri de coeur* as he brought the nascent conservative movement out of the intellectual shadows that their job was to "stand athwart history, shouting, 'Stop!' "

The "conservative movement" that first clumped around the person of Barry Goldwater in 1964 and finally jelled around Ronald Reagan in 1980 featured diverse groups with divers (and at times contradictory) concerns.

There were the religious conservatives, who were terrified by the powerful forces rapidly secularizing the United States in the 1960s and 1970s, when in a matter of a few years school prayer was found unconstitutional, pornography was decriminalized and abortion was given legal and social sanction.

There were the anti-Communists, hurled onto the defensive by the fashionable support for Castro's Cuba and Ho's Vietnam, and the simultaneous decision by the supposedly McCarthyite Richard Nixon to open relations with the country they called *Red* China and seek cooperation they considered alternately foolish and morally noxious with Brezhnev's Soviet Union.

There were the economic conservatives, shaken to the core of their being by the once-unthinkable notion of the 1960s that it was perfectly all right to run the country at a loss and build up a large deficit. That idea, which allowed for the drastic expansion of the federal government and the Great Society, they believed to be a stab at the heart of the American polity, which Jefferson and Tocqueville had argued could survive and prosper only if the central government was weak and local communities strong.

There were the libertarian conservatives, who did not simply find the expansion of the state a worrying fiscal trend; as enemies of state action altogether, they believed the growing size of the federal government was a threat to civil liberties and democracy itself.

Three of these four camps had slowly made their way out of the Democratic party in the 1960s and early 1970s and finally fled to GOP safety after the one-two punch of presidential candidate George McGovern in 1972 and President Jimmy Carter in 1977. And they became the intellectual engines for the party that, in one of the most delicious ironies of the age, was to become the chief beneficiary of the growing public disaffection with American institutions—institutions whose legitimacy had been called into question not by the Right, but by the ideological Left.

The idea, prevalent thirty or forty years ago among the masses, that national leaders and national institutions were worthy of respect because they were the pillars of a great nation had by the early 1970s all but vanished—mainly under the combined influence of the Kennedy assassination, the civil rights movement, the Vietnam War and Watergate.

The slaying of John F. Kennedy awakened a nation living with a complacent sense of its own immortality to the fragility of the social contract. If, as Hazlitt said, "No young man ever thinks he shall die," America moved from a happy and mindless adolescence into a difficult and confused twenties. The civil rights movement had similarly awakened complacent Americans to the fact that in much of the country the very institutions that protected them existed in part to quash an entire race of people. When the villains in the United States changed from foreign influences and the criminals of the 1960s TV show "The Untouchables" to Southern law-enforcement officials and government bureaucrats as well as clergymen and other segregationist community leaders, the whole idea of community leadership itself began to seem illegitimate. The Vietnam War, of course, shattered the American sense of inviolability and also created an all-too-understandable sense of alienation from leaders who told you everything was great and then couldn't get the job finished. And Watergate combined all these disaffections—the idea of a hostile government, the idea that there was something corrupt at the heart of the American experiment—in the collapse of a presidency, which would have to rank as the ultimate institutional crisis.

Liberals and radicals were the prosecutors in these cases. They attacked the validity of the Warren Commission's establishmentarian report that found only one Kennedy assassin and no conspiracy. They made villains out of segregationist governors Orval Faubus and George Wallace. They created the protests against the Vietnam War, and engineered the national response to the Watergate scandal.

But they never benefited from their assaults. Conservatives did. Why? Because the conservative movement attacked the very institution of government itself—in conservatives' account, the root cause of the institutional malaise in the rest of the society. Liberals *believe* in government; belief in the positive value of large-scale government action is the centerpiece of American liberal ideology. Liberals believe that through institutional action—the creation of gigantic governmental systems like Social Security and Aid to Families with Dependent Children, better known as "welfare"—you change America for the better.

For a long time, everybody in America basically agreed with them.

But something changed with the assault on the institutions of the American polity, especially the presidency. The liberals began to undermine their own case.

If the political system were as rotten as they were saying, then expanding its size didn't make any sense. In fact, it even seemed kind of malign; maybe rather than helping all the people, the liberals were actually serving the interests of their own constituencies. Maybe the do-gooders had turned into another set of pols whose goal was lining the pockets of their "special interests." Since Roosevelt's time, Republicans had had to carry the crushing burden of being called the Party of Big Business; now Democrats had to bear the weight of Big Government on their backs.

The liberal critique of institutions robbed the American people of any real assurance that the programs the liberals wanted were going to help them or those less fortunate than they. The country itself, liberals maintained, had profound problems at its core and was in need of substantial overhaul. If they were right about that assertion, however, then new programs weren't going to accomplish anything but the perpetuation of a status quo opposed by the very people who were advocating their passage and implementation.

That was the big-picture problem with American liberalism in the 1970s: It became pessimistic. The liberals fragmented into environmentalists, who said American society was poisoning itself; feminists, who said American society trod on the ambitions of the majority of Americans; rights activists of every stripe, who said America was not a melting pot but a pot full of white sauce. The underlying liberal message from the 1960s onward was not liberalism's traditional belief in unending progress toward a utopian goal. It was, instead, that there was a cancer at the very root of American society itself.

This idea had been more a tenet of classic antidemocratic conservatism than anything that had previously been given the name of liberalism. Its popularity meant that no positive spin could be put on government actions except insofar as they could be claimed to be a form of reparations toward all sorts of groups of people crippled by the unjust American order.

Gone, then, was the Great Society promise of eradicating poverty, of creating social harmony through Supreme Court edict and just law, of an American utopia that would be majoritarian in approach and egalitarian in fact. Liberalism lost faith in itself, so America lost faith in liberalism. And losing faith in liberalism meant losing faith in government and government programs.

And while all this was going on, government just grew larger and larger, taxes rose and rose, and all to support what even its supporters believed was a basically ineffectual set of extremely expensive Good Works.

The three successful presidential candidates between 1976 and 1988—Carter, Reagan, and Bush—all campaigned as people who understood that the liberal government experiment was a failure. Carter talked about the need to make the government "as good as the American people"—a betrayal of the principle of New Deal liberalism, which was that government was actually better than the American people and had to take a primary role in society to force the people to *be* better. The Reagan 1980 campaign was based primarily on the idea that it was not the American people who had failed in the late 1970s—as Carter had notoriously insisted in his "malaise" speech—but the activist government in Washington that had failed them. And Bush's entire 1988 campaign was a referendum on the very idea of liberalism, converting the very term into a dirty word that even Michael Dukakis was afraid to speak for fear that it would raise his "negatives" so high he would never come down again.

Carter had won the presidency by posing as an outsider, but as president he busied himself by worrying over who was using the White House tennis courts and accusing the American people of not being cheerful enough for him.

Reagan also ran as an outsider, but unlike Carter he really was an outsider. He wanted to smash the state, not enhance it. That is why Reagan managed to remain an "outsider" even though he effectively ran Washington for eight years. Like the core of people who voted for him, he never believed government was the answer to anything except the provision of a common defense. *Government isn't part of the solution, it's part of the problem,* he said famously. And that was insulation enough against being tagged a Washington insider, because with those words Reagan did inspire the members of Congress and the state and local leaders who despised him to defend the very government workings and programs that their own philosophers had determined were ineffective at best.

Reagan never promised to manage government better; he only promised to get government off our backs. For that reason he was not tagged with the blame for scandals that occurred on his watch. They somehow only *proved* Reagan right; they were proof of his contention that the system was out of control.

That explains why he was, as his critics constantly complained, "the Teflon President"; the outrages and failures of his administration and Washington in general never stuck to him.

By contrast, at some point in 1991, George Bush became the Velcro president—people blamed him for everything that Washington did badly, or did not do at all. Everything stuck to him. And it was his own fault, because he reveled in the fact that he was king of Washington, the insider's insider.

The day after he was elected president, Bush gave a press conference in which he signaled his willingness to play by inside-the-Beltway rules as president. "I start with a great respect for the institution," he said of Congress—words that would never have come out of Reagan's mouth unless a punch line followed them.

"The American people did not send us here to bicker," he said in his inaugural address. By allying himself with Congress even before his swearing-in and by continuing to work with Congress not as the representative of the people but rather as a kind of supercongress-man, just a little loftier in role than the Senate majority leader and the Speaker of the House, he was unable to protect himself from the fury of the voters when Congress was hit with scandal after scandal and later when Congress simply refused to pass any of his programs.

Nor was it just Congress he made nice with. He declared himself chief clerk of the United States in a little-noticed speech during his first week in office that almost literally declared an end to the Reagan revolution four years before the press would give Bill Clinton credit for doing so.

The speech was delivered on January 26, 1989, when he traveled a few blocks west of the White House to Constitution Hall and addressed the career members of the Senior Executive Service. The members of the SES are the permanent bureaucrats of the executive branch, career officials who attach themselves and their careers to the public trough with glue as strong as barnacles. SES jobs are, without question, among the cushiest in America. They are positions of high rank and relatively little authority. The members of the SES are among the last nine-to-fivers in the country (they work nine to three on Fridays, generally), but unlike other white-collar wage slaves, they take in, on average, a yearly income in excess of $100,000.

They are, in sum, the very demons who populated the nightmares of every Reaganite—the fat, happy, lazy paper-pushers of Reaganite fantasy whose power and comfort lay not in less government and bureaucracy but in more, more, more. Since Reaganites believed that politics, like economics, was a matter of self-interest, they assumed that the permanent bureaucrats who worked for the president either were fundamentally unsympathetic to Reagan's cause or were working actively to subvert it.

Bush and Sununu chose the Senior Executive Service for the new president's first speech outside the White House grounds for a very specific reason. "You are one of the most important groups I will ever speak to," Bush told the dazzled audience, which could barely believe its ears. "What we really have in common is that each of us is here to serve the American people. *Each of us is here because of a belief in public service as the highest and noblest calling* (emphasis added)."

Hold the phone! A Republican president in the late 1980s praising public service as the highest and noblest calling? Celebrating *government workers*? A religious Republican would no doubt consider preaching the gospel the highest and noblest calling. A supply-side Republican would consider job creation the highest and noblest calling. An anti-Communist would consider the sacrifice of the American fighting man the highest and noblest calling. But these . . . these comfortable, do-nothing, block-everything, useless, overpaid, underoccupied, self-regarding, self-perpetuating, taxpayer-defrauding clerks?

Well, of course. Because who was the biggest clerk of them all? None other than George Bush himself, who had spent thirteen of the previous seventeen years working in the government in a series of jobs, in none of which he had performed with special distinction. He had been an unmemorable UN ambassador, a faceless and powerless ambassador to China, a tentative director of the Central Intelligence Agency and a far less impressive and less politically savvy vice-president than the much-maligned man who in turn served as his vice-president. He had proved that you could be a clerk and still, if you played your cards right, become president of the United States.

No wonder he was so eager to take the trip to Constitution Hall. These were the people who could best appreciate the astonishing turn his career had taken, not the Reaganites whose hero had had four different careers (as sportscaster, actor, union president and corporate representative) before he even thought of turning toward politics. Reagan had treated his final and truest vocation as if it were a painful and dirty duty that had been thrust upon him, and whose responsibilities he was willing to shoulder because the American people were nice enough to ask him to.

Nobody paid any attention to Bush's January 26 speech, but it was one of few genuinely meaningful addresses he gave as president. Having jabbed away at the sore spots of the Reagan coalition during his campaign and the transition, while simultaneously declaring his fealty to the principles of the Reagan revolution, he chose that speech to declare his independence from the Republican majority and his intention to throw in his lot with his true fellows.

In the weeks before the 1992 election, when it became clear that Bush was going to be brought low, Reaganites tended to react to Bush's misfortune with a kind of cold glee. And in the week before Election Day, a story began circulating in Reaganite circles from Los Angeles to New York. The details were a little sketchy, but it seemed that the Old Man himself had been having dinner with members of his "kitchen cabinet," the California brain trust and financial backers who had turned him from actor into governor and financed his three races for the presidency. As they discussed the coming electoral disaster,

Reagan said, "I guess I really effed it up in 1980." Meaning, if he had chosen a better vice-president, none of this would have happened. Phones rang all through Reaganland with news of the dinner party.

Reaganite One: Did you hear the story? The Old Man said he had, and I quote, "effed up" by picking Bush in 1980.

Reaganite Two: Where did you hear that?

Reaganite One: From John. He said he heard about it from one of the guys in the kitchen cabinet. Justin Dart or somebody.

Reaganite Two: I don't buy it. Sounds apocryphal.

Reaganite One: No, no. He said "effed" instead of "fucked." *I* heard him do that once in the Oval. It's got to be true!

Reaganite Two: I still don't believe it. Listen, I have to go. (Picks up phone, calls a third Reaganite.) Hey, Peter, did you hear what Reagan said about Bush? He was having dinner with Justin Dart and some of those guys . . . Yeah, the "effed-up" thing. . . . No, I heard it from somebody there. . . .

The Reaganites believed all of Bush's humiliations—losing the election, finally pinning a medal on the Old Man—were rough justice for a man and his followers who had turned their backs on the One True Republican Religion and indulged in heresies and pagan rituals with Beltway Infidels.

Those heresies flowered once the 1988 election was over, as Bushies got the word out that their man was going to be a better president than Reagan—more engaged in issues, not as lazy, and less ideologically driven. In a hundred media stories between November 9, 1988, and January 19, 1989, the same line was repeated over and over as the Bushie spin doctors convinced the press corps that the big news of the incoming administration was how superior Bush was in most ways.

First, the spinners played into the press's long-standing criticism of the Reagan administration's staginess. "Unlike his scripted mentor Ronald Reagan, Bush has displayed spontaneity," wrote *The Washington Post*'s David Hoffman on November 26, 1988. Maureen Dowd of *The New York Times* made the same case on January 15, 1989, when she wrote: "He will be a very different sort of chief executive from Ronald Reagan. . . . He says he will be engaged, peripatetic and responsible. . . . Since his election, Mr. Bush has shown a serene confidence that while he may never match Mr. Reagan's performance in some areas he can easily outpace him in others." Translation: Reagan okay, Bush good.

Second, they went so far as to use Michael Dukakis's rhetoric against Reagan. Dukakis, Bush's Democratic rival in the 1988 election, had said that the election was not about "ideology" but rather about "competence." Dukakis hoped to use the media image of Reagan as disengaged and even a little gaga to scare the electorate by tarring Bush with the same brush. Bush successfully convinced the American people that Dukakis was merely attempting to hide his ideological liberalism from them; he turned the election into a referendum on liberal ideology, and won it.

But that was over the minute the election was. A Bushie told *The Washington Post* that Bush was going to "make a determined break with Reagan's relaxed management style. . . . [Reagan] was a 'macro manager,' but Bush wants to show he is a 'competent' manager." Translation: Reagan bad, Bush good.

This attack on Reagan's legacy was politically incomprehensible and yet all too understandable as a matter of human nature. It was the Washington version of sibling rivalry. For Reaganites and most of the Republican party, Bush was like the kid brother of his high school's greatest quarterback (now graduated) who takes his kinsman's place. The kid is damned if he does and damned if he doesn't: A successful season, and everybody will say, "Well, what do you expect? He's Ron's little brother." A bad season, and everybody will complain: "What's the matter with him? Ron was so much better."

Bush brought those expectations on himself by choosing to run in 1988 as Reagan's True and Only Heir. While his mainstream Republican rival Bob Dole worried over the deficit and his Reaganite rival Jack Kemp worried over the policies of the Fed, Bush had a plain message. "Stay the course," he said. The course he was referring to was Reagan's: The nation had had a terrific five years on that course and he was going to keep in place the policies that had brought the boom of the 1980s about.

But by the time he accepted his party's nomination at the 1988 convention in New Orleans, Bush was already beginning to hint at his desire to follow a new course even as he was promising to stay the old one.

He wanted a "kinder, gentler nation," he said—implicitly endorsing the notion that the 1980s had been excessively harsh on the have-nots. This view was not, to put it mildly, the majority view in the Republican party. Far from it; the party's aggressive conservative intellectual leadership considered the talk about the 1980s being "a decade of greed" to be an ideological assault by statist economists and Democratic interest groups on Reagan's effort to reduce governmental control over the economy.

He wanted to be the environmental president, he said—implicitly embracing the notion that Reagan had abetted and encouraged the plunder of natural resources. This, too, was something the Reaganites considered a libel fashioned primarily by environmental interest groups. They called environmentalism "the new socialism," and charged their foes with seeking a complete overhaul of the American way of life.

He wanted to be the education president, he said—an implicit acknowledgment of the Democratic criticism that the federal government had done too little to improve American education. This was especially galling to Reaganites, who believed their administration had sounded the clarion call about the decline of American education. They were committed to the principle that education could only be fixed at the local level, with parents and taxpayers taking an activist role in getting teachers and administrators to take responsibility for truly educating their children.

The Bushies were deploying inside-the-Beltway criticisms of the Reaganites in an effort to make their boss and themselves look better by comparison. And the Reaganites caught on quickly. They found themselves in a kind of spiritual exile in Bush's Washington.

The Bush recession hit the Reaganites first. Always unpopular in mainstream Washington, they found themselves almost unemployable out of the government. Law firms were not that keen on Reaganite lawyers. Lobbying firms wanted specialists, not ideologues. The Republican minority on Capitol Hill was shrinking, not expanding, which meant that there were more Republicans chasing fewer jobs. Unlike the Carterites, they could not go into the academy or the media, both of which were hostile to them.

That left the Bush administration, but the Bush administration wasn't all that interested. Reaganites were not considered for the best jobs, although over the course of the four years many Reagan administration officials found their way back into the government they claimed to hate so much *because they needed the work.*

But they were treated by the Bushies like once-rich relations who had gone broke, and they acted that way too—desperately desirous of approbation and yet irritated that they needed it from those boring Connecticut cousins.

They came to hate Bush with the bottomless rage of a shy and awkward straight-A coed who, courted aggressively by a Big Man on Campus she does not trust, receives flowers and candy and love poems, and with some misgivings allows herself to be taken to bed; whereupon, the seduction complete, he rises quickly and is out the door to spread the word that she is easy, she is anybody's for the taking.

For that is precisely what Bush had done to them. He had courted the party's conservatives for years and, once his seduction was successful, abandoned them. In 1980, Bush had been the candidate of the party's fading liberal wing. He was selected by Reagan only because the California conservative wanted to balance his ticket both geographically and ideologically. The colossal Reagan victory in November 1980, which gained the Republicans control of the Senate and de facto control of the House, convinced Bush that the center of Republican and American politics had shifted so far to the right that he was bereft of a meaningful base. The remaining liberal Republican voters would move to the Democratic party because they had no home in the world of Reagan, and anyone who wanted to be a Republican president henceforth was going to have to be the candidate of, or acceptable to, conservatives—who were no longer merely a wing of the party but its dominant majority.

His courtship of the Right took place on two fronts. First, he became Reagan's most strident public supporter. "I am for Reagan—blindly," he said in 1986 in a classic demonstration of the principle that no gentleman is to be trusted who protesteth too much. The party's most prominent supporter of abortion rights in 1980, he almost immediately became a prolifer and never veered away from this position. The author (or utterer, rather) of the damning phrase "voodoo economics," with which he described Reagan's economic plan simultaneously to cut taxes and balance the budget, Bush later said he was wrong and said it and said it and said it.

Second, he trained his laser sights on conservatives, using his considerable charm and grace to win them over. He went to their conferences and gave fire-breathing addresses, using the words drafted for him by speechwriters Joshua Gilder and Peter Robinson and Clark Judge, all three of whom would go on to write for Reagan.

He went to fund-raisers and Republican dinners in conservative states like Michigan and Indiana, attempting to demonstrate his bona fides and establishing personal relations with local politicians for use later, when he would have to charm them into supporting him and not someone for whom they would have more natural ideological sympathy. He raised money for them and did them favors in Washington and wrote them notes—hundreds and hundreds of notes, countrywide, in his own glad hand, a brilliant form of politicking because it showed the truest and best side of his character while creating a correspondence between him and the recipients in every sense of the word.

When the conservative candidates in 1988, primarily Jack Kemp, failed to ignite the passions of the Iowa or New Hampshire electorates, the Reaganites had nowhere to go but to Bush. Over the course of the months between the February New Hampshire primary and the August convention, they talked themselves into believing that Bush had had a political conversion.

Their view of Bush and his presidency then went from modestly hopeful (transition) to disappointed (early administration hiring) to aghast (Tiananmen Square) to disgusted (sticking by Gorbachev) to enraged (1990 budget deal) to impressed (Desert Storm) to dismayed (no economic growth package in 1991) to outraged (supporting the Serbs in Bosnia) to traitorous (some supported Pat Buchanan in early 1992) to darkly amused (badly run campaign) to grudgingly supportive (realistic fears of Democratic takeover) to self-satisfied in their prophecies of doom (knew he would lose and he deserved to, too).

Reaganites professed themselves especially dismayed and disgusted by Bush's failure to pay proper obeisance to his predecessor. He never invited Reagan to Washington; he never called Reagan to ask his advice. It was as though Reagan were Lear and Bush some combination of Goneril and Regan: By his obsequious devotion to the king Bush was given the kingdom, whereupon he proceeded to belittle Reagan, retroactively criticize him and go to war with the old king's most devoted followers.

As the Bush years proceeded along, Reaganites began looking back on the Reagan years with a nostalgia that threatened, if they weren't careful, to progress very quickly into uncontrolled sobbing. At a party, somebody would mention that he had been in Los Angeles the week before and had "stopped by" to see the former president—which was far more difficult to arrange than the insouciant tone might imply—and related that the Old Man was the same as ever. And the other guests would stop whatever they were doing and sigh a collective sigh of regret for "their" moment, "their" time, "their" place in history, and for the fact that they were now adrift without a clue about what they were going to do or accomplish for the rest of their lives.

But despite the roseate gauze through which they gazed on the recent past, in fact the Reaganites had frequently been disappointed with the Reagan administration and its actions and often said so in ways that infuriated both Reagan and his staff. For example, they had found their administration far too willing to throw controversial Reaganites overboard without a life raft in order to limit the political damage. They had thought Reagan talked a better game than he played.

So during the Reagan administration and even afterward, the Reaganite defense of the Old Man and his reputation was not quite as selfless and loyal as it seemed. Truth be told, many Reaganites were less upset at the liberal criticism of Reagan, or at his treatment at Bush's hands, than they were at Bush's treatment of *them*. They used Reagan and his name as cover for wounded pride.

The effort to distance Bush from Reagan and the estrangement of the Bushies from the Reaganites was perfectly conscious, but the Bushies claimed they meant no offense. Privately, they explained it was merely a matter of strategy. They even had a name for it: They called it "the emerging suburban strategy." Their polling data supposedly proved that the suburban voters who had benefited from Republican economic policies in the 1980s were fiscally conservative but socially moderate. Those voters were said to be environmentally conscious— hence "the environmental president." And Teeter's suburban women were offended by the Republican propsensity for social-Darwinist rhetoric about the glories of market competition—hence the phrase "kinder and gentler."

The Bushies believed that "the emerging suburban strategy" was the key to winning over the electorate of the future. They somehow never explained how it was that in just four years the electorate had changed so profoundly. In 1980 and 1984, Reagan won landslides not by appealing to young Republican suburbanites, but by adding middle-aged urbanites to the Republican mix—the famous Reagan Democrats, who were economically moderate but socially conservative. The construction of that coalition destroyed the New Deal coalition, which had been the single most potent force in American politics.

In the 1988 election season, the Bush campaign used Ronald Reagan to appeal to the Reagan Democrats while Bush went after his emerging suburbanites. When Bush won, the Bushies believed the key to their success had been the emerging suburban strategy. The Reaganites, for their part, believed Bush had won by wrapping Ronald Reagan around himself like a blanket.

Who was right? There's no way of proving, but think of this: When people abandon a proven formula in favor of an untested one, as the

Bushies did in 1988, they are either visionaries or fools; they do so either because they see something other people can't see or because they want to see something that isn't there. The visionary looks at sand on a beach and sees a computer chip; the fool looks at the world's most successful beverage and sees . . . New Coke.

The Bushies saw a changed electorate because they wanted to believe that the electorate had changed, that it had turned into something they could recognize as easily as Reagan had recognized his fellowship with the Reagan Democrats. ("I didn't leave the Democratic party," the onetime union boss told them. "The Democratic party left me.") The Bushies looked at the poll data and chose to see an electorate that looked remarkably like themselves and held opinions like theirs: nothing too strong, not too much this way, not too much that way. "We don't have ideologies," one senior official told *The Washington Post* during the transition. "We have mortgages."

That was a pretty good line, and it spoke to the central Bushie belief that conservative ideology had been a hindrance, not an aid, to the success of the Reagan administration. Once again they were accepting the Beltway criticism of their predecessors; only when a bunch of conservative ideologues got some power in Washington did the word "ideological" become a pejorative and "pragmatist" an endearment.

But all the word "ideological" means is that you are governed by ideas and principles, not by the desire to make deals and do business. The ideology of the Reagan administration may have caused it no end of trouble—few Reaganites actually enjoyed the battles over Star Wars, the nomination of Judge Robert Bork and the nearly murderous disagreements over the contras—but it was a very effective organizing principle. Reagan's stated convictions provided a road map for his administration. It was not always followed in every detail, but those who worked for the Reagan administration generally were going in the same direction.

The same could not be said of the Bush administration, which had no ideology and therefore no sense of direction. Even when there was a stated policy, written in stone, it was not necessarily followed—don't forget "Read my lips." As a result, the Bushies had to reinvent the wheel every time a major new issue came up. This was exhausting, and made for ugly policy disputes inside the administration that were basically pointless.

Perhaps the most comic example of the adminstration's crisis of ideology came in a poisonous nine-month debate over the question of whether to grant the state of Oregon a waiver from Medicaid restrictions. (It sounds incredibly boring, but give it a chance—it's actually a good story.)

Oregon had come up with an innovative plan to solve its spiraling health-care costs. The plan guaranteed full coverage for all state residents, with one major trade-off: The cost of certain treatments had to be taken into account when doctors considered them. This meant that Oregon wanted to attempt a system of "rationed" health care for all patients—the uninsured, the privately insured and those insured by Medicaid, the federal plan.

Under current law, doctors treating a Medicaid patient are obligated to attempt every available medical intervention. What the new plan meant was that in order for Oregon to be able to insure everybody, some patients were not going to be treated. To put it most harshly, they were going to be allowed to die naturally instead of being kept alive artificially.

The plan could be implemented only if the state of Oregon received a waiver from Medicaid rules. And by law, only the president could grant such a waiver. Although the proposal was basically completed in 1989, it took Oregon more than two years to get its ducks in a row. Finally, at the end of 1991, it submitted its request for a waiver to the White House.

Chief of staff Sam Skinner appointed a working group inside the White House to study the matter and make a recommendation. And study it the members of the group did. For a full seven months. It took that long because the group quickly splintered into a prowaiver faction and an antiwaiver faction, and could not reach a consensus because while the prowaiver forces thought it a nifty experiment, the antiwaiver people thought it morally questionable at best, and possibly even state-sanctioned murder.

The prowaiver faction was led by OMB associate director Tom Scully, and soon his hand was immeasurably strengthened when Gail Wilensky, who had been in charge of administering Medicaid at the Department of Health and Human Services, joined the White House staff to honcho the health-care issue. Scully and Wilensky argued along these lines: The Bush administration believed that things were best done at the state and local levels. Well, here was an innovative state proposal, a test program of an important new approach to the national health-care crisis. The administration had just recently agreed to a Medicaid waiver for the state of Wisconsin to support its innovative welfare-reform proposal. No reason not to do the same here.

They had a strong political argument as well. In November 1991, Democrat Harris Wofford had won his smashing victory over Republican Richard Thornburgh in the Pennsylvania Senate race by using health care as his sole issue. Bush had a rather weak record when it came to health care. By endorsing the Oregon plan, he could claim he was looking for ways to change things. What was more, Oregon's two senators, Mark Hatfield and Robert Packwood, were Republicans and they were both absolutely committed to the plan. Bush could not turn his back on two Republican senators, could he?

This was a classic GOP good-government argument of the sort favored by the Bushies: Interesting plan, don't cost nothing, let's give it a try.

The antiwaiver group consisted of Lee Liberman of the White House counsel's office, Leigh Ann Metzger of Public Liaison and Jay Lefkowitz of Cabinet Affairs. They considered it horrific. The state deciding who shall live and who shall die? There was a name for that: It was euthanasia, and euthanasia was simply unacceptable, not only as a matter of morality, but as a matter of law. Good government be damned—this was not only a stab at the heart of modern humanistic philosophy since Kant but a profound violation of the traditional religious idea of God-given life.

The antiwaiverites had a strong political argument, too. First, the party's prolifers were already up in arms because they believed the notion of rationed health care was another way to get at the unborn child. Bush had failed to solidify his conservative base in the first half of 1992, and if he granted the waiver, the prolifers might well just decide to sit out the election. Since they constituted a solid 25 percent of the Republican electorate, that was not a particularly good idea.

The working group met, and met, and met. Skinner asked Metzger why he was getting so many letters from prolifers about it and she said, with some exasperation, "Sam, they think it's murder. They think it's Auschwitz." What he did not know was that Metzger was actually encouraging the prolifers, and anybody else she spoke to, to write Skinner so he would understand the political costs of a favorable decision on the waiver. Meanwhile, the prowaiver people were getting Hatfield and Packwood to call Skinner and Bush to lobby for it.

So frustrated were the prowaiverites by what they saw as the obstructionist tactics of the antiwaiverites that the usually pleasant (if excitable) Tom Scully took to screaming in meetings at the stolid Lee Liberman. "It doesn't matter what we think," she would say calmly. "It's a matter of law."

Skinner wanted to grant the waiver, but he was completely flummoxed by the passion of the conservatives on the matter. He asked Quayle chief of staff Bill Kristol, who was the Great Reaganite Hope in the White House, to explain it all to him. "The only rationale for granting the Oregon proposal is a theory of federalism that argues in favor of all state experimentation that doesn't violate federal law," Kristol (or rather he and Lefkowitz and Liberman) wrote in a June 12 memo. "It is a little late in the day, however, for us to embrace such a rigid conception of federalism principles. . . . It is one thing to approve certain details of a federally financed state-run program even if they are objectionable. It is very different to fund a state program that offends deeply-held Administration principles."

It was a complete standoff between the managers and the ideologues, and it was finally settled by letting the lawyers decide. As the time came to make a decision, Liberman came up with a new argument: The very notion of rationed health care might well violate the precepts of the Americans with Disabilities Act. The ADA was a far-reaching piece of civil rights legislation whose purpose was to end all discrimination against handicapped Americans.

This was a brilliant ploy on her part, because Bush and Skinner and the whole campaign kept mentioning the ADA almost obsessively whenever anybody asked what the hell Bush had actually done as president. Along with the Clean Air Act and the Civil Rights Act of 1991, it was one of the few pieces of legislation Bush could take real credit for. When Skinner heard that the disability-rights community was furious about the waiver, and, what was worse, that the waiver might actually violate the ADA, he was utterly at a loss about what to do.

White House counsel Boyden Gray, Liberman's boss, had an idea. Why not send it over to the Justice Department to decide whether the waiver violated the ADA? After all, wasn't that what we had a Justice Department for? Great idea, said Skinner.

But what Liberman (and surely Gray) knew was that the opinion would go right into the Office of Legal Counsel at the Department of Justice. And OLC was a hotbed of ideological conservatism. Within two weeks, OLC made the call: Oregon waiver unacceptable. In violation of the ADA.

And so, at the beginning of August, almost eight months to the day after it was requested, the Bush administration said no to the Oregon waiver.

Suppose, hypothetically, that the state of Oregon had requested the waiver during the Reagan administration. The chief of staff would have called a meeting. He would have asked what the substance of the issue was. Somebody would have explained the plan and praised its virtues as an example of Reagan's New Federalism. Then somebody else would have explained that it meant rationed health care, which not only would upset the prolifers but was potentially a form of euthanasia and as such a violation of deeply held conservative philosophical and religious beliefs.

"Oh," the chief of staff would say. "Well, we'll have to say no, then."

Elapsed Reagan standard time: five minutes. Ten, tops. Same

result. And all because the Reagan administration had an ideological barometer that could guide even those (like his chiefs of staff) who were not ideologues themselves.

When it came to ideological questions, Bush understood the words but not the music. His idea of pleasing the Right was to push for a constitutional amendment banning flag-burning after the Supreme Court ruled it an act of free speech. This was not deep conviction; it was kitsch, the defense of a symbol rather than a principle. But when it came to something the Right really did care about, he turned a pointedly deaf ear. Given a choice between conservative ideology and moderate practicality, he always chose the latter.

In the spring of 1989, a major ideological fight erupted in Washington over the federal funding of art. The Corcoran Gallery decided to cancel Robert Mapplethorpe's homoerotic photography exhibit, which would have been indirectly paid for by the taxpayers, because its director feared the wrath of congressional conservatives led by Senator Jesse Helms. This decision was greeted as the Second Coming of Kristallnacht by the art world and by cultural liberals. They grabbed hold of this outbreak of Political Oppression and wrung every polemical drop they could out of it.

Their caterwaulings awakened the Right, which actually hadn't been paying all that much attention but, once conscious, knew a good, attention-grabbing issue when it saw one. Here was something on which almost all Reaganites could agree, albeit for different reasons. "The government is paying for dirty pictures taken by homosexuals" brought together people who opposed arts funding as a matter of principle, people who opposed it because they considered it wasteful spending, people who opposed it because they thought it obscene that their money was going to pay for this bilge and people who opposed it because they considered it, basically, the work of Satan himself.

The arts war broke out in the first few months of Bush's presidency, and should have alerted him to the fact that regardless of what he did there was going to be a major culture war in the United States during his time in office. He was not going to be able to stay out of this one, because it was being fought by members of his party over the funding of an agency, the National Endowment for the Arts (NEA), he ultimately had to administer.

Bush had to select a general to command one front in the culture war, a new head for the NEA. He turned not to the conservatives for help in finding someone, but rather to the party's last unabashed liberal in the Senate, Mark Hatfield of Oregon—considered the Tokyo Rose of Washington for those Republicans whose passions ran high about issues like arts funding. Hatfield's candidate was John Frohnmayer, whose brother David was the attorney general of Oregon. Hatfield had been pushing Frohnmayer for the job ever since the beginning of the Reagan administration.

Frohnmayer must have seemed a canny choice to Bush and chief of staff John Sununu for the same reasons they would use privately to defend their selection of David Souter to the Supreme Court two months later: He was a nobody, a mediocre nonentity, which meant there was nothing in the public record to suggest what kind of NEA chief he would be. That would make it difficult for Democrats to oppose his choice while Sununu could assure conservatives that Frohnmayer would tend to their concerns.

The selection sent a clear message to the Reaganites: The Bushies were more interested in telling themselves and the rest of Washington that (as Bush said in his inaugural address) "a new breeze [was] blowing" in American politics than they were concerned with the passions of the Reaganites.

But those who felt passionately about the issue on both sides were not going to shut up just so Bush could avoid trouble. The arts world, doubly radicalized by both the gay-rights movement and the supposed threat posed to them by the Helms gang, produced ever more scandalous material under government subsidy and demanded ever more money for it. For its part, the right wing, especially the Christian Right, were genuinely shocked by the stuff they were seeing—and were raising millions of dollars complaining about it.

Frohnmayer found himself with the most thankless job in Washington. When he canceled NEA grants on the grounds that they were

ADVENTURES IN REPUBLICANLAND

unsuitable, he was assaulted in the press as the moral equivalent of a book burner. On the other hand, his utter lack of relish for the task turned the right wing against him; it wanted somebody more like onetime National Endowment for the Humanities head William Bennett, who had canceled grants he considered politically motivated with enormous gusto and utter conviction.

In short, for the most controversial and difficult job in Washington, Bush picked a liberal Republican concerned about his reputation in Democratic circles, someone who had everything to lose by siding with the outspoken members of his own party and everything to gain by siding implicitly or explicitly with his own political opposition. And as the administration wore on, Frohnmayer gave up on any pretense that he was following the party line and began, instead, to Grow.

The verb "to Grow" applies to a Republican official who departs from the line of his party and his president and, instead, becomes politically correct. "Growing" is also known as "pulling a Koop," in honor of the journey of Reagan surgeon general C. Everett Koop from hated prolife maniac to AIDS Warrior and Nationwide Condom Distributor in just five years. When a Republican acts as Koop did, he is given immense credit all over town for "Growing" while in office—in other words, coming to see the true liberal light. Reaganites have another term for it: They call it selling out.

Frohnmayer called a press conference to defend in the strongest terms the endowment's funding of a lousy little movie called *Poison*, which was certainly very gay but not at all obscene. "The film obviously had serious artistic content," he announced, "dealt with a serious societal issue, namely violence, and how that tends to destroy relationships."

As Frohnmayer surely knew, this sort of talk was even more offensive to the Reaganites than the grant itself. He might have been forgiven by them if he had said, "Look, this thing makes me sick, but there's not a legal reason on earth I can think of not to fund it." That would have been true. Instead, he used the occasion to pick sides, to go with the gay arts guys instead of the antihomosexual Right.

Who could blame the man? Frohnmayer would have to have been

some sort of superhuman freak to withstand the torrents of abuse flung at him from the most articulate and culturally significant people in America without core conservative beliefs to give him strength.

Fearful of the embarrassment Frohnmayer might cause and concerned that right-wingers on Capitol Hill would do something to the endowment that might embarrass the president, Sununu began spying on Frohnmayer. We have to "get control" of the NEA, he said. He used Quayle chief of staff Bill Kristol, who established an independent relationship with Frohnmayer's second-in-command, Al Felzenberg. Kristol tried to keep the Hill Republicans calm by passing word to Felzenberg about what they would and would not accept. When Frohnmayer discovered the conspiracy behind his back, he fired Felzenberg. Whereupon the White House immediately established another back-channel relationship, this time with another Frohnmayer deputy, Anne-Imelda Radice.

Increasingly paranoid about the White House, albeit with good reason, Frohnmayer started making speeches and decisions that led him right "off the reservation," as politically incorrect Washington lingo has it. For these betrayals alone he could have—indeed, should have—been fired, but he kept his job at the pleasure of the president.

But Bush, who could certainly sympathize with somebody excoriated by the conservative wing of the party, resisted all efforts to dismiss Frohnmayer. He listened not to the Reaganites, but to Roy Goodman and Jocelyn Levi Strauss instead. These were two liberal Republicans who served on the council that oversaw the NEA and, not coincidentally, two of Bush's oldest friends. They defended Frohnmayer against the depredations of the Republican Right. And so Bush stood behind Frohnmayer, who was personally loyal to the president but professionally disloyal to the party Bush led.

Frohnmayer was not Bush's worst appointment—that honor would have to go to Education Secretary Lauro Cavazos—but he was in every possible way unsuited to the job. The manager of a tiny and rather insignificant government agency, Frohnmayer so outraged conservatives that Pat Buchanan made him and the agency a major campaign issue in his insurgent effort to unseat Bush in 1992.

Buchanan's success in New Hampshire so spooked the Bush campaign that the president finally gave Sam Skinner the okay: Fire Frohnmayer. Thus an action that Bush could have taken on high ground—dismissing a disloyal or inept employee—became instead merely a crass political move. The dismissal did not satisfy conservatives, who saw it merely as a bone he was throwing to them. And the chorus of denunciation it earned Bush all over Washington proved that his initial effort to make nice with the other side by picking somebody uncontroversial had ended up backfiring every which way.

Bush's almost pathological efforts to avoid controversy always had terrific short-term results but disastrous consequences in the long run. A choice like Frohnmayer or Souter allowed his administration to avoid the kind of day-in, day-out, constant trouble that had plagued the Reagan White House. The dearth of controversial Bush appointments meant there were fewer bloody confirmation hearings before the Senate, while the lack of controversial policy pronouncements kept the Bush administration off the front pages for the most part.

The problem for Bush, though, was that gains like this were only brief. His refusal to take strong conservative stands ultimately created the Buchanan and Perot candidacies. And his conciliatory efforts toward Reagan's enemies only caused them to perceive and exploit his considerable weaknesses long before he even knew they were doing it.

Bush's failure gave the Democrats an unearned political opportunity. During the 1992 campaign and afterward, Clinton and the Democrats kept hammering at "the failed policies of the past twelve years," or "the policies of the Reagan-Bush administrations." But in truth, with the exception of abortion, the two presidencies had almost nothing in common. Reagan had at least slowed the growth of government; Bush sped it up again. Reagan had cut tax rates and simplified the tax system. Bush agreed to tax increases and compromised the integrity of the Tax Reform Act of 1986. Reagan reduced government regulation; Bush doubled the number of regs. Under Reagan, the Reaganites believed, America prospered. Under Bush, America had a double-dip recession.

And George Bush's recessions and ineffective leadership allowed the Democrats to succeed in 1992 at something they had failed to do throughout the 1980s—invalidating Reaganism in the eyes of the American people.

It was Bush's final betrayal of his old boss, and the final humiliation of the Reaganites at the hands of the Bushies.

FREEZE FRAME:

THE QUEST FOR
GOOD RECEPTION

AUGUST 17–21, 1992

Nobody in Houston has gotten any sleep. Why sleep here? You can sleep on the charter planes that will carry White House staffers back home to Washington Friday, the day after the close of the Republican National Convention. There is just too much going on, too much to do, to sleep. Every minute of every day, from 5:30 A.M. onward, brushfires ignite that must be doused, volcanic tempers erupt that must be soothed, prima donnas must be stroked one moment and put in their place the next.

This is pretty much what you are at the convention for—to warn your superiors of impending crises, to get instructions on how to handle them, and to execute the plans to defuse them before they make real trouble. At the crack of dawn Wednesday morning, after his successful speech to the convention faithful, HUD Secretary Jack Kemp lets you know that he is canceling all his media and personal appearances that day unless the president right now, this second, makes it clear he isn't being fired.

You swing into precrisis mode, which has become a tradition when dealing with Kemp. The night before, Bush went on "MacNeil/ Lehrer" and started talking about how he was going to make some changes in the second term. So Kemp's two chief longtime Bushie enemies—Dick Darman and John Sununu—spent the evening telling their contacts in the press that Kemp would be the first to go.

So you get in touch with Marlin Fitzwater, and Fitzwater realizes the gravity of the situation. Next to Dan Quayle, who is making a dizzying twenty-four appearances in four days and knocks everybody's socks off with an extraordinarily polished prime-time performance on Thursday, Kemp is the undisputed star of the convention. Several polls of delegates indicate that Kemp is their choice for 1996, but you don't need a poll to see the frenzy of support for him on the convention floor when he speaks. Hordes of College Republican girls have his name painted on their faces, and there is a look in their eyes half lustful and half worshipful.

He's so rock-star popular here that at the series of cocktail parties thrown in his honor he could have stage-dived into the crowd and they would have borne his body aloft like Peter Gabriel or Bruce Springsteen. It not only seems that everyone knows and likes him, but that he reciprocates personally; Kemp has a positively freakish memory for names and faces, and nothing is more flattering to a political junkie than when somebody more famous recognizes and says hello to him by name.

He is just having the best time, relaxed and joking. And Kemp didn't even *want* to come. Just because he did, Kemp is receiving obsequious phone calls from the president and is the subject of an obsequious public statement by Fitzwater. Crisis averted.

What about Secretary of Labor Lynn Martin, who is nominating Bush Wednesday night? From the moment she arrives at the convention she makes demands. She insists on a two-bedroom suite at the Omni. She wants the campaign to fly down her hairstylist from Washington. Nothing is right, nothing works, and she is driving everybody absolutely nuts.

So there is more than a little pleasure to be had when she finally gets to the podium and bombs big time. She has so lost control of the convention audience by the time the speech lumbers toward its conclusion that she is screaming into the microphone, and still nobody is paying her any attention. "You know," says a friend of yours, "she

THE QUEST FOR GOOD RECEPTION

may have been a pain in the ass, but after a performance like this, all I can say is, it sure was worth it."

And with all of this going on, you and the rest of the White House staff are in a state of flux, because the Thursday night before the convention began Sam Skinner was fired and the news came that Jim Baker was taking over at the White House. Which means there are at least five new people to impress, and probably a whole lot more. Smart folks are spending time in Houston buttering up Baker's number-one son, Jamie, who's hanging around; when Baker's assistant, Karen Groomes, arrives at the airport, a relatively senior White House staffer is there to meet her to help her advance Baker's arrival the next day, but also to make sure that Karen Groomes knows who he is and if given the opportunity will speak well of him.

It's not enough merely to work, however; it is also important to go to as many parties and events as time will allow. These are the real meat and potatoes of the convention for the people there, since the convention itself is basically a gigantic four-day television show for which the assembled Republicans are either extras or stage managers, gaffers and best boys.

There are dozens of events during the day and another dozen at night after the gavel comes down, and at least three must be sampled daily. Not just because the partying is fun, although it is, and free food and drink are just that—free. No, you must attend the parties because the primary commodities at a convention are access and visibility—meeting, schmoozing, being schmoozed, getting close for a few days to some very rich people who are jazzed to be talking up somebody at the White House, making these contacts for later on, should it become necessary to seek a job in, oh, God, the private sector.

So you are constantly in motion, moving through all 246 acres of the Astrodome complex and throughout the city of Houston for two weeks, on two or three hours of shut-eye a night. And what is the central issue on the minds of many of these exhausted, exhilarated folks? Good reception. Not from the press and the general public. From Comsat.

For this is the first fully Cellular Convention, and everybody who is anybody has a phone at his hip. But the most frequently uttered sentence is "I can't hear anything on these fucking things." The lines crackle and buzz as though you're making a trunk call from Antarctica. Throughout the Astrodome, the Astrohall and the Astroarena—the three huge indoor spaces that make up the convention grounds—and elsewhere in the city, Republicans are making strange figure-eight patterns as they seek a clear channel on their cellular phones. They bob and weave, turning their faces to the wall and then out again toward the mobs of people approaching them on foot. They walk right past friends and strangers alike with faraway looks in their eyes, talking into thin air. "You're breaking up! You're breaking up!" they scream helplessly, as though the person at the other end were on the *Challenger*.

There's very little difference between their demeanor and that of a psychotic homeless guy on Broadway. The psycho homeless guy thinks he's having a conversation with people from outer space; a Phone Guy is literally receiving transmissions from twenty-three miles up. And, like psychotics everywhere, a Phone Guy cannot make real eye contact with a Normal Guy; he looks through you like you're a ghost even though in truth he's the one who isn't there, not really, but is instead floating metaphysically between his limited corporeal form and a satellite in geosynchronous orbit above the earth.

And you have not one phone, but two! One is being paid for by the White House. The other is being paid for by the convention. It would be illegal for you to transact convention business on a White House phone line, but the trouble is that when a phone rings, you're never sure which is the one going off, and you always go for the wrong one.

The other problem is that as work expands to fill the time allotted, this terrific convenience proves to be a new kind of headache. Instant communications requires instant response; a nervous phone call from your superior can now be placed immediately, and hysterical demands can be made. In the old days—four years ago in New Orleans—such hysteria was often allowed to die out by itself, but cellular communications allows it to find its immediate expression. Things that weren't problems in the precellular days are now problems;

things that previously could fix themselves must now be repaired by hand.

This all fits in with the extraordinarily studied nature of the convention, whose masters hope to bleed out every possible surprise or spontanous incident in favor of Total Control. In the Astrodome itself, the convention is being run from an area behind the podium that is like an indoor trailer park, a dark cavern filled with dozens of trailers from which Big Republican Brother can control all that he surveys. In the rehearsal trailer, speakers are practicing their performances with a hack television director and a hack speech coach. Other trailers are filled with television equipment, as cameras latched to the dome's roof stare down on the convention floor, and those surveying the action can send messages to their floor agents, known as "whips," telling them to clear a certain aisle or get the New Jersey delegates to start raising high their Bush/Quayle '92 signs. The whips are equipped with earpieces through which Big Brother sends them messages and little wrist mikes through which they can talk back, turning each of them into a cross between a Secret Service agent and a villain on "Batman."

On the other side of the podium are the convention floor itself and the stadium seating and skyboxes above it. In many ways, these are the least important places at the convention; they are merely the staging area. All the work goes on in the trailers or in the Astrohall, across the way from the dome's south entrance. Here, 15,000 working members of the media as well as the 250 employees of the Bush campaign are located. The news stories are filed here, the spin doctors roam around giving little preconvention poop to media acquaintances, half a dozen wordsmiths are homogenizing the remarks of the convention's eighty-odd speakers to make sure they say exactly what they need to be saying at the moment they're saying it, while the campaign people stand around and worry.

In the Astroarena, at the south end of the Astrohall, another gigantic indoor space is filled to the brim with vendors selling T-shirts and buttons and little elephant sculptures at preposterous prices next to a makeshift food court. Here the true nature of the convention comes out: All this bears the same relation to real politics that the

Universal Studios Tour has to the movies. It turns a practical place of business into an entertainment center, complete with knick-knacks for the kids.

You and a White House colleague are stationed on the concrete steps directly up from the convention floor in section 270 of the Astrodome, two rows over from the presidential box. But you don't stay at the base for long. Your colleague feels a vibration at his left hip, indicating that a message is coming over his beepless beeper. He leans over, reads the electronic missive and responds immediately, taking the stairs at a speedy but controlled clip. You remember something you forgot to tell somebody about, and whip out one of the phones you are carrying with you.

You love your phones. In less than a week's time you have decided you cannot live without them, and ply everybody you encounter with questions about *their* cellular phones, what brands they have, how much power they store. Your colleague doesn't like his so well, and keeps having weird experiences, like the time he had to call another convention staffer but found himself in the path of a marching band in full swing making its way from the Astroarena out to the Astrohall. And every move he made to get out of the band's path was hopeless; it followed him around for a good ninety seconds, until he was collapsing with laughter.

The most novel use of cellular technology: You are standing about twenty yards away from your colleague. His beeper goes off. He looks down to read the message. It says: "Turn around. [You] wants to show you something." You could not get his attention, and you were stuck in place, so you got out the phone—the White House phone—called the White House operator, gave the operator the message, and in twenty seconds he was spinning on his heels.

"You won't believe this," your colleague said in a tone of conspiratorial pleasure on the Sunday night just before the convention began. He was in his room at the Omni Houston, the "overflow" hotel for White House staffers directly across the street from the Houstonian, wherein George Bush has supposedly lived for twelve years. "I am sitting on floor passes to the convention with a street value of one point two million dollars." Not only do you and he have your own passes granting you total access to all areas at the convention, but you have been given control of hundreds of others as well.

This makes you very important, because floor passes are the most hotly desired commodities at the convention. For every session, and there are five, a person must have an individual pass. The floor pass allows its bearer to wander about on the floor. With a Guest pass, which allows a conventioneer only to sit in an assigned stadium seat, you are an onlooker, a bystander, but with a floor pass you can feel as though you are a player, part of history in the making.

People without floor passes—people who are not delegates, campaign officials, White House officials or members of the press—seek them avidly, unashamedly, like one of those junkies in bad movies seeking a fix while the heat is on. "Hey, man, I *need* a pass, man, I need it *bad*, man."

There's nothing so exciting about being on the floor—in fact, it's just a lot of plywood covered by a carpet, and if you aren't a delegate you don't have a chair, and after about twenty minutes of walking on it your feet start feeling like they're on fire. But the fact remains that at the convention there are two kinds of people: floor people and nonfloor people.

And there is your colleague, sitting on a hundred floor passes and another hundred really good seats, all of which are theoretically designated for specific people. Craig Fuller, who is running the convention, had given him every single pass for the cabinet departments and gave him explicit instructions not to hand them out all at once. Instead, he was to parcel them out session by session so that the convention personnel could be sure they knew where the cabinet officials were at all times.

So when Attorney General Bill Barr doesn't show up, your colleague suddenly has possession of a bunch of floor passes meant for Barr and his security guys. And Clayton Yeutter, who was told in the pages of *The Washington Post* in the stories announcing Baker's arrival that he was "expected to return to private life," also doesn't show. And some cabinet officials don't come to some sessions. So your colleague has got seats and passes to dole out. He has passes that read, "Security Personnel." He has passes that read, "COA

Official"; "COA" means "Committee of Arrangements," which means nothing. He has passes that read, "Podium Work Area," which allow their bearers to head on backstage to the trailer park. He himself has a White "Officer of the Convention" pass round his neck, which gets him everywhere. So he's going to be the object of some serious ass-kissing this week. And at the thought of that, he laughs at the absurdity of it all.

He may have the passes, but you have Bruce Willis. On Wednesday, Willis makes an unexpected appearance arranged by A. C. Lyles, an elderly Paramount executive and old friend of Reagan's. After Willis spends a few minutes in the president's box with Barbara Bush, you are tasked with the arduous detail of escorting Willis from the box up to the skybox reserved for the president on the ninth level. Though Willis has a reputation as a difficult and creepy guy, he is excited to be here and chats amiably as you and he and his security detail arrive at the one elevator in the Astrodome that is still working.

The elevator is a nightmare; everyone who has had to use it has a horror story to tell about it. This is yours: You and the Willis Brigade get in, the doors close . . . and nothing happens. No movement for a couple of minutes. "I'm sorry about this, Mr. Willis," you say, whereupon Willis makes like John McClane in *Die Hard* and says, "Don't worry. If it goes on too much longer, I'll just break through the ceiling and climb up the shaft."

That isn't necessary, and at last you do get up to the presidential skybox. Following your success with the movie star, you are appointed to bring all sorts of people up to the box—which has a living room and full bar and lavishly stocked taco and dessert table. The place is reserved for members of Team 100, the big donors who have thrown $250,000 into Republican coffers so that they can get treated nicely at conventions and the like. You bring Malcolm Forbes, Jr., up in there, with his two daughters, and Fred and Cheryl Halpern and George Klein, the foremost rich Republican Jews. And somehow you talk the guard at the door into letting some of your buddies in as well, even though they do not have the right credentials. Who needs credentials when you've got pull? And what good is pull if you don't pull with it?

The best part is the car. You have suddenly become important enough to rate a full-time car and driver—even though back in Washington you would be lucky to get a White House car to drive you half a block.

You make great use of this car and its driver, a middle-aged fellow named Ned who in the off-season is the very well-heeled and established executive director of Houston CrimeStoppers. Ned is there at the hotel in the morning when you need to get to the Hyatt downtown for a meeting with the convention leadership. He takes you for a late lunch to Otto's, Bush's favorite rib joint in town. He brings you to the J. W. Marriott hotel for a National Jewish Coalition reception followed by a Dan Quayle reception. He waits for you after the convention is over, driving you over again to the Hyatt bar or to the Hilton Southwest, where Fox News is having a party. Ned also has a phone in his car, so you consult him too about brands and time of battery charge.

As the Astrodome fills up during the third week of August, it seems like GOP Heaven and Media Hell. The press people are all acting like they are trapped in their idea of a political horror show: *Night of the Living Republicans,* perhaps. But embattled Republicans are relieved at last to be coming together after a nightmarish year. Twelve months earlier they were part of an invincible political juggernaut; now they're riding on the back of a physically challenged horse that could use all the help it can get from the Americans with Disabilities Act, that landmark piece of legislation you are getting to hear so much about from the droning speakers on the platform.

And the good cheer—and there is plenty of it—comes from being at last with allies, even ones with whom you are quite uncomfortable.

The Astrodome has turned into Republicanville. Imagine a town square the size of a football field covered with bright red carpet laid over plywood with a ceiling towering twenty-four stories above the ground and you get some idea of the animating spirit of the convention floor. It is even laid out a little like a town, with one main avenue—call it Broadway—about twenty feet wide making a semicircle from the dome's west end to its east. Several side streets come off perpendicular to Broadway, and are fronted on either side by blocks of chairs where the state delegations make their homes.

These side streets lead right into the heart of the town, the podium, which serves the convention much as the gazebo served the people in a million different Norman Rockwell paintings. In front of the podium there is a shorter semicircular avenue we can call the Strand.

In Republicanville, it's Sunday right after church, and everybody in town is on promenade, nodding to one another on Broadway, walking together down a side street to get to the Strand, and all along the way stopping to chat with old friends, old acquaintances, new acquaintances. Broadway is as crowded as the Beltway at rush hour, only the traffic here is all on foot and nobody seems to be going anywhere special. They're just roaming and mingling, guests at the world's largest cocktail party.

And with all this comity, you are amazed that the media have decided to portray the convention as Nuremberg II. Monday night they are crazed with fury at the supposedly unacceptable tenor of Pat Buchanan's "religious war" speech. But the story of Monday night is not Buchanan but rather Ronald Reagan, who positively knocks the crowd out with his sunny valedictory. The media are also suggesting that there is open warfare in the place on the subject of abortion, but the mood on the floor reveals no such thing. Though some of the more radical members of the two camps glare at each other's buttons and signs—over by the Pennsylvania delegation a woman with a big sticker that reads, "Barry's right," referring to a statement by Barry Goldwater that abortion shouldn't be discussed in the party platform, looks wide-eyed at a baby with a sticker on her cap reading, "I'm glad my mommy chose life"—by and large the assembled seem very happy to come together at last in a strange and glorious world in which everybody is a Republican and everybody pretty much wants to see George Bush reelected (or at least see Bill Clinton defeated).

Everybody is having a great time, but you can tell that with the exception of Reagan's appearance, Dan Quayle's surprisingly stirring speech and the sight of Barbara Bush with the Bush brood behind her, the convention is hardly engaging anyone's attention. Keynoter Phil Gramm dies like a comic on an off-night; Lynn Martin hollers her way into oblivion. There's a little rush of feeling when the pretty lady with AIDS makes her emotional speech Wednesday night—like the zing you get when you bite into an unexpectedly hot pepper—but that dissipates as quickly as the pain from the pepper. Even Bush's speech Thursday night holds the attention of the assembled only because the dictates of the show demand it.

Everybody talks about family values but nobody can define them except that you know them when you see them and we have them and so do the American people but the Democrats don't.

But from Monday to Thursday, throughout the parties and the sessions and the T-shirt buying and the hotel bars, there is a feeling of ease in the air. Unless you are from Utah or Idaho, and probably even there, it is usually a bit of a burden to be a Republican. Republicans are constantly under assault by the national media and by the doyens of popular culture, who see them as too white, too well off, too uncaring, too male, and—horror of all horrors—too square. They see their politicians get very little friendly treatment and a lot of rough questioning and have the impression that the politicians they don't like are treated with kid gloves by the unfair and biased media.

And yet the media are the celebrities on display here. When Dan Rather, or Connie Chung, or Andrea Mitchell does a report from the convention floor, people make a semicircle around the reporter to watch. And what Rather does is this: He whispers into his microphone. It may sound on television like he's shouting, but if you are standing two feet from him you cannot hear a word he says.

Thursday night, after the final gavel comes down, you and your colleague suffer your only real disappointment of the convention. Jim Pinkerton, whom you used to work with in the White House before he moved over to the campaign, mentioned a private party for Arnold Schwarzenegger in some suite at the Ritz Carlton sometime after midnight. Pink gives you *his* cellular phone number and tells you to call around midnight to find out where the party is. But Pink has slipped up, because when you make the call it goes to somebody else on the campaign, who has no idea either what Pinkerton's true number is or where the Schwarzenegger party might be.

Still, you are granted one last coup. As you take your seats on board the charter plane from Houston back to Washington, a stewardess comes by and says there are two open seats in first class for the two of you. How or why you got them, you have no idea, but you ignore the glowering faces of fellow staffers and assume your very comfortable new seats.

"Oh, no," you say.

"What?" your colleague says.

"I feel naked without my phones," you reply. *"Where are my phones?"*

SIX:

THE EMPTY BOX, OR, WHY BUSH RAN POORLY AND SPOKE BADLY

David Tell could not chain-smoke backstage in St. Louis—the Secret Service men told him not to, with their customary officiousness, as though his Camels posed more of a risk to the president than this first presidential debate, which Bush was just in the process of botching. In his anxiety Tell weaved his cancer-stick-free fingers through his newly grown red beard. The beard gave Tell's face the aspect not of a hotshot young political operative, but rather of a sensitive graduate student.

He was listening to the president begin his attack on Bill Clinton for helping to organize a protest against the Vietnam War in London in 1969. "I just think it's wrong to demonstrate against your country in a foreign land," Bush said—and Tell tensed, awaiting Armageddon. Because if the Clinton campaign had just found this one little clip from a London newspaper, Clinton himself could right now deliver the *coup de grâce* that would level the Bush candidacy for good. The clip was a story about the demonstrations dated September 22, 1969, and one of the Americans who spoke critically of his country's role in the Vietnam War was "Michael Boskin, 22, of Stanford University."

Boskin, now 45, was currently serving as the chairman of Bush's Council of Economic Advisers, in a grand office on the third floor of the OEOB.

For a week, ever since he had come upon the clip, Tell had lived with a low-grade existential dread the way others live with a low-grade fever. As opposition-research director of Bush/Quayle '92, he had come to bear on his slender shoulders the increasingly desperate hopes of a critically injured Republican political establishment. For surely somewhere in Bill Clinton's past there was a silver bullet that could pierce Clinton's armor and bring down the Democratic candidacy. The 1988 Bush campaign had found so many in Michael Dukakis's past—the rampage of furloughed convict Willie Horton and the pollution of Boston Harbor, just to name two. Tell had to find it, somewhere, somehow.

But what could Tell do after the revelations of Clinton's liaison with Gennifer Flowers and the clear inconsistencies in Clinton's draft record? What did people want, exactly? News that Clinton was an axe murderer? And anyway, nobody really understood the job of "oppo" director. It was, he said, "partisan political science"; the opposition-research team spent its time poring over public records and news clips, searching for inconsistences and disastrous mistakes in Clinton's political past.

But the only silver bullet they had uncovered so far was the fact that the president's CEA chairman had been a leader of the very demonstrations the president had been blaming on Clinton.

The Clinton campaign apparently never found the Boskin clip, nor did they need it; Bush's assault on his rival's patriotism failed to sway the voters and there was no need for the Clintonites to counteract it. Tell could only relax about it the minute he found his president voted out of office.

The irony of Bush's assault on Clinton's behavior and conduct as a graduate student twenty-three years earlier in London was that Bush had begun the campaign season insisting he was not going to "go negative." He had wanted to do things differently from 1988, when he not only defeated Michael Dukakis but ran him out of politics altogether. This time he could be nice; he could stress his accomplishments and merely disdain discussing the pip-squeak, draft-dodging, adulterous little boy running against him.

But nobody wanted to hear about what a good president he had been; the American people hadn't heard much from Bush until he wanted their vote again, and they were in a pretty lousy mood when he showed up at their door with hat in hand. For three years he had avoided them, and those had been a momentous, world-historic three years, too. The fall of the Berlin Wall, the end of the Soviet Union and the biggest military victory since Agincourt had all happened, and they hadn't gotten so much as a clue from their president about what to think about it all.

Bush had proved so stingy in providing the voters with information about the nation's direction and purpose that by the fall of 1992 an unprecedented *ninety million* of them were tuning in to watch the very debate at which the Secret Service would not allow David Tell to smoke.

In truth, Bush did not tell them how the world had changed, and why, because he did not know and did not understand it himself. For the most part (with the exception of the Gulf War) he had been a bystander as the world changed startlingly around him, and all he could do was gawp at it dumbly and then, when it was convenient to do so, turn around and try to take credit for the whole thing.

The worst-run campaign in presidential history began and ended right there—led by a man who believed he deserved a second term because, damn it, he just did, that's all.

In the spring and summer of 1992, White House staffers had various theories about why the president was doing so badly. They went like this:

(1) He's had a total nervous breakdown.
(2) He doesn't really want to win.
(3) He has an amazing master plan according to which he will come out of the box at the Republican convention in August and crush Clinton and Perot beneath his shoe.

Now let us examine these theories individually.

(1) **The nervous breakdown:** Bush's staff physician, Dr. Burton Lee, gave an interview to *The Washington Post* in March during

which he said the president was "tired" and really should spend more time resting. Lee had already prescribed the tranquilizer Halcion for the president to take as a sleeping aid on foreign trips and whenever he found it necessary.

Staffers studied Lee's words the way Kremlinologists once studied photos of the Soviet leadership at the May Day parade. Was Lee saying that the president was falling to pieces? That he couldn't hack it? The Bushies clucked their tongues sympathetically; any emotional difficulties the president might be having would only be proof of his essential saintliness. He just cared too much about people, about his family and about his staff. Look what a difficult life he had been leading the past three years: his beloved wife ill with Graves' disease; his son Neil in trouble over his directorship of a Denver savings and loan; his daughter Doro's divorce in 1989; his favorite uncle dead and his mother dying. And he was just taking the most unmerciful pounding at the hands of the press and that awful Pat Buchanan, who were both accusing him of not caring about the sufferings of the American people and (in Buchanan's case) of being the next thing to a pornographer for keeping the National Endowment for the Arts in business.

How dare they talk this way about a man who flew fifty-eight combat missions in World War II? Who had given his life to public service? It was just outrageous. Oooh, it made them so mad. As angry as they got, though, the president himself never complained about the treatment. He said it was just the give-and-take of politics. But the Bushies just knew he was dying inside from the unfairness of it all. They certainly were.

So was it any wonder the president was stressed? All that was going on, and still he felt it necessary to keep a stiff upper lip and good cheer so that the lesser mortals who worked for him didn't have to worry.

That was the sentimental Bushie attitude. The cynics in the White House who had lost whatever faith and confidence in the president they once possessed thought the nervous-breakdown idea made sense because his conduct was otherwise inexplicable. They were completely puzzled by his continuing refusal to go after Congress for the way its leadership had obstructed his political agenda; by his

stubborn insistence that everything was just fine and he was completely convinced he was going to win in November; and by his
inability to take advantage of the bully pulpit provided to every president to speak directly to the American people without the filter of the
media.

These failings made no sense to them; after all, Bush had spent
eight years working for Ronald Reagan, and even a mentally impaired
denizen of the Reagan White House must have picked up a few simple
tips about how to seize and maintain the public's affection and support. Bush's inability to do so could only be explained by the misfiring
of his synapses and hallucinations perhaps brought on by the Halcion.

In fact, Bush had not had a nervous breakdown. He had simply
been sandbagged by his doctor. Lee was one of the singular figures
of the Bush White House; as the president's doctor, he was on call
twenty-four hours a day for four years, he traveled everywhere the
president went, and he basically had nothing to do. But like doctors
everywhere, he believed he knew everything, and he made no bones
about lecturing his fellow workers about their fields of expertise. Lee
spent his time trying to interfere with administration abortion policy,
and soon became one of those people from whom others flee when
they see him coming down the hall. As a result, he was a reporter's
dream: He leaked like a sieve and said whatever was on his mind. He
wanted the president to slow down, and said so, and thereby began
months of fruitless speculation and gossip within his boss's shop.

(2) He doesn't want to win: According to those who ad-
vanced this opinion, the president believed his main mission in life
was to protect and defend American national interests against foreign
enemies. He was the consummate Cold War politician, having served
in three foreign-policy posts in the Nixon and Ford administrations,
and he believed the worldwide chess game against Communism was
the central issue of our time. When Soviet Communism ceased to
exist, it was a wonderful step forward for world peace, but it robbed
George Bush of his reason for being president. Politics at the end of
the Cold War were entirely domestic in nature, and Bush (like Nixon
before him) had no deep interest in domestic questions. In contrast
to his sophisticated and layered ideas about foreign affairs, he had

little experience and little sense of direction about where he stood on domestic issues. He was at different times a tax cutter and a tax raiser, a deficit cutter and a big spender, a deregulator and a reregulator—all because he just followed the fashion of the moment or the opinion of the last person he talked to.

A president was going to have to be a policy wonk like Bill Clinton to care about the issues that would matter to voters in the 1990s, they said. But once again for selfless motives, ran the theory, Bush had decided to run for a second term because so many Republicans depended upon him for their livelihoods, and as head of his party he really had no choice—especially since his designated heir apparent, Dan Quayle, was unsuitable to take his place at the top of the ticket in 1992.

The weakness of this whole notion is that, contrary to Bushie and Washington cliché in 1992, Bush was *not* an especially competent foreign-policy president. He certainly liked the foreign stuff more than the domestic and was better at it too, but he was not exactly a creative and inventive steward of the American national interest, as his role model, Richard Nixon, had been. Given a choice between doing something obvious and uninspired and doing something interesting, he invariably chose the former. He went for the desiccated Communist leadership of China instead of the Jeffersonian Chinese students, and for the hapless Mikhail Gorbachev over the brave Boris Yeltsin; more troubling, he unwittingly gave sanction to the genocidal Serbians by indicating his preference for the continued Serb domination of Yugoslavia.

Even his most impressive diplomatic accomplishment, the formation of the coalition to defeat Saddam Hussein, was motivated by a cover-your-ass instinct: He made sure every other world leader was on board so that they could all share the blame if the whole thing went badly.

Since his record as a foreign-policy president demonstrated so clearly that he did not understand how the world had changed in world-historical terms, how could he understand that America had changed as well? The answer is, he didn't—understanding was not really his strong suit. That was one of the reasons he decided to run for reelection. He did not understand he would lose.

Of course he wanted to win. Nobody who has ever been president willingly gives up his duties, with the possible exception of George Washington, and George Bush was no George Washington.

(3) He has a master plan: Of all the theories about the campaign's evident weakness, this was the most seductive for worried and confused Bushies. It meant that the enterprise was not without direction or hope, but was instead guided by a superior political intelligence and the steely nerves of a veteran fighter pilot. Bush understood that he had to play his own game his own way and not change his plans to satisfy the demands of a voracious media or a staff too weak and stupid to grasp his Machiavellian scheme. It was also the only one of the theories supported by textual evidence: the man's own words.

Time and again, word would come down from Sam Skinner to the White House staff: *The president is confident. He is sure he is going to win. He knows what he is doing; he won in 1988; there's no reason to worry.* Bush even showed up a few times at the senior staff meeting or at gatherings of campaign workers to tell them so himself. Almost everybody in the place had worked on the 1988 campaign, and they spoke incessantly about how Bush had been 17 points behind Dukakis until the Republican convention in August, at which point he had overtaken his Democratic rival and left him in the dust. The words "in '88" were intoned like a mantra around the White House—the very fact that Bush had won in '88 surely meant that he would win in '92 as well. If you've won one presidential election, you've won them all.

Bush himself evidently believed this one, but once again he and the Bushies were operating from a false premise. The successful two-term presidency is not the norm in the modern world. It is an aberration. In the postwar period only Eisenhower and Reagan have actually served two full terms. Kennedy had been assassinated, Johnson could not win a second term in 1968, Nixon was forced to resign before completing his, Ford could not even win one and it's a wonder Jimmy Carter made it to 1980 without being torn limb from limb.

Bush knew this one thing: He had worked for Reagan. Reagan had won two terms. According to the polls, he was more popular than Reagan had been. Therefore, he would—he should—win two terms. And he should win on his own terms.

And here were his terms. On August 3, 1991, George Bush had surveyed the thirty months of his presidency and seen that they were good. Not only had he defeated Saddam Hussein in the desert, he had also: ousted and arrested Panamanian strongman Manuel Noriega; engineered upcoming peace talks in the Middle East; overseen the overthrow of Communism; negotiated cuts in U.S. and Soviet nuclear arsenals; guided the passage of the Clean Air and Americans with Disabilities acts; and been party to a far-reaching package that would cut the deficit in half in five years and restrain Democratic spending.

When he and his close advisers met at Camp David that August day to talk about his reelection, they quickly agreed on a nice and happy model: They would design the 1992 Bush effort on the 1984 Reagan campaign. Reagan had won forty-nine states using a feel-good approach that stressed the renewal of American confidence after the nation's crisis of self-doubt in the late 1970s. "It's morning in America," said the announcer at the beginning of Reagan's most successful 1984 ad.

The Bushies believed that not only could they duplicate Reagan's success, they might even be able to better it. After all, at a comparable point in his tenure Reagan was not quite at 50 percent in the popularity polls, while Bush was still in the 60s. And people really *liked* Bush in a way they hadn't liked Reagan; he was a real guy, with a real family. He had a secret weapon, too: Barbara Bush was the single best-liked person in the country. The Bushes were the perfect subjects for a well-designed Madison Avenue campaign selling them as the ideal Americans and Bush as the ideal leader in a freer and safer world.

Rather than attack the Democrats, the Bush campaign would instead focus on good and nice things. Bushies were especially excited about promoting the president's role in getting Arabs and Israelis to sit down together in one room—"for the first time in three thousand years!" claimed one early and never-aired commercial, whose authors apparently did not know that Israel was only forty-three years old and the term "Arabs" to describe the non-Jewish peoples of the Middle East came into existence only after the death of Muhammad in the seventh century A.D.

Bush did not want just to be reelected; he wanted a coronation. But those plans ran into trouble when the economy refused to rally in the fall of 1991. Reagan's "morning in America" campaign was designed to take advantage of the fact that in 1984 the nation had just emerged from a recession into an unparalleled spurt of economic growth. The Reagan model obviously would not work in a weak economy. Time to change the game plan.

Or so you might have thought, but you would have been wrong. The game plan did not change. Nothing did; not the campaign plans, not the economic plans. Bush and his advisers believed the best thing he could do about the economy was absolutely nothing. Political interference would only confuse and delay the certain recovery.

That opinion might have been defensible economically, but politically it was suicide. The obvious political play going into an election would have been to do anything the Bushies could think of to try to stimulate the economy and persuade the American people that the president was really on their side. It was the obvious play because most of the sensible Republicans in Washington were pushing the administration to do precisely that. But the Bushies were immovable.

Having decided not to seek an economic stimulus package, Bush had another obvious play: Go on television and explain to the nation what was going on, why the economy was suffering, what he was doing about it and how and why people should take heart because things were on the verge of getting much better.

He would not do this, either, instead instructing his troops to tell the press and the voters to wait until he delivered the State of the Union on January 28 to hear all about it. The Bushies began pushing this line in October, clearly hoping that the economic news would improve so much that Bush could tell the nation in the big speech that things had already begun to turn around.

The delaying tactic was unsuccessful; the economy continued to float in the doldrums. The voters were unhappy and getting nervous, which made perfect sense; things did not seem to be going right and the man they had elected to steer the ship of state was hiding in his cabin. Now and then Bush would come up on deck, waving at the camera on his way to a helicopter, buying those notorious socks at JC Penney, barfing on the Japanese prime minister.

Why was Bush so silent? Here's a clue. After he had been replaced by Sam Skinner, John Sununu attended the weekly breakfast meeting of the "empowerment" boys in the White House Mess. One of empowerment's most enthusiastic supporters, Richard Porter of Dan Quayle's staff, asked Sununu why Bush hadn't gone on television in the fall either to seek support for emergency economic legislation or to give the nation some confidence that the troubles were only temporary.

"They wouldn't listen," Sununu said of the American people.

"What do you mean?" Porter asked.

"The president *gave* a big speech on the economy at the time of the budget deal. He asked the people to support the deal. And do you know what happened?" Sununu made a Bronx cheer. After Bush's October 2, 1990, Oval Office address to the nation, the Capitol was flooded with millions of calls urging Congress to *defeat* the budget package.

"Maybe that had to do with what was in the budget deal," Porter said.

"Bullshit!" Sununu replied.

Were Bush and Sununu and everybody else just being remarkably stupid? Well, they certainly were, but idiocy this pronounced can only be the result of careful planning or a deep psychological need. In this case, it was both.

Bush wanted to run a happy-face campaign in 1992. That would not have been possible if instead he had to spend a few months locked in a bloody political struggle with Congress over an economic stimulus package. That would require him to go negative, to stop being nice—to get in the way of his campaign's message.

So unhappy were the Bushies at the thought of doing battle with Congress going into a campaign year that John Sununu made the amazing claim that the administration had achieved its domestic political goals for the first term and would be perfectly happy if Congress just adjourned itself until 1993. Sununu's offhand remark convinced the Democratic leadership on Capitol Hill that they had nothing to fear from the then immensely popular George Bush, who was going to do nothing with his popularity except hoard it. And it would serve as evidence to anybody who wanted to look that Bush believed the best thing he could do as president was . . . nothing. And that is not a good image for a president.

Bush stubbornly hewed to his strategy—act like everything's fine, don't make trouble—until December 17, two weeks after Sununu was fired and Skinner began as chief of staff, when the White House finally admitted in a written statement that "for all practical purposes, the recession continues."

Did that admission mean Bush was ready to suggest a major package of economic stimuli? Did it mean he was ready to speak to the American people about their fears and worries? Did it mean that he was willing to do battle with Congress?

No. He continued to wait until the State of the Union five weeks later to have a conversation with the nation about its woes. Whereupon he announced a couple of insignificant economic proposals and dared Congress to pass them by March 20. Three days before March 20, when not a single one of those economic measures had been brought to a vote in a House or Senate committee, the Bush White House did not even have an event scheduled to commemorate the ultimatum and remind voters of Congress's complicity in the political gridlock afflicting Washington. And when Republicans from all over later advised him to go on the warpath against Congress, which had become the most unpopular institution in America according to some polls, he said no.

Why? Because it was morning in America!

*   *   *

The fact that Bush/Quayle '92 was going to be a campaign bereft of ideas was not a matter of policy. Nobody ever sat down and said, "Let's say absolutely nothing for nine months and win in a landslide." In fact, the campaign's managers were just dying for Bush to say something. They just didn't know what, exactly.

In the third week of June, George Bush's speechwriters met with Robert Teeter in the Roosevelt Room. Teeter passed around an elaborate chart he had generated on his Apple computer that tied some ideas—about education and values and jobs and crime—together in a structure he hoped his audience would later follow when drafting Bush's speeches.

Each major idea had its own box on the chart. The first box, on the chart's far left, read:

I have been president for 3 1/2 years.
Major accomplishments/record:
*Foreign & Domestic
*Tremendous benefits for all Americans
*Some disappointments.

The second one, right next to it, read:

Various serious problems facing us at home.
Must solve these problems if we are ever to
fulfill our promises [sic] as a country.
Describe problems using examples that connect.

On the right-hand side of the chart, boxes four through nine listed the main arguments in favor of the president's stands on the major issues.

But it was the third box, at the center of the chart, the box from which all the other boxes flowed, that was the subject of the meeting.

It read:

Theme/Slogan/Name

There was nothing else in the third box.

"What I want from you," Teeter told the speechwriters, "is to help me fill this empty box."

Teeter was worried, but Bush was not. After all, he had said nothing from January 1989 onward and had by some reckonings been the most popular president in history. So why mess with success?

No president had ever spoken more frequently than Bush; no president had ever said less. By the end of his four years in office, Bush had given more speeches and made more public appearances than Ronald Reagan had in eight years' time. And yet if people were asked what memorable things Bush had ever said, they could think of only three: "Read my lips: no new taxes," "a kinder, gentler nation" and "a thousand points of light." All three came from his acceptance speech at the 1988 Republican convention. Once he was president, he never uttered a phrase worth remembering.

This was certainly not the fault of his speechwriters, many of whom were exceptionally talented—among them Tony Snow, Dan McGroarty, Curt Smith, Jennifer Grossman and especially Andrew Ferguson, who was and is one of the best writers in America. But they had no power and their work had no authority. Reporters who covered the White House learned early on in the Bush administration that they did not even have to attend presidential addresses because they offered not a clue to policy.

Instead of having a continuing conversation with the American people, Bush spoke solely to small groups, praising himself and his administration. Speeches were gimmicks, not efforts to disseminate information. For the first six months, speechmaking was organized into "theme weeks," according to which Bush would spend exactly seven days talking about one matter before proceeding to the next. One week was "drug week," another week was "national service week," and so on. The theme weeks put the administration on rhetorical record: It cared about drug abuse, it believed in national service, and so on. And once a subject's week had passed, so had the administration's interest in it.

Everybody knew that real administration policy was being made in secret, in negotiations between Sununu and Darman and Congress, or between Bush, Scowcroft, and Baker and whatever tyrant was their buddy that month. And by the time Bush broke his campaign pledge about not raising taxes, the American people, like the press before them, had come to understand that Bush's public statements were essentially meaningless.

So for three years Bush and his men had systematically devalued the very notion of presidential speaking and speechwriting. Then, when they got into trouble, they looked around for somebody to blame and picked . . . *the speechwriters*! The speechwriters weren't getting the "message" out. What message? Why, the message that George Bush was a good president!

But the speeches had *always* been about George Bush's exceptional job as president, and *only* about that. They had not offered a benchmark, a way of understanding the American future; they were solely about the Bush administration's recent past—what it had proposed in the last three weeks, what it had done in the last three months.[1] The speeches restated endlessly the favored clichés of the Bush White House—gobbledygook about "letting the market work" and "meeting the challenges of our technological future" and "making sure that every child begins school ready to learn." They cited administration programs whose very names and conceptions were themselves cliché—programs called Workplace 2000 and America 2000 and Job Training 2000, praised in sentences that invariably began, "It's hard to believe, but the year 2000 is just nine years away, and as a nation we need to look ahead to the opportunities of a new century and, yes, a new millennium."

The speeches had, in fact, always been exactly what the campaign wanted, but that did not matter. The speechwriters were to blame because (a) George Bush was a wonderful president, but (b) his poll

---

[1] Cam Findlay, who was Sam Skinner's aide-de-camp, complained that whenever the Bushies got together to discuss how to raise the president's positives in the early months of 1992, they invariably decided to produce a pamphlet, or a booklet, or a fact sheet, or a handout, whose purpose was to describe the Bush administration's successes. "It was all about the past," he said. "Never a word about the future. It was defense, not offense. It was all about how wonderful they were."

numbers were bad, so (c) the problem was entirely due to the people who were supposed to explain why the president was so wonderful and why his poll numbers should be better.

So in February Skinner removed chief speechwriter Tony Snow and put him in an office across the hall. Nothing else changed in the office. Same people, same speeches. Not until July was a new chief speechwriter hired, and not until August were other speechwriters let go.

In the meantime, the speechwriters, who had grown used to being ignored, were suddenly being told weekly by campaign chairman Bob Teeter that they and only they held the key to turning around the faltering campaign and saving the president. Every single major speech the president gave in 1992 was going to be "the one," Teeter would say. "This is the one, the one that's really going to turn it around." First the State of the Union was going to be "the one." Then the March 20 speech attacking Congress for not passing the economic stimulus package was going to be "the one." Then a speech before College Republicans. Then a speech in New Jersey. And on and on. Teeter believed that there was some magic spell the speechwriters could weave to seduce the nation—after all, it had worked that way in '88, with the convention speech.

But there was little the White House speechwriters could do, because they were writing not for the mostly unknown Vice-President Bush, as Peggy Noonan had been when she worked on the convention address, but for the very well-known President Bush, with whom the nation had lost patience and sympathy. And they were completely flummoxed by the comic disorganization of both the White House and the campaign.

In April, Andrew Ferguson was assigned a speech for Bush to deliver before the Detroit Chamber of Commerce. Ferguson wanted some color detail for the speech, so he had his researcher call the Chamber of Commerce to find out who its members were and what the business situation was like in the Motor City. The Chamber of Commerce person said, "The president is coming to speak here? Before us? This is the first we've heard about it."

It turned out that there was no speaking engagement at the Detroit

Chamber of Commerce. Rather, the speech was going to be given at a machine tool company in a Detroit suburb called Fraser. But the man in charge of the president's speaking schedule did not know that.

For the event now in Fraser, deputy chief of staff Henson Moore wanted Ferguson to rework a previous speech he had liked on the president's "reform agenda"—welfare reform, campaign-finance reform. But Ferguson began getting calls from the Labor Department and members of the White House's policy development staff. They said they heard he was working on the big job-training speech in Fraser the next week and wanted to brief him on the administration's job-training proposals.

Ferguson called his boss, Dave Demarest, who said, no, it's a reform speech, not a job-training speech. Demarest double-checked it with Moore, who said, no, it's not a job-training speech, but a reform speech. Ferguson finished his draft, which then circulated to all White House offices. It was edited, completed and about to go to the president for his comments when Ferguson received a call from domestic policy's Roger Porter. Porter's staff had already read through and cleared the speech, but Porter called Ferguson because, he said, "We need to talk about the job-training speech."

Ferguson went across West Exec to meet with Porter in his office. Porter said, "It's really terrific that we're giving a big speech on job training next week, because we really have some news to make here."

With a comically hangdog expression that belied his fierce wit, the mustachioed Ferguson was one of the best-liked and most even-tempered people in the White House, but this incessant back-and-forth caused him to lose his cool a little bit. "The speech is *done,*" he said. "It's been through staffing. It's on its way to the president. It's a *reform* speech, *not* a job-training speech. I told your staff that two days ago."

"But this was supposed to be a Job Training 2000 speech," Porter said in his customary whisper. "We have important information that will make news. First, we'll be transmitting our Job Training 2000 initiative to Congress that morning. And we've included a real incentive for the governors of all fifty states—all of them—to pass it: a thirty-thousand-dollar grant!"

Stop the presses.

Porter called Henson Moore, who immediately joined him and Ferguson. Moore heard Porter out, then said, "I find myself on the horns of a dilemma. Some people are saying we should be going out there with our speeches and just say one thing in each one over and over. On the other hand, there's all these stories in the press about how we're not getting anything done, not moving the agenda. So I think we need to blend the two together in this speech. Let's keep the reform stuff, but also put in the stuff about job training so we can make some news."

Ferguson right away realized that the speech, which Bob Teeter had designated as that week's "thing that was really going to turn us around," was going to be a disaster. Moreover, the decision to rewrite it meant he was going to have to work all weekend, for the fourth time in the last month. And finally, it turned out that (a) the job-training stuff wasn't news, because Bush had already cited all its details in a January speech in Atlanta, and (b) the White House couldn't transmit the Job Training 2000 package to Congress that day, because Congress wasn't even in session.

Porter's response to all this news was to say, well, we can just transmit it anyway. But someone on his staff said, no, Roger, really, we can't.

The speech was to be given on a Tuesday. On Monday morning, the job-training material was removed from it. But Moore and Teeter had decided on Friday that Porter was right; the speech must make some news. So instead of job training, they decided the speech should make a big deal out of the proposed Youth Apprenticeship Act of 1992.

And, of course, not a single major news organization covered it.

These organizational woes were nothing next to the intellectual vacuum at the heart of the White House. For when Ferguson tried to fulfill Teeter's mandate and turn things around with a more effective approach to talking about the issues, the president himself would either reject it or corrupt it.

A perfect case in point came in July 1992, when the new chief speechwriter, Steve Provost, asked Ferguson to come up with some ideas for a speech in Michigan the campaign wanted to focus on CAFE standards—the laws that compel the U.S. auto industry to produce fuel-efficient cars. Al Gore, among others, was talking about raising the CAFE standards to forty miles per gallon, which would be extraordinarily expensive and cost thousands of jobs in Michigan.

Ferguson came up with an inspired idea: Bush should use the occasion to talk about "trust." The speech would go as follows: *Elections are about trust, about the man the voters trust to sit at the big desk and make the big decisions. But this year, trust is a two-way street. We politicians have to learn to trust you, the American people. We must trust you to make decisions about your schools, which is why I am for school choice. We must trust you to raise your families, which is why I oppose condom distribution in the schools. And we must trust you to make decisions about the environment and not force ruinously complicated regulations on already troubled industries. We must trust you enough to get out of your way and let you live your lives.*

Provost shared Ferguson's ideas with Skinner and Teeter, and they were dazzled. They talked to the president, who was similarly impressed. Trust! Yes! A theme! They could build a whole "theme week" around trust!

Only one little change, though. All Bush wanted to say was that this election was about trust: Whom do the voters trust to sit at the big desk and make the big decisions? None of that other stuff. Too confusing.

In his vanity, Bush had taken a very clever libertarian message about taking power away from politicians and putting it in the hands of the people and turned it back into his own smiley-face campaign. He wanted to talk about how the voters should vote for him because they trusted him. That was it. That was all he wanted to say.

It seemed never to occur to him that perhaps it was the worst possible message for him. Because the voters had no reason to trust him; he had lied to them. And because the voters didn't like him any more, no matter what he might want to believe.

FREEZE FRAME:

LOSING

OCTOBER 15–NOVEMBER 3, 1992

There is a corridor in the basement of the West Wing that leads into the White House Mess—a combination lobby and schmooze-on-the-fly room. When you come in at 1:15 P.M. on Wednesday, October 28, for the second seating (first seating is at 12:00) and wait for a table to open up, staffers who are coming in and going out are generating a hubbub in which the words "two points" are everywhere audible.

"Two points. Did you hear? Gallup has us down two points. Two points. . . . I knew it. . . . Two points. . . ."

In a few hours, the Gallup organization is set to release a tracking poll that has Bush at 40 percent and Clinton at 42 percent—a narrowing of 6 points from its poll a few days before.

"Two points. . . . They must be shitting a brick in Little Rock . . . What I always said, the closer it gets the more people are just going to look at Clinton and say, 'This guy can't be president.' . . . They're calling it 'startling' on CNN. . . . I can't wait to hear how Dan Rather deals with this one . . ."

The Mess corridor is giddy, people talking to each other, shaking hands, grinning as though it is Easter Sunday after church. The poll is a lifeboat for drowning souls, and you and your colleagues clamber onto it almost hysterically.

It is, quite literally, the first piece of good news to hit the White

House in a year. You cannot think of another. The happiness that first greeted James Baker's takeover of the White House and the campaign in August was quickly tempered by your fears that he might fire you and everybody else. And though you had prayed devoutly for Baker's arrival in June and July, you soon learned that there is no such thing as a *deus ex machina*. Baker has no magic powers. Once again, an inflated Washington reputation is punctured by its proximity to the reality of the Bush White House. Baker's influence is felt nowhere. This is still Bush's White House, still indecisive, still ideologically confused, still "reactive" instead of "proactive," to borrow the inelegant terminology of the New Paradigmers.

The only good laugh you've had came when somebody handed you a piece of paper and said, "Have you seen this?"

It had a White House letterhead, and was addressed to "Mr. John Hinkley, St. Elizabeth's Hospital, Washington D.C. 06969."

"Oh, my God," you said. "The correspondence unit sent a letter to Hinckley?"

"Read it," your friend said, so you did:

> Dear John:
> Barbara and I hope you are making good progress in your recovery from the mental problems that made you try to assassinate my predecessor, Ronald Reagan.
>   The staff at St. Elizabeth's tells me that you are doing just fine and may be released soon.

"This is a disaster!" you said. "What if Lois Romano at *The Washington Post* gets ahold of this?"

"Go on," your friend said.

> As you probably know, I have decided to seek a second term of office and I hope I can count on your support and the support of your fine Republican parents in my re-election campaign.
>   I hold no grudge against you, John, and I hope that if there is anything you need at the hospital, you will let Barbara and me know.

By the way, did you know that Bill Clinton is fucking Jodie Fos-
ter?
 Sincerely yours,
 George Bush

Pranks like this and the happy lift you get from the way the polls
are closing force you to come to grips with just how depressed you've
been these past few weeks. You've been having all these unusually
somber conversations in which you and your colleagues have prepared yourselves for disaster. Well, no more of that. Even your dour
friend on the campaign is cackling with glee, the guy who recently
said to you, "You know, I had a fight with my father. He's a lifelong
Republican, and he said to me, 'I don't see how I can vote for Bush
after the budget deal and the way he's talked about Israel.' And I said
to him, 'Dad, I have a wife who doesn't have much of an income and
two kids and a mortgage and I am cut off with no salary on November
fourth if we lose. I can't believe you're saying this to me!' I mean, it's
bad enough my own *wife* is voting for Clinton! But my *dad*?" You are
single, and you rent, but you understand. The month of October has
been horrible, an endless series of dashed expectations.
 Everybody agreed that Bush simply had to hit a home run in the
first of the three presidential debates, held on October 11. Well, he
went out there and he hit a towering pop fly that barely made it out
of the infield.
 Instead of going after Clinton on the inconsistencies in his record
and the outright lies of his campaign, instead of talking about the
future, the president launched into a defense of all the piddling little
stuff he had done in the first term—again, "first-time credits for
home buyers" and "investments in civilian R&D" and other equally
catchy ideas. The purpose of this wildly uninspiring public performance was to correct the American people who insisted on believing that the Bush administration had done nothing in domestic
affairs.
 It was clearer than ever that Bush simply would not accept the
disappointment of the electorate about his unwillingness or inability to
act more decisively to improve the economy. *I have* too *done things,*

lots *of things*, Bush was telling his bosses. *You're all just wrong. Wrong, wrong, wrong.*

How could he have made such a blunder? Well, look at the staffer chosen to prepare him for the debates: Richard Darman. All the stuff Bush talked about in the debate was Darman's stuff—all the proposals Darman had squeezed into the budgets he sent up to Congress, which Congress simply ignored when it passed the thirteen separate bills that make up the federal budget.

Bush wasn't defending his record; he was defending Darman's.

You could see how it was going to happen the day of the debate, when the president left the Oval Office to the cheers of his staff and headed toward *Marine One,* the helicopter that would take him to *Air Force One* at Andrews Air Force Base eight miles east of the White House for the flight to St. Louis. Right there at his side was Darman, and in Darman's arms was the thick, heavy white plastic briefing book—the bible of the debates. Inside the briefing book was every single thing the administration had ever proposed to Congress or said to the public about those proposals, and everything the campaign had on Clinton as well.

The briefing book was one of those thick three-ring-binder jobs, the kind that the best-organized students in high school always had with them in class. The guys with the three-ring binders run Washington. You've seen them in the cabinet departments you worked for before joining the White House. Every agency of the federal government has such a guy.

While his colleagues in the second tier enjoy the trappings of power—meeting famous people, glad-handing, talking on the phone to reporters—the Three-Ring-Binder Guy literally keeps tabs on everything. He writes down everything that is said and done and gives each item its own sheet of paper. He assigns each page to a subsection, and each subsection to a larger section that is marked by a colored tab.

The Three-Ring-Binder Guy is the functional equivalent of a eunuch in an imperial Chinese court; nobody there would want to be him, but because he has no interest in hedonistic pleasures he can spend all his time controlling everybody else.

Like the ever-flattering, sweet-tongued eunuch, the Three-Ring-Binder Guy is there to ease the uneasy spirit of his superior. If a cabinet secretary suddenly wakes up in the middle of the night and thinks, "What the hell am I doing here? I don't know what the hell I'm doing!" he can call his Three-Ring-Binder Guy. And his Three-Ring-Binder Guy will assure him that he's done a lot and is doing a whole lot more. Why, just look at this tab, and this one, and this. The binder itself is incredibly thick and unreadable, which is by design. Its purpose is to intimidate anyone who picks it up, to impress the boss with its sheer bulk and allow him to conflate the physical weight of the binder with the weightiness of his actions and policies. Three-Ring-Binder Guys use the three-ring binder because every day it just gets bulkier and bulkier, more and more intimidating. It's an egalitarian binder, too, because everything from the most serious matters to the most trivial literally weighs the same.

Darman, the king of the Three-Ring-Binder Guys, has triumphed yet again.

The relationship between Bush and Darman is a subject of endless speculation among your colleagues. One of them has lately been going around telling a story about an encounter between the two of them in 1987, when Bush was veep and Darman was working as Jim Baker's deputy at Treasury. Bush had an old friend visiting in his West Wing office and decided to walk his friend down to the lobby. As the two men left Bush's office, Dick Darman came down the narrow hallway, looked up—and did not acknowledge Bush. "Hey, Dick," Bush said, and Darman just walked past. Bush turned to his friend and said, "God forbid something should happen to the president [Reagan], but if I took over here the first thing I would do is fire that asshole."

During the '88 campaign, Bush was openly cool to Darman. But somehow, nobody knows how, Darman changed Bush's mind about him after the election. "He's Rasputin or something," the friend says. "He's got the president in his evil power." You don't think Darman is evil at all—in fact, you think he's one of the few people in the place who knows what he is doing, even if what he is doing has been calamitous—but it's true that Bush's continued reliance on Darman is impossible to understand. Especially since the gasp-inducing act of treachery Darman was responsible for just two weeks before the first debate.

He was the star and hero of an amazingly damning four-part *Washington Post* series about Bush's economic policies by his very dear friend Bob Woodward. The articles never quoted Darman directly except in the recounting of anecdotes, but everybody knew it was The Bush Administration According to Dick. Darman criticized Bush for disavowing the budget deal in March 1992, called it cowardly, even. He said he had thought the "Read my lips: no new taxes" line in the 1988 convention speech an act of the grossest demagoguery.

Like everybody else, you did not just want Darman to be fired for his disloyalty; you wanted him to suffer, to be stretched out on a rack for a few hours. You had witnessed Darman's ill-mannered behavior in meetings with your own eyes, but despite his reputation as a creepy back-stabber in the early Reagan years you had never seen any evidence here that he was a worm. Now you had. There was simply no precedent in Washington history for a sitting official to work with a hostile journalist on an exposé of his own administration to be published in the middle of a life-and-death reelection drive. The morning the first piece appeared, your friend on the campaign called. "Teeter went this morning to tell Bush that Darman had to be fired right now, right this minute. Can't have Bush's own chief economic adviser publicly deserting the ship."

"So what did Bush say?" you asked.

"He told Bob he wasn't happy about it, but Darman told him Woodward had sandbagged him. Darman was really upset about it, apparently, since the guy is such a close friend of his. Told him the series was only going to be published in a book next year sometime."

"You mean, Bush thought it would be okay, talking like that for a book by one of America's best-selling writers?"

It had to be true, then: Darman had the president hypnotized. And under his Rasputin's tutelage, Bush was tentative and defensive in the first debate, and allowed the loose and funny Ross Perot to reestablish himself as a potent political force while Clinton did absolutely nothing to embarrass himself and kept guarding his lead.

The morning after the debate, the place was abuzz. *That fucking Darman*, you heard again and again. "He has the heart of an abacus," somebody said. The Darman fixation was so intense that one of the staff assistants in your office came in to tell you about a nightmare he had had the night before: He was in the crowd in St. Louis, and Bush walked right past him to get to the stage. He stopped the president suddenly because he realized he had figured out the silver bullet, the killer question, the perfect issue with which to nail Clinton and destroy his chance of winning. Whereupon Darman interceded and said, "*I* prepared him for the debate. He knows everything he needs to know." And the president went on ahead, and the staff assistant woke up bathed in sweat.

"Oh come on," you said in response. "You didn't have that dream."

"Yes, I did," the staff assistant said, and you know he was telling the truth. "It was so sad."

Some people tried to look on the bright side. Quayle speechwriter Lisa Schiffren told her boss, Bill Kristol, that she thought Bush had done well and that the American people must have hated Clinton as much as she did. "Lisa," said Kristol, "take my advice. Go into your office and start getting your résumé ready."

When you and your colleagues weren't busy denouncing Darman, you were flying into rages at the media all day. Never *seen* such bias. It's unbelievable. Clinton can do no wrong, we can do no right. They never quote the president's speeches, they only talk about how it's raining when he talks, or the fact that there was a heckler in the crowd.

And never did you consider the bias more pronounced than two nights after the first debate, when Dan Quayle and Al Gore tangled. You watched it in your office with about ten people from your staff. Political events are communal experiences in Washington. Elsewhere in America, men gather to watch sporting events, but most of the people you know don't care about sports. Politics is their sports. Debates, presidential addresses, conventions—these are occasions for beer-and-chip parties in front of a large-screen television, complete with audience participation. Cheap rhetorical shots are greeted with the same howls of fury as a late hit in football or a deliberate beanball in baseball, and a corresponding insistence that the ump—in this case, the American people—must declare the blow illegal and penalize the offender if there is any decency left in the world, if there are any standards at *all*. At the same time, you want your guys to play it as mean and tough as possible, just to show a little life and self-confidence.

"Hit him!" you screamed as Quayle lit into Gore again and again, accusing him of "pulling a Clinton."

"Yaaaaaaah!" you cried when Quayle cited Gore's own contention in his book *Earth in the Balance* that it would cost $100 billion to put all his environmental plans in effect. You hissed when Gore denied it, and cheered again when Quayle cited the *page* number.

You heckled Gore with a delighted frenzy, so contemptuous of his humorless eco-piety and innate pomposity. You mimicked the kinds of questions you would like to hear with the bad taste common at these sorts of things: " 'Senator, if a tree broke into your house and raped Tipper Gore, would you be in favor of chopping it down?' " You mocked his cigar-store-Indian posture and the mirthless laugh. Every time Gore said something you all believed to be untrue or thought went too far, you and your colleagues would make a loud and obnoxious buzzer sound, as though you were all judges on a game show.

The worriers among you feared that every time Quayle opened his mouth he was overdoing it—like the guy in the stands who questions the manager's strategy every two minutes and drives the people sitting behind and in front of him crazy. But the common consensus was that Quayle won the debate hands down; he bashed Clinton and raised all the character questions that needed to be raised and really juiced up a pathetic public performance so far by the Bush campaign in the home stretch.

And as the debate came to an end, the commentators came on and . . . *declared it a draw*. You channel-zapped from CNN to CBS to ABC to NBC to PBS and they were all saying, yes, Quayle certainly was lively, but Gore really held his own—and then went on to spend oodles of time discussing Perot's sidekick, Admiral James Stockdale, and his embarrassing performance.

"This is bullshit!" you shouted. "This is shameless! Do they really hate Quayle so much?"

At the same time, there was something a little unseemly in your enthusiasm for the vice-presidential debate—Quayle did show some signs of life, but that really meant very little. Everybody in the place was saying, *This will really get Bush pumped up for the second debate two nights from now. He'll see how vulnerable Clinton and Gore really are and go right for the jugular like he did with Dukakis in '88.*

The glee you took in Quayle's scrappy performance and in the brilliant strategy you hoped and believed had been at work led you to go down to the South Lawn the next morning to meet his car, together with about three hundred other staffers and campaign workers who screamed with enthusiasm at Quayle's wave and held up signs reading, "We ♡ Dan." Finally, after four years, the White House found itself unambiguously celebrating the vice-president.

Your views on Quayle have shifted weekly—one moment you believe he's the only politician in the building with a feel for the American people and the next you think there's something seriously wrong with the guy, a connection missing between his left and right brains that allows him to do the strangest and dumbest things. After this year's biggest political gaffe you ran into Kristol at the men's-room door and said, gently, "How's it going, Bill?" To which he replied, glumly, "Potatoe."

Your ambivalence reflects the opinions of the two Republican camps within the White House. To the extent that Bushies think about Quayle at all, it is to feel a little sorry for him and at the same time to wonder whether he bears some of the blame for the president's troubles even though there isn't a single poll to prove that. The Reaganites in the place think he is a true-blue stand-up guy but don't really know whether that's Quayle himself or merely Kristol's brilliant job of political positioning. But at last Quayle has earned his stripes in the Bush White House as the Official Pit Bull of the 1992 Campaign.

You and your friends are desperate to believe that there is an entire strategy for the debates that is working out perfectly, a Machiavellian scheme consistent with Baker's reputation as a behind-the-scenes schemer: Knowing there were four debates, Bush and Baker didn't want Bush to peak too early and bash Clinton too much the first time: they understood that it's better to wait and land the blows as close to the election as possible.

To get through the day, you have to believe Baker and Bush know what they're doing and you will take any scrap of evidence as proof. The day *The Washington Times* revealed that Clinton had taken a trip to Moscow as a student in 1969, deputy chief of staff Bob Zoellick was absent from the senior staff meeting. His secretary reported he was out sick.

Out sick! Bob Zoellick was famous in the Bush administration for being quite possibly the most intense workaholic in Washington. He worked eighteen hours a day, seven days a week. None of his friends had ever known him to take a sick day, especially in the homestretch of the campaign. Obviously something was going on. . . . He had gone to Moscow. That was it. That *had* to be it. Zoellick had gone to Moscow because they had found the goods on Clinton and Baker needed his right-hand man to get the information himself.

It turned out that Zoellick was, in fact, sick—so sick he had gone to the George Washington University Hospital and had been admitted immediately. He was there two days, and then was back at his desk.

The rumor mill is on a twenty-four-hour-a-day schedule, producing smoking guns against Clinton that never materialize. The favored source of rumors is "a friend in the Secret Service" who himself has a friend in Bill's or Hillary's security detail and thus has inside information on the couple's peccadilloes. Bill is having an affair with a wire-service reporter. Bill and Hillary have separate rooms when they are on the same trip. One of Bill's Secret Service guys begged to be transferred when the Democratic candidate made a crude reference to a woman's anatomy in his presence. You would think every single person in the White House did nothing but go out and have coffee with Secret Service agents from the way dozens of staffers bragged about their intimacy.

The night of the second debate, Thursday, you travel across the Potomac to an apartment in Arlington whose panoramic view of the city stretches from the Washington Cathedral to the west and RFK Stadium to the east, the night sky interrupted by the planes taking off and landing at National Airport. There are seven of you from OEOB, including a couple who met and fell in love in the building. You settle in with your beer and your chips and your dip.

You know you're in trouble when moderator Carole Simpson describes the proceedings: All the questions will be asked by 209 "real people" in the audience. "That's it," someone says. "The complete and total Oprah-ization of American politics."

The candidates should feel free to leave their lecterns, do whatever they want. "Why did Baker agree to that?" you say. "This is Clinton's dream format."

A friend points out that Bush is used to this format; during both the 1980 and 1988 campaigns he traveled around the country doing question-and-answer sessions called "Ask George Bush."

"Yeah," you say, "but those were handpicked Republican audiences. Who knows who these people are?"

Whoever these people are, from the first question Bush looks like he's the president of a different planet. He has nothing to say to a guy with a ponytail who begins the session by asking the candidates only to talk about the "issues" and not to engage in discussions of character. This is bad news, because the word "issues" is shorthand for "attack Bush's handling of the economy," while "character" has become shorthand for "Clinton is a liar and a cheat." Bush begins, haltingly, once again to defend the administration's record, gets lost in his own sentence, looks a little tired. Meanwhile, Perot continues to throw out bon mots and Clinton stands there like the Terminator, his robotic brain whirring for a second as it searches the database for the answer that has been preprogrammed there.

Clinton brags about a program in Arkansas. Bush does not respond, and a frustrated wife in the room speaks: "His Arkansas record is *terrible*. In his twelve years as governor nothing has improved there. He can't let Clinton get away with *that*."

A woman in the audience asks the president what effect the deficit has had on Bush's life—he does not understand the question because she has misspoken and said "deficit" instead of "recession," and he stumbles around trying to explain that a large deficit has an unfortunate effect on the amount of money in the economy going to productive investment.

He is so uncomfortable up there it makes you uncomfortable watching him. You get up and go to the window, watching a 747 pass in front of you, going down.

"He really needs to hit Clinton," whispers a speechwriter. His girlfriend, who also works in the OEOB, smokes cigarette after cigarette and does not take her eyes from the screen.

Then he is asked whether he has any women as his close advisers, and he responds not with the name of his labor or commerce secretay, his cabinet secretary, Ede Holiday, or his personnel director, Connie Horner, but his former secretary-typist Rose Zamaria. Watching the television's reflection in the picture window, as though watching a reflection will be less painful than the real thing, you let out an involuntary sound that is half sigh, half groan.

"Jesus," somebody else says.

A few people go over to the bookcase and start thumbing through the volumes there.

You all know now that there had been no strategy. Quayle's performance had done nothing to stir the president up. He hadn't been playing possum in the first debate. This is it. There is not going to be a surge. It is lost.

The party doesn't last a minute beyond the debate's conclusion. Everyone gathers his things together and goes home—you can't bear to listen to the commentators and their ready-made analyses. The next day back at the White House, the denunciations of Darman's debate prep continue, but the truth is, people are so heartsick they cannot bear to talk about it.

God is not finished with you pessimists, however. In the third debate, finally, Bush puts in a good performance, telling America that Clinton "says one thing and does another" and warning taxpayers that when Clinton talks about "investment," "watch your wallet, because he's talking about taxes."

Bush becomes manic in its aftermath, hitting the campaign trail not only with vigor but with a sloppy enthusiasm that is matched by the rhetoric he is cooking up with his speechwriter, Steve Provost. Provost is ladling pop-culture references over the speeches, giving Bush one-liners that make reference to 1960s television programs he not only never saw but surely never even heard of—calling Clinton and Gore "Rocky and Bullwinkle," for example.

The speeches sound out of tune, silly, to you, but you feel defensive every time you watch the news and hear Susan Spencer of CBS or John Cochran and Lisa Myers of NBC sounding subtle notes of disapproval when Bush talks about "nutty pollsters" and quotes the bumper sticker popular in Republican circles that reads, "Annoy the media. Reelect Bush."

You chide them as you watch them debate the propriety of Bush saying, "My dog, Millie, knows more about foreign policy than these two bozos." "Oh, come on, have a sense of humor," you say aloud, but it rings hollow; it is off-putting to hear a man in his late sixties going in for this kind of juvenilia, especially when he is the oldest and most distinguished person in the race. It's even more amazing when you consider the fact that his own campaign chairman, Bob Teeter, is a pollster by trade.

You are made angrier by the attention given to the supposed scandal of a State Department search of Bill Clinton's passport file, which had been begun in response to a Freedom of Information Act request by *The Washington Times*. If this didn't prove the media were completely in the tank, what would? Usually the media complain when the executive branch doesn't move fast enough on FOIA requests; now they're complaining because this one was expedited.

Of *course* the search was expedited. The information would be meaningless after the election. And why *isn't* Clinton's trip to Moscow a legitimate news story? He won't talk about it, says he doesn't remember, then says he remembers a little. Clearly the guy is lying again. You don't think he was a KGB agent or anything, but why shouldn't the American people know what's in that passport file?

And yet your hot defense of Passportgate, like the president's talk of bozos, doesn't convince even you. After all, the Baker people are behaving as though it was wrong, very wrong. They are saying they were nowhere near it when it is impossible that Betty Tamposi, the State Department official who coordinated the search, would have done the whole thing on her own. If the search had been kosher, why were the Baker people behaving as though it were a crime?

You find you feel dizzy all the time, as though you are on a roller coaster that refuses to let you off and keeps taking unexpected turns and dips. First debate—down. Quayle debate—up. Second debate—way down. Third debate—up. Passportgate—down.

And when the Gallup folks report the president within 2 points, it's too good to believe, but you can't help believing it. The mood lasts exactly forty-two hours, until Friday, when the new news hits the White House that Iran-contra maniac Lawrence Walsh has indicted Reagan Secretary of Defense Caspar Weinberger anew and in the indictment cites a note taken in Weinberger's hand saying that Bush supported the arms-for-hostages swap.

Your friend on the campaign calls. "We're dead," he says. "They're all over us. The Clinton people got tipped off in advance."

"Come on," you say. "The voters don't care about this."

"We're dead," he repeats dully, and his attitude is shared by Bush himself and his people on *Air Force One,* who react to the press's questions as though they have been kicked foursquare in the balls.

There's a part of you that thinks this Walsh business is a kind of rough justice for Bush, and even for Ronald Reagan. Bush had had the opportunity, time and time again, to announce he was pardoning the Iran-contra defendants. Though he, like you and most other people in the White House who cared about the issue, believed Walsh's prosecutions had become an unwarranted criminalization of political differences, Bush still let it all stand because people like Marlin Fitzwater made it clear he would be beaten to death with a lead pipe by the press if he interfered.[1]

The days following all this are anticlimax; by Monday only the especially crazed Bushies and the ideologues who simply cannot imag-

---

[1] With his customary perfect timing, Bush pardoned Weinberger, George, CIA operatives Duane Clarridge and Alan Fiers and State Department official Elliott Abrams on December 24. In the interests of full disclosure, I should mention here that Abrams is married to my sister Rachel.

ine that an electorate might choose those traitorous villains the Democrats persist in believing that Bush can pull this thing out.

You and the guy in the office next door to you set up a previctory party in your suite and invite people in the building and elsewhere in government to come by for beer and egg rolls (courtesy of the catering service of White House Mess) at 6:00 P.M. There are five television sets, one each for CBS, NBC, ABC, PBS and CNN. A full-size cardboard cutout of Bush stands in the doorway, and on its label is a button: Al Gore's name with a *Ghostbusters* slash through it.

The mood is neither depressed nor elegiac. There is about it, rather, the calm and peace of the terminal patient as he readies to die. Cheers erupt occasionally as the early popular vote numbers tilt toward Bush—with 3 percent of the national precincts reporting, he is ahead by 2 points.

"Two points! It's a two-point race!" shouts one mordant guest, mocking the buzz from the Mess corridor just six days before. Word has already filtered over from the campaign that the exit polls have Clinton winning 43 percent and 368 electoral votes. At least it's no landslide.

Since there is no suspense, you talk little about the election. Rather, the discussions are about things people rarely talk about in the White House: the kids, and the family, and cars; a staffer brings her newborn baby and everybody coos over the little girl.

You and your colleagues are testing out real life again, seeing what it is like to behave like normal, ordinary people with normal, ordinary jobs instead of the eunuchs and fops of a palace court.

The only flash of anger comes from Leigh Ann Metzger. She swirls on her toes, her blond locks swirling as well, as she looks around at the Bushies—the Twinkies and Ken dolls who populate the room. "They don't know what's going on," she says fiercely. "They don't even know. They don't even have the foggiest idea that the country is about to go to hell in the next four years and maybe more."

People wander out onto the balcony, which faces the Winder Building, home of the Office of the U.S. Trade Representative. Somebody says that under Clinton the building will grow four stories and have its name changed to "the Office of the U.S. Trade War."

The party breaks at about 8:30, and you go out to dinner at an Indian restaurant with a fellow staffer and two civilian friends. You talk about nothing—a visit to an Italian restaurant in New York, a pesty friend, the dating habits of somebody else—and you fall silent.

It has actually happened. The loss has actually happened. Now all you have to hope for is that Bruce Herschensohn, the conservative intellectual running for Senate in California, beats the very liberal Representative Barbara Boxer. You go to sleep and wake up the next morning to the news: Boxer won too.

You haven't really considered what a loss might mean until now. You have just turned thirty, and your entire adult life has been lived under Republican rule. And after college and graduate school and one job in conservative intellectual circles in New York, you have spent your professional life working in the executive branch. You knew the minute you began that this was what you really wanted, what you liked—being part of the process of governing, helping to manage things, getting to watch the mechanics of government up close and keep the machine greased and well oiled. You are really good at it, too, and took to the work with the comfort of a man who had found his proper place.

You are not interested in making money (it would be nice, but not necessary), and even if you were you don't know how, exactly. Other people in the White House can "go home," back to the companies or law firms they previously worked at or back to their hometowns and home states, where they can get involved in local politics and maybe even run for office themselves.

You, on the other hand, are a rootless cosmopolitan. You have no home to go back to. This is your home. Washington. The OEOB. After all, you spend more time there than you do in your apartment.

Your debate-watching friends are in much the same predicament. You and your fellow clever young conservatives who came of age in the 1980s with a consuming interest in politics did not want to go to law school like your more ideologically liberal college classmates or to business school and Wall Street like your more materialistic peers.

You wanted to write for the conservative intellectual journals that gave you sustenance and pleasure, but by the time you attained your majority there was almost no way to support yourself as an intellectual. You might have become a college professor, but you found universities and faculties hostile, and the prospect of spending your life among people who considered themselves your enemy was not especially pleasant.

The truth is, despite the much-discussed conservative ascendancy in the 1980s, there were precious few institutions in which you could make a life for yourself. There was, however, the entire executive branch. Now *here* was a remarkably fertile field to plow with a remarkably varied set of opportunities working for people who were, if possible, even more perfervid about these things than you. You needed no special expertise. You just needed entrée, and one article in *Commentary* or *The American Spectator* was it. If you could write, you could be a speechwriter. If you had a government degree, you could be a special assistant and factotum.

Interested in education? Go work in the Department of Education, where your belief in a Great Books curriculum was not only shared, but where the secretary himself, Bill Bennett, spoke of little else.

Concerned about judicial activism and a believer in a strict reading of the Constitution? You would find no closer and passionate allies than in the nooks and crannies of the Department of Justice.

Hate Commies? You had your chance to fight them over in certain corners of the State Department with Elliott Abrams or the Defense Department with Richard Perle.

The other departments weren't as interesting, but people like you found easy employ there too.

And though you fought the good fight in the Reagan years, working in the cabinet departments was still a job like any other, and maybe a little worse, because the closer you got to the boss the more you became a valet rather than a policy guy, and truer words were never spoken than "No man is a hero to his valet."

The Bush White House was smaller, more collegial—intimate, even. And working there, even if you were relatively junior and stuck in the OEOB, was genuinely pleasant. Nothing quite like telling somebody you work "in the White House" and getting that surprised, impressed "Oh!" in return.

Bush's loss is more than a confusing layoff, especially for you, since you don't have a family to support. As you watch the debate wind down, you begin to understand the emotional impact of "going into exile"—a phrase you have heard often in your life and never really thought about before. "Going into exile" means losing your home and your familiar surroundings and being cast upon unfamiliar waters without any assurance that your vessel is going to land somewhere.

It means finding that the world around you is nowhere near as stable and permanent as you imagined; instead, it is unstable, impermanent, and you can take nothing for granted ever again.

SEVEN:

THE SOLIPSISTIC PRESIDENCY, OR, MESSAGE: I CARE

Two weeks after the 1992 election, senior staffers dutifully trooped into the Roosevelt Room at 7:30 for the morning meeting. Even though they had lost, and thus the only real issue they had to address was how exactly they were going to make a living come January, the members of the Bush senior staff still conducted themselves as they had previously—still getting into petty fights, still ordering their underlings in the OEOB around, still imagining that they were people of importance because they attended the morning staff meeting in their lame-duck White House. They were like the agents of the East German secret service who continued to show up every morning at their headquarters even after the secret service was disbanded and the doors locked. They did not know any different.

The only person who did seem to know different was chief of staff James Baker, who barely bothered to show up for work. But this morning even Baker came to the staff meeting, because right behind him was the outgoing president of the United States, who proceeded to deliver a twenty-minute monologue.

Bush wanted everyone to know that he was not depressed, contrary to press reports. Sure, it had been hard to lose, but he was doing okay. So was Bar. They'd taken a couple of days off to unwind;

Bar was going down to Houston to scout out a good place to rent for a while.

He was sure everybody had heard all the rumors about how he might be asked to serve as president of Yale or commissioner of baseball, but he wasn't interested in any of that. Not really his cup of tea. Like he had said on election night, he wanted to get heavily into the grandkid business. He was really looking forward to it.

He knew, he said, how hard everybody had worked in the past couple of months, so he wanted them to know that for the next nine weeks, until it was time to go, they should really take care of themselves. Take the time they need, look for a good job. And listen, if there's anything he can do for anybody, a letter of recommendation or a phone call, don't hesitate to ask.

And then he got up and went down the hall to the Oval Office.

George Bush ended his tenure the way he began it—comically self-obsessed. The essentially solipsistic character of George Bush has been little noted except by the voters of 1992, who noted it all too well. For most of his years on this earth, Bush had succeeded in keeping a lid on it. In her book, *What I Saw at the Revolution*, Peggy Noonan talks about how Vice-President Bush was uncomfortable talking about himself, as though the use of the word "I" were somehow tacky and tasteless, ill bred. She helped find a rhythm for his speeches by restricting the use of the word. He said things like "Went west, had a family," and held back on the use of the first person until he needed to make a serious point, as in "The Congress will push me to raise taxes, and I'll say no. And they'll push, and I'll say no. And they'll push again, and I'll say to them: 'Read my lips: no new taxes.' "

That may have been true about the George Bush who preceded the 1988 election, but it bore little resemblance to the man who became president. Never has a public figure used the first person so often. In his breathtakingly revealing first press conference as president-elect—the one in which he rejected the possibility that he had received a mandate in the election—he began talking about himself and never stopped. He lovingly interpreted his own feelings and motives:

Q: How does it feel?

A: Somewhere in between total exhilaration and recognition
that the challenge ahead is going to be awesome, that I
need to get some rest, and I think everybody involved
in this campaign needs to get some rest. And I will do
that. But I can't use the word "exciting." I can use the
word "gratified" at the outcome, better than many of us
thought. But I will not underestimate the challenge
ahead. And there's a seriousness that takes over right
this minute.

Q: How are you going to communicate with the American
people?

A: Reach out and touch someone, use a telephone. And I'm
not going to change in terms of my belief that the
more personal contact you have, the better. I recognize
there's, the parameters of this job are quite different,
but I will continue to do what I've done in terms of contact. And I'm one who works with, closely with the
people that I've, you know, associated with on my staff,
not just one person I talk to. . . . It's a little bit of a
departure, but that's the way I'm going to do it. . . .
But I'll try to keep in touch as best I can.

"I" was a word you rarely heard Ronald Reagan use, either in
press conferences or in speeches; Reagan instead relied on the democratic "we" (as opposed to the royal "we") in referring either to his
administration or to the country at large. He did not separate himself
either from the people who worked for him or from the people he
worked for—the voters.

Bush did, all the time. He made it very clear that administration
policies were *his* property, and said nothing that would lead the press
or Congress or the people to believe he was acting not as George
Bush himself but as the elected representative of the American people. In the course of his presidency, he would on eighty-four separate
occasions indicate administration support for a program or policy with
the words "I'm for that," a small but significant rhetorical trope. He
could discuss policy questions only by inserting himself into them,
using the first person even when it was inappropriate. In September

223

1991, when he was asked about a controversial and possibly unconstitutional plan to send black boys in Detroit to all-male schools, he
said: "I'm for as much innovation as possible. . . . I'm going to be
respectful of the law. If somebody says that's not right, might try to
fight to change that one, and a few other things. But let's not go
overboard on this stuff, for heaven's sake."

Bush was not attempting to rally support for an idea, to defend a
position or to advance an argument; he just wanted to talk about
himself for a little while.

Comedian-impressionist Dana Carvey of "Saturday Night Live"
captured Bush's self-obsession perfectly when he picked up on Bush's
incessant use of the word "prudent," lampooning it in the oft-invoked
phrase "It wouldn't be prudent at this juncture." In his first year in
office alone, Bush used the word "prudent" or some form of it four
dozen times when describing how he was approaching a policy matter. Explicate the text: Someone who is obsessed with "prudence" is
less concerned about what is going on around him than he is about *his
own response* to the activity and how it will be perceived. He was
"prudent" about the democracy protests in China, "prudent" about
the leadership situation in the Soviet Union, "prudent" about the
Berlin Wall, all because he was unable to grasp the enormity of these
events and could only focus on his own halting reaction to them.

Or about the reaction of others to him. He went campaigning in
New Hampshire in February 1992 and, reading off a card in his
pocket, spoke the words: "Message: I care." He was supposed to ad
lib words of care and concern, but instead he read his stage directions. That was in keeping with his persistent habit of trying to tell
people how best to analyze him and his ideas, rather than just going
out and doing and saying things worthy of analysis.

He would cease using the word "I" only when he wanted to talk
about himself in the third person and make himself sound grand,
formal, important. He frequently treated the public to the strange
spectacle of a president of the United States talking about the "president" as if "the president" were someone else.

He talked about what a president ought to do and not do: "If the
president misspeaks or sounds euphorically optimistic or overly pes-

simistic [about the economy], you send the wrong signals," he said in November 1991. A couple of months earlier, signaling to Saddam Hussein that he was getting ticked off by the Iraqi dictator's refusal to allow UN teams to do weapons inspections, he said: "I am determined that he comply with these [UN] resolutions. And when a president makes a statement like that, he ought not to do it without being willing to back that up." At the end of February 1992, when asked if he was tired of getting attacked by Pat Buchanan, he said: "I don't think a president should get down there in that level. I think, just keep trying to do my job."

When he got a little more informal, rolled up his sleeves and talked politics, he was able to discuss only one thing—the ever-present "I." The day after the New Hampshire primary, in which he as incumbent president had won only 58 percent, he might have thought it necessary to use precious television time to win some support from other disgruntled voters; instead, Bush took the time to praise and criticize and analyze himself: "I must say I feel good today. . . . With an eighteen-point win, most people say, 'Hey, that's not bad.' . . . The other thing I've got to do, though, I do think I have to do better, is get this message to the country about what we're trying to do. . . . And so, I've got to get this—what I really want to do is get something done in terms of stimulating the economy. . . . I'm not going to give up on trying to get the Congress to move. . . . I'm going to focus on what I think is best for this country and proclaiming, hey, fifty-eight/ forty [the Bush-Buchanan percentage count], a lot different than I heard some of you guys talking about earlier last evening. . . ."

Once again he could not talk about programs themselves or about their merit, but only about how well or poorly he was doing getting votes and getting the sympathies of voters.

Is it any wonder, then, that the Bush White House was the center of a potent cult of personality in which every issue afflicting the body politic was reduced to its impact on the president's popularity or his chances of reelection? Throughout the building, from the walls of the West Wing basement to the walls of every office, were thousands of photographs of the man himself in various poses and guises. Those in the common areas were changed biweekly to keep the photographers occupied and the staff dazzled by the handsome visage of their leader, always surrounded by adoring crowds, accompanied by his adorable wife, and if you were at an event and looked really hard, you might even be able to spot your tiny face in a sea of hundreds of other tiny faces.

Bush was left after the election with only his cult of personality intact, which was what led him into the Roosevelt Room that November morning to reassure the people he had so seriously let down that *he* was all right, they really shouldn't worry about him.

He had his cult of personality, and now, for the next ten weeks, he had all the pleasures of the presidency with none of the burdens; did not have to concern himself with the pesky ideas of the American people or the U.S. Congress. Until January 20, when Clinton kicked him out, he could make lots of decisions—to bomb Iraq again, send troops to Somalia; anything he wanted. He was no longer the people's representative; he was, instead, the government caretaker, which was what he really always wanted to be.

Bush so personalized his presidency that in his final months he made an enormously consequential decision essentially to make nice with one of his favorite cabinet members.

The issue was food labeling, and stick with it for a little while. In 1990, Congress passed a law requiring more extensive nutritional information on food packages by summer 1993. It did not, however, specify what sort of information should appear, but if the most restrictive form of regulation was imposed, it would cost the U.S. food industry big. Very big.

In time, there were two camps in the administration. The first was the Department of Health and Human Services, which had bought into the idea that all of America should be placed on a low-fat diet, and the lower in fat the better. It wanted the labels to detail every ounce of everything in every product and how it conformed to an ideal American diet (for women, two thousand calories, 30 percent from fat; for men, twenty-five hundred calories, 30 percent from fat).

The second was the Department of Agriculture, which wanted less detailed labels. It had been fighting with HHS over the very concept of the ideal diet because the HHS's concept essentially declared war on the two most profitable areas of American farming: beef and dairy products. The two departments were at daggers drawn on the issue of whether, in fact, the ideal diet even was an ideal diet. Ag claimed that the ideal diet for women was really good only for post-menopausal types, while HHS claimed it was now a matter of common knowledge among health people that fat was the cause of every single problem on the face of the planet.

The two camps could not come up with a compromise, and finally the matter landed on the president's desk. A complicated, almost Solomonic decision involving regulation, and Bush had to make the call.

Bush stood in a strange relation to the issue of the effect of government regulations on the economy. In the Reagan administration he had chaired a task force that eliminated a million or more regulations from the *Federal Register*. As president, however, he presided over a regulatory frenzy, mostly as a result of the the environmental promises he had made during his 1988 campaign. His "no net loss of wetlands" policy gave the Environmental Protection Agency wide latitude in regulating American commercial real estate. His Clean Air Act added hundreds of thousands of pages of regulations on the economy. So did his Americans with Disabilities Act.

"The Re-Regulatory President," he had been called in a 1991 cover story in the *National Journal*. When he saw and read the story, Bush was shocked to discover all this regulating going on. He was against that! Overregulation? Was his administration overregulating? Why hadn't anybody told him?

If Bush had truly been against regulation and in favor of the freest market economy possible, the decision was a no-brainer: Ag's less restrictive food label was the clear winner. But of course the president wasn't really "for" or "against" anything so abstract; his mind didn't work that way. Sure, he was "against" excessive regulation. But he was also "for" health, and nobody could say he wasn't. And Lou—meaning Louis Sullivan, his HHS secretary—was a doctor, so he must know about these health things.

This was how Bush made the decision:

The previous week Agriculture Secretary Edward Madigan had

received Bush's permission to void a 1937 regulation that had established a truly Stalinist system of production quotas for California citrus growers. The "marketing orders" system, as it was known, was one of those amazing programs that compelled the destruction of millions of perfectly good oranges; if their number was restricted, prices could remain high. And any farmer who did not go along with the marketing orders was committing a felony.

So when the time came to make his decision on food labeling, this is what the president said: Ed won one last week. We should probably let Lou win one this week

Cost of letting Lou win one this week: $4 billion.

White House officials enraged by the move on food labeling said it proved that at the end of his political career, Bush was returning to his roots. He was, once again, a liberal Rockefeller Republican— someone who basically believes everything a Democrat believes but thinks he can manage it better.

In truth, there was no consistent ideological approach in Bush's last two months. One moment he agreed to restrictive food labeling; the next he pardoned the Iran-contra defendants. He went into Somalia for liberal humanitarian reasons, and threw billions of dollars' worth of cruise missiles at Iraq in defense of his no-fly zone.

It was the logical conclusion to the beginning of his presidency, when in his inaugural address he spoke of all the things he cared most deeply about. Cared about the environment and cared about business. Was concerned about education. Wanted to stop the scourge of drugs. Understood that education was the key to a brighter future. Believed that we should help our fellow humans and make this "the age of the outstretched hand." Knew the American people didn't send the president and Congress to Washington to bicker. Other things were added later: Loved the flag, hated to see it burn. Believed in art but didn't like obscenity.

He didn't mean any of it. Or, rather, he meant it the way a Polonius would mean it: He was in favor of good things and against bad things. As though good things were so easily come by; as though bad things were easily gotten rid of by merely stating your opposition.

Consider the sorts of poll questions his deeply held convictions would seem to answer:

• Are you for the environment or against it? *For it. Sure. Environment. Very important.* Who would say, "No, I'm against the environment"? Nobody. Literally.

• Do you support the efforts of American business to grow more competitive with foreign imports? *For them. Vital to our future.* But what if your concern for the environment as expressed above gets in the way? What if regulations you support increase the cost of doing business in the United States and make competition that much more difficult? When you have to choose, which do you choose?

• Do you think education is the key to a brighter future? *Absolutely. Can't get anywhere without a good education.* Although Bush certainly had. The only book anybody thinks he read during his four years in office was Tom Clancy's novel about the drug war, and there's no evidence he finished it. No one who ever flew with him as vice-president saw him with a book. He grew bored reading a four-page speech. Given his thirty thousand handwritten notes, it's entirely possible Bush wrote more than he ever read. But again, who would disagree with the idea that education is important?

• Must the drug scourge stop? *You bet. Gotta stop that drug scourge.* Well, this one is maybe a little tougher; there are some people who believe in legalization of drugs. So he gets maybe a little credit for this one. But there are two different ideas about how to do it: You need to focus your energies on cutting the supply or focus your energies on cutting demand. There is simply not enough money to do both. Which should you do?

• Should the president and Congress bicker? *Of course not. They should join together to do good for all the people.* Again, nobody sane would disagree. But what if the president and the Congress strongly and passionately do disagree on exactly how to do good for all the people? What if they stand mortally opposed on, say, how to make education the key to a brighter future—Congress wants to increase funding for lousy public schools while Bush wants vouchers so poor people can send their kids to private schools? There's no compromise here. The two of you are parallel lines that can never meet, both aiming at the same mystical goal of "better education" but with wildly contrasting notions of how to get there. Shouldn't you bicker *then*? Isn't it a little stupid—or at best naive—to imagine that people of good-will can bridge these chasms just because you *want* it to be the case?

• Should Americans help each other? *Helping each other is one of the best things in this country. We must love one another or die. When I see Bar holding an AIDS baby in her arms* . . . Who could deny the truth of this? But the fact is, Barbara Bush doesn't have a job and never did. It's all well and good for Bush to talk about how this is the age of the outstretched hand, but most people in America make less than $40,000 and must support a family of four on that. They want to send their kids to college and own a home and go away on vacation and have a car that runs. They stretch out their arms plenty—for their own kids and for the people they know. They watch a neighbor's kid when she has to work the night shift. They run a scout troop. They drive their daughter around to sell Girl Scout cookies, and buy more boxes than they need so she can make her quota. They don't have time to join the Junior League. If they are not do-gooders, it's because they don't have time. And they don't need some rich panty-waist from Maine telling them to volunteer their time as though they would just go to Elizabeth Arden all day if they didn't go ladle out soup at a homeless shelter. Besides, Bush loved to talk about the impor-tance of families. Doesn't spending a lot of time with your family in order to help your own children preclude spending a lot of time helping others who are not members of your family?

He didn't mean it. He didn't believe in anything very much except that he wanted to be president, and finally, somehow, through some fluke of nature called Ronald Reagan, he made it. In the final analysis, George Bush's presidency was a kind of cosmic joke.

Fortunately, somebody up there liked us; a man with no core became the president of the United States and, just to keep us safe, Communism collapsed and a psycho bully in Iraq with no decent airplanes tried to make a big war against our big military.

Gives you a good reason to believe in God.

FREEZE FRAME:

"WE WILL BE BACK"

JANUARY 11–20, 1993

A Monday morning, and you go through the double doors in your second-floor OEOB office out to the balcony overlooking Seventeenth Street. You are carrying a white banner, eight feet long and two feet high, an expensive piece of work that has been handsomely printed and layered in plastic. It reads, *"We will BE BACK!"*

The banner was given to you by a friend "in the private sector"; you will not say who it is, because your friend and his friend's lobbying group will have to work with the Clinton administration and you have sworn to die with the secret of their identities.

You hang the banner off the balcony so that everybody who looks up at the OEOB can read it while walking or driving along Seventeenth. You go back into your office and wait, killing time by playing the golf program on your computer, which you bootlegged from a friend down the hall. You and he and a few other people have gotten into a ferocious computer tournament as you sit around, not much to do, waiting for your headhunter to call with news of another job prospect.

Forty minutes later, a woman storms into your office. She is from the General Services Administration, which oversees the office buildings of the executive branch. Its offices are down the street from the OEOB.

"Who authorized this?" she sputters.

"Nobody," you say in your affable, slow-talking way. You are in your midthirties, and came over to the White House from one of the less significant cabinet departments a year before.

"Well, *I* think it is in extremely poor taste, and I demand that you take it down immediately," she says.

"I don't think you have the authority to tell me to do that," you say, ever pleasant.

"I think I should call my supervisor," she says.

"I think you should," you agree.

"May I use your phone?" she says.

"Certainly," you say.

She cannot reach the supervisor, so she says she will go back to her office and call you from there. Fifteen minutes later, the supervisor calls. You are correct; GSA has no authority over these matters at the White House. Only Tim McBride, the White House director of administration, does. The supervisor also thinks the banner is in poor taste, but suggests you call McBride to see what McBride thinks.

You call McBride and explain the situation. McBride is the person in the White House literally closest to the president; he was his military and personal aide for three years, which means he was at his side whenever the president set foot out of the Oval Office.

If any single White House employee reflects the views and spirit of the outgoing president of the United States, it is McBride.

He listens to you and says, "You know what? I think you'd better take the banner down."

Elapsed time: one hour, thirty-seven minutes.

You are no fire breather. You are a gentle fellow—pretty conservative, but no one would take you for a crazed ideologue. But you've worked in government for years; you know the score. You knew you were going to get lip from GSA. After all, most everybody in GSA is a career employee, which in Washington means chances are eight to one you're talking Democrat. And somebody at GSA would certainly fear trouble if some Clinton person saw the banner and it made him mad.

But you had hoped for better from McBride, even though you had guessed McBride's reaction beforehand. After all, the banner was not in the least offensive; said nothing hostile about the Dems; was merely a high-spirited denial of the prevailing mood in the capital that the natural order had been restored with the complete Democratic dominance of the Congress, the media and now the presidency as well. A mild rallying cry, a whistle in the dark, good for a wistful photograph in *The Washington Times,* maybe.

But Bush said he wanted this to be the best transition ever and shadow-baby-Bush Tim McBride was going along. So here Bush is, once again and for the final time disappointing you and your fellow embattled Republicans who want to feel as though you are not fighting a losing and lonely battle. Instead of rallying you, helping you feel better, Bush is playing nice with the Democrats, which is the last thing you want.

The best transition ever—what the hell did that mean? It was one thing to ensure the orderly transfer of power, but it was entirely another to kiss Democratic ass when the Dems are doing everything they can to turn Bush's very name into a late-century version of Herbert Hoover's—the bogeyman image of the evil and uncaring Republican.

Bush seems most concerned about salvaging his own reputation as a *decent* guy, a *gracious* guy, especially after the end of his campaign when he called Clinton and Gore "bozos." Okay, so, unlike you, the president *was* publicly rejected by sixty million people, which means his reputation is in need of some salvage work. But still, Bush gets to go back to Houston with a big pension while you and the hundreds and hundreds of younger Republicans whose jobs and careers he threw away because he didn't have a clue how to be president now have to stay on in a Washington in which you will be as popular as the economists of Kirghizia's finance ministry.

Standing in this office, which has been emptied of all its files so they can be carted away to the future Bush library, where no one will ever look at them, the feeling comes over you in a nihilistic rush—he is the reason that things were never quite right, never, ever. George Bush, empty man.

You hear that Andy Ferguson and Bob Zoellick were set to work on a farewell address, the farewell address of George Herbert Walker Bush, forty-first president of the United States. Zoellick wanted to know what the president wanted to talk about in his final message to the American people. The president thought a little, thought a little more. Said he wanted to say something about family. The family is very important. But, he said, none of this right-wing agenda stuff. Don't want any of that right-wing agenda.

The family is important—that was it after sixty-eight years on the earth, thirty of them in public life, twelve of them in and around the White House. *My fellow Americans, I want to speak to you tonight about the family. It is very important. Thank you, God bless you, and may God bless this wonderful country.*

He gives no farewell address. Instead, he spends the last couple of days of his presidency bombing Iraq again and putting everyone in his senior staff on various boards—the Southern Pacific Railway Commission, the Micronesia Commission—all boring assignments that can bring in an extra five to ten grand, and if you get the Micronesia thing you get a free trip to the South Pacific.

He makes 111 executive decisions that Leon Panetta, Clinton's budget director, will void with a dash of a pen January 21. Then he gets on a plane that used to be *Air Force One* but is no more because he is president no more, and before leaving says, "It's been a hell of a ride."

Hell of a ride. He is right about one thing, at the very last.

some words of thanks and explanation

In the early months of 1992, my friends and acquaintances who worked for George Bush began pouring out their woes and fears and mordant witticisms in countless and endless conversations at breakfast, lunch, dinner and on the telephone. These were White House staffers and Bush campaign officials with whom I had worked and played poker and spent a lot of my spare time in the eight years I had lived in Washington.

I understood them because I was one of them. I too had moved to the capital in the early 1980s because for conservative Republicans like us, Washington was what Paris was to the expatriate Americans after the First World War: the center of intellectual, social and ideological ferment. The only difference was that they mostly came to work in government, whereas I was a writer and a journalist.

But there is no way to avoid a tour of duty when you live in Washington, and so for nine months between August 1988 and May 1989 I ended up working in the White House myself—first as a speechwriter for Ronald Reagan and then as a special assistant to William Bennett when he was drug czar. It was in large measure because I feared that government service was a path to nowhere that I left it to go back into journalism. And with the decline of George Bush so pronounced in the early months of 1992, my friends similarly looked around and wondered where they could go and what they could do to make a living if Bush went down to defeat.

In their despair and anxiety, they were narrating a classic Washington story nobody had ever really chronicled before: the tale of a mortally wounded presidency whose wounds were almost entirely self-inflicted, with considerable collateral damage inflicted upon them as well.

When I decided to write a book about the inner workings of the Bush White House in April 1992, the working title was *Suicide/ Attempt*. If Bush lost, as I believed he would, the completed tome could be called *Suicide*; if he won, the victory would have been so unimpressive that *Suicide Attempt* would have been accurate as well.

Although my friends and sources constantly compared the troubles of George Bush to a Greek tragedy, the stories they were telling were far more farcical than tragic. As they talked, the image of silent-film comedian Harold Lloyd dangling from the arm of a clock fourteen stories over Los Angeles kept flashing through my mind, except that in place of Lloyd's calm Yalie face was the visage of Yalie supreme George Bush.

The final product is the result of more than two hundred hours of interviews and the perusal of some ten thousand pages' worth of documents, speeches, statements, and memoranda that came out of the Bush White House, conducted and compiled over a period of nine months.

The central characters in the "Freeze Frames" are not composites; they are, rather, abstractions. Each character was a real live White House staffer. I am afraid that several of them did not know they were posing for portraits, and if they can determine who they are and are unhappy, I apologize. If they are happy, then so am I.

The "Freeze Frames" are so written in large measure because most of those who spoke to me and shared paper with me did so on the explicit condition that their names and the information they supplied be kept confidential. (In at least two of the cases, the "Freeze Frame" subjects could have been named, but since it was necessary to obscure the identities of some, the formal style demands of the book took over.) The subjects feared retaliation at some later date, feared hurting the feelings of others, or just were afraid in general.

There are some staffers, though, whom I get to thank publicly simply because they cannot escape their association with me. Foremost among them is my good friend and business partner, Daniel Casse. He disagrees with many things in the book but nonetheless served as a selfless and meticulous editor of the manuscript.

Andy Ferguson, now of *The Washingtonian,* shared his time and thoughts and stories with me even though we both knew his own book on the subject would have been not only more incisive, but twice as funny.

Jay Lefkowitz became a pal in the course of this work, and I hope he remains one in spite of it.

Though Bill Kristol's father is often confused with mine, I doubt anyone could confuse my understanding of the Washington scene with Bill's sheer political brilliance; he taught me more about the workings of Republicanism in a series of conversations over the course of a year than I had learned in my previous thirty-one.

Others proved terrific company, like David Tell, the nicest opposition-research director you would ever want to meet. Shane Schriefer and Carie Stevens were the sweethearts of the OEOB.

Outside the White House complex, Mike Joyce of the Lynde and Harry Bradley Foundation and Jim Piereson of the John M. Olin Foundation were remarkably generous when I let them know that the more scholarly project they had initially funded was going to have to wait until this more timely enterprise was done. Les Lenkowsky of the Hudson Institute was a prince, but that is nothing new.

Gregg Kenyon did spectacular research work.

Bob Tyrrell of *The American Spectator* gave me my start as a writer, and has done something almost unheard of in my experience: He has returned good for ill. I owe him more than I can say, and the same is true for his right hand, Wlady Pleszczynski.

Tony Dolan and Mari Maseng are partly responsible for this book, since they gave me my chance to work in the Reagan White House. Bill Bennett and John Walters did the same for me in the drug czar's office at the beginning of the Bush years. Don't blame the four of them, though; if you must blame somebody, blame Alice Mayhew of

Simon & Schuster, whose enthusiasm for the project carried me through some rough patches. I am equally grateful to my agent, Cynthia Cannell.

Clark Judge had to live through the gestation process in the office we shared. He was endlessly encouraging, always free to bounce an idea off or grab some lunch with our third office mate, Rett Wallace, when the last thing I could imagine doing was sitting down to write. I profited as well from the musings of Eric Felten and Peter Robinson.

Special thanks and profound apologies are due Rick Marin, George Russell and my sister Rachel Abrams, who patiently listened to my incessant complaining when they all had far better things to do.

One final caution: Any and all errors perceived herein are purely subjective.

Index

INDEX

John Podhoretz was born in New York City in 1961. He is a partner in the White House Writers Group, a speechwriting consortium, and a visiting fellow at the Hudson Institute. He was a speechwriter for Ronald Reagan and also served as special assistant to the nation's first drug czar. He has held editorial positions at *The American Spectator*, *Time*, *The Washington Times*, *U.S. News & World Report*, and *Insight*. He lives in Washington, D.C.